Globalization in the Asian Re

Globalization in the Asian Region
Impacts and Consequences

Edited by

Gloria Davies and Chris Nyland

Edward Elgar
Cheltenham, UK • Northampton, MA, USA

Published by
Edward Elgar Publishing Limited
Glensanda House
Montpellier Parade
Cheltenham
Glos GL50 1UA
UK

Edward Elgar Publishing, Inc.
136 West Street
Suite 202
Northampton
Massachusetts 01060
USA

A catalogue record for this book
is available from the British Library

ISBN 1 84376 627 2 (cased)

Printed and bound in Great Britain by MPG Books Ltd, Bodmin, Cornwall

Contents

Contributors

John Ballingall: New Zealand Institute of Economic Research (Inc.),
P.O. Box 3479, Wellington
john.ballingall@nzier.org.nz

Gary D. Bouma: School of Political and Social Inquiry, Faculty of Arts,
Monash University
gary.bouma@arts.monash.edu.au

Phil Briggs: New Zealand Institute of Economic Research (Inc.), P.O. Box
3479, Wellington
phil.briggs@clear.net.nz

Gloria Davies: School of Languages, Cultures and Linguistics, Faculty of
Arts, Monash University
gloria.davies@arts.monash.edu.au

Vi Meghnad Desai: Centre for the Study of Global Governance, London
School of Economics
Contactable through Rita Field: R.Field@lse.ac.uk

Jane C.Y. Lee: Hong Kong Policy Research Institute
Contactable through Nora Leung: noraleung@hkpri.org.hk

Richard Lee York Wo: First Eastern Investment Group, Hong Kong
rlee@first-eastern.com

Ross Mouer: School of Languages, Cultures and Linguistics, Faculty of Arts,
Monash University
Ross.Mouer@arts.monash.edu.au

Chris Nyland: Department of Management, Faculty of Business and
Economics, Monash University
chris.nyland@buseco.monash.edu.au

Robert C. Rice: Department of Economics, Faculty of Business and

Economics, Monash University
Robert.Rice@buseco.monash.edu.au

Joanna Smith: New Zealand Institute of Economic Research (Inc.),
P.O. Box 3479, Wellington
joanna.smith@nzier.org.nz

Russell Smyth: Department of Economics, Faculty of Business and
Economics, Monash University
russell.smyth@buseco.monash.edu.au

Idris F. Sulaiman: Partnership for Economic Growth Project, USAID
Idris@pegasus.or.id

Tham Siew-Yean: Institute of Malaysian and International Studies
(IKMAS), Universiti Kebangsaan Malaysia
tham@pkrisc.cc.ukm.my

Marika Vicziany: Monash Asia Institute, Monash University
marika.vicziany@adm.monash.edu.au

Vivienne Wee: Center for South East Asian Studies, City University of Hong
Kong
v.wee@cityu.edu.hk

David Wright-Neville: School of Political and Social Inquiry, Faculty of
Arts, Monash University
David.WrightNeville@arts.monash.edu.au

Preface

Gary D. Bouma

This volume is a product of researchers associated with the Monash University Institute for the study of Global Movements (MUISGS). Established in 2002, MUISGS promotes interdisciplinary research that seeks to both describe and understand the causes and consequences of newly emerging patterns in the global movements of people, ideas and capital. MUISGS draws together researchers from five faculties of Monash University (Art and Design, Arts, Business and Economics, Education, and Law). Deliberately seeking to break down the barriers between disciplines, faculties and schools that inevitably emerge concomitant with the organizational structure of a university, MUISGS organizes lecture series and seminars and funds several major research teams.

The key questions to be addressed by projects of the Institute are: What are the nature and implications of the global movement of people (migrants, tourists, labour), resources (capital, goods and services) and ideas (knowledge, culture and fashion/style)? What institutions, systems and structures are evolving to facilitate global flows and movements and heightened global interdependence? and what are the implications for national and local institutions? What is the impact on security, human rights and national identities in an increasingly mobile or even borderless world? Current MUISGS research teams are examining the following issues: global markets, human mobility and well-being; the effect of global movements on health and well-being; sustainable governance of international trade, finance and investment: 21st century challenges; and labour implications of the re-location of capital.

Globalization refers to a bundle of processes that continue to change the world we live in and the way we live in it. There are historical antecedents to some of the processes described by globalization, times when people moved more freely and capital moved in even less fettered ways, and when there appeared to be a limited number of transnational totalizing discourses shaped by the empires that sustained them. However, these antecedents are inadequate to the task of understanding and managing global change as currently experienced.

As ever in social science, ideologies abound as researchers bring to bear on contemporary phenomena the tools they were trained to use to describe and analyse earlier phases of the social, cultural and economic order.   For some, freedom from controls on capital brought by globalization will bring good things, while for others there is no good to be seen in the consequences of globalization.   Desai's chapter on poverty is a welcome corrective to such ideologically driven views, pointing out the failure of both capitalism and the welfare state to answer the challenge of poverty in a globalized world.   The editors of and contributors to *Globalization in the Asian Region: Impacts and Consequences* have sought to avoid ideology, seeking first to describe accurately contemporary changes in the patterns of global movements and their consequences.   In doing so they update our understanding of the processes of globalization and move the discourse beyond notions of internationalization, liberalization, and Westernization, using Scholte's concept of supraterritoriality (see the Introduction by Davies and Nyland) and by squarely facing the implications of post-September 11 changes in US foreign and economic policy.

The processes of globalization constitute the most active current site of fresh information about the reality of social, cultural and economic systems. They are real in that they are experienced as limiting and shaping human action, being beyond human control; and changes in these systems occur only to a limited degree as a result of human action, whether individual or collective through the policies of nation states.   Globalization is encountered – run into – in the course of living, and is experienced as something 'out there', yet objective and largely unyielding.   The changes associated with globalization are not the result of deliberate human engineering, nor are they merely the sum of the decisions of individuals, or the products of psychological processes.   To live in a globalized world is to live in a very different world from the world of encapsulated nation states with national identities, cultures and economies.   For example, we not only know what is happening in every corner of the world, we are also aware that it either affects – or has the capacity to affect – our lives.   In ways such as this, a globalized world is palpably different from previous socio-cultural and economic systems.   Differences in the patterns of the movement of people, ideas and capital produce describably different contexts for human decision making, policy formation and planning.

Moreover, the processes of globalization themselves are changing at what appears to be an accelerating rate.   These changes and their accelerating pace require a re-examination of the conceptual tools for describing and understanding them.   For example, discussions of 'level playing fields' so popular in the early 1990s have been replaced with much more realistic appraisals of the role of power gradients in reshaping the playing field and the knowledge that the ebb and flow of global movements are not random and are certainly not equal in their consequences. Following the collapse of the USSR, there are no sufficiently powerful countervailing ideological or economic forces to qualify the dominance of the USA.

Similarly, the optimism of some early analyses of globalization has been replaced by fearful attempts to promote security in a world rendered anxious following the September 11 terrorist attacks. The influence of two cultural forces not globally present before this event is central to understanding globalization now. Terrorism is now a global phenomenon in an entirely new way, making everyone vulnerable and transmitting to every locality both the negative ideologies supporting various forms of terror and the technologies of terrorism (recipes for bombs, networks of economic support and capacities to communicate intensely at a distance about terror). The mirror-image cultural force is the fear, anxiety and security fixation of many nations, most particularly the US, which is placing security ahead of economic agendas and hard-won human rights. These two forces have changed the face of globalization and may have the effect of undoing many of the gains associated with globalization, with no measurable positive outcome.

The processes of globalization and their consequences described in this volume are eloquent testimony to the vitality of social, cultural and economic systems. Far from being static structures supporting long-term predictability, these systems are at once highly structuring of the pattern of opportunities shaping the human decision-making frame and also quite volatile. This volatility might suggest that globalization processes are too transitory to be worthy of study since the patterns are not as persistent as might be desired for law-like description of them. However, to take this view would be a serious error. Rather, different methodologies are required — not so much to trap as to glimpse, and not so much to control as, through awareness, to shape the human response.

Asia provides a particular lens through which to examine globalization. On the one hand, Asia seems to be very much the brunt-bearer of the processes of global movements. Many of its people would move to the West in even greater numbers if permitted to do so; its products are archetypical of the movement of goods; and its employment structures have been profoundly changed through the movement of jobs (not people) to Asia from the West. On the other hand, Asia may be in a cultural and economic position to be better able to cope with and respond creatively to the changes brought by globalization.

Australia, which is essentially marginal to both the West and to Asia but is dependent on the West for much of its culture and on Asia for its economic well-being, provides a very different vantage point from either Asia or the

West of Europe or America.   Nyland and Smyth describe the complex ways in which this nation has negotiated involvement in Bush's wars, emerging free trade policies and domestic policies.   These complexities point directly to the fact that the effects of globalization cannot be categorized as those felt by 'the West' and those felt by 'Asia', but require much more nuanced and careful description and explanation.

The contributors to this volume speak directly to current issues of great importance to the whole world, opening up new vistas, raising new concerns and pointing tentatively to ways forward.

Gary D. Bouma
Monash University

Acknowledgements

The editors would like to express their gratitude to the Monash Institute for the Study of Global Movements and the Committee for the Economic Development of Australia (CEDA) for the kind assistance they provided to this project. Both these institutions liaised with the Asian Region International Association of Co-operating Organisations (ARIACO) on our behalf and provided advice on various aspects of the project. In this regard, we owe a special debt to Professor John Nieuwenhuysen, Director of the Monash Institute for the Study of Global Movements, for his sustained and critical support of this project. Financial assistance from the Institute was also crucial in expediting the project's completion.

We would also like to thank Professor Gary Bouma who, in his capacity as Chair of the Institute's Board, kindly agreed to write a preface for this book. We are especially grateful to Dr Miriam Lang for her editorial assistance and to Mrs Lyn Vinton for helping with the production of this volume. Their professionalism and efficiency has enabled this project to be completed in good time. We also thank Dr Felicity Rawlings-Sanaei and Mr Andrew Fernando of the Monash Institute for the Study of Global Movements for the assistance and support they provided with various matters related to this project.

Finally, we thank our contributing authors for their willingness to participate in this project, and for bringing a diverse range of perspectives to bear on the impacts and consequences of globalization in the Asian region.

Gloria Davies and Chris Nyland

Views of Globalization, Empire and Asia: An Introduction

Gloria Davies and Chris Nyland

The Asian financial crisis of 1997-1998 removed some of the gloss that, for many observers, had accumulated around the concept of globalization within Asia through the first half of the 1990s. During this time, globalization had been understood to mean the free movement of goods, services, capital and ideas (though not people) across international boundaries. Thus understood, by the mid 1990s the concept was being embraced with increasing enthusiasm even by many of those who had helped situate their countries on a sustained development path that carefully balanced economic openness and state intervention. In the wake of the crisis, there was much allocation of blame. Those who had argued that to capture the benefits of the global movement of resources nations must allow firms maximum freedom to relocate their investments were accused of undermining their national economies. It was held that advocates of this form of corporate flexibility had rendered large (poor to lower-middle class) sectors of populations and even whole nations vulnerable to the growing volatility of the global economy. This volatility was and continues to be blamed, in part, on the very corporate flexibility that advocates of thoroughgoing market liberalization had championed. Within the national context, state officials in developing or newly industrialized countries that were hardest hit by the crisis (such as Indonesia, South Korea and Thailand) were further accused of having collaborated with non-nationals in the removal of instruments and practices that had previously insured these societies against the worst forms of global instability. Corporate globalizers, on the other hand, countered that it was in fact their critics who should bear the main responsibility for the crisis. They insisted that the root of the problem lay in the corruption of globalization by the 'cronyism' associated with the 'traditional' Asian approach to global integration.[1] The cure that they prescribed was more openness to global markets and the removal of the remaining restraints on the free movement of resources. Given that the inadequacy of social protection for the poorest and most disadvantaged was assuming crisis proportions in several Asian countries (most notably China), this proposed 'cure' rang increasingly hollow.   Nonetheless, the chorus of corporate voices calling for greater market liberalization harmonized with the national interests of the world's richest countries, especially the United States. It also melded well with the transnational interests of International Monetary Fund (IMF) programs. These, as Joseph Stiglitz (2002, p. 24) observes, 'are typically dictated from Washington and shaped by the short missions during which its staff members pore over numbers in the finance ministries and central banks and make themselves comfortable in five-star hotels in the capitals'.

Associated with these mutual recriminations was much talk on opposing 'sides' of the debate over globalization of the need to reform core policies. Indeed, for a period it was even mooted that it would be necessary to establish a new 'global financial infrastructure' and create social institutions that could limit the costs imposed on populations should the existing infrastructure prove inadequate. Six years on, it is clear that much of this discussion was little more than the immediate knee-jerk response that normally occurs with the onset of natural or human-made crises. This is not to denigrate the importance of these spontaneous reactions, for they are an important part of the process by which capitalist communities establish sustainable regulatory structures over time (Braithwaite and Drahos 2000). This process has tended to follow a standard form. Shocks induce a demand for reforms, some of these demands are ceded and institutionalized, and then the socio-economic game continues along a path that has been changed, though not transformed, until the next crisis. This was the situation that veteran observers like Stiglitz would reasonably have expected would occur in Asia at the beginning of the new millennium.

In the period following 1998, however, it has become clear to many that anomalies and inequalities in globalization were the direct product of a very uneven playing field, in which the United States occupied an unrivalled position of dominance. Opposition to the 'one size fits all' doctrine of the IMF – which reached a peak with street violence in Indonesia in the late 1990s – led grassroots organizations and governments like the Mahathir regime in Malaysia to reject many of the global practices and structures that had been established as the norm of what the economist John Williamson (1990) has dubbed the 'Washington Consensus'. At first those who opposed this so-called consensus sought to expand direct participation in the decision-making processes of globalization.   These Leftist critics loosely unified themselves as a different form of consensus that became known as the 'global justice movement'.[2] This movement initiated a pattern of activity that had its first and arguably most spectacular success at the 1999 Seattle Ministerial Meeting of the World Trade Organisation (WTO). Following the Seattle debacle, popular rallies and discontent in the streets became a standard feature of the meetings of the major global agencies. This development appears to have had a significant impact insofar as agencies such as the World Bank and the IMF began, in the wake of these protests, to call for an expanded global dialogue that would involve increasing the number of 'seats at the table' of global forums.

The discomfiture on the part of leading representatives of the world's richest nations, corporations and transnational agencies became highly public when the WTO was placed in the embarrassing situation of having to hold its 2001 Ministerial Meeting in authoritarian Doha to avoid attracting street protests and hence bad publicity via global television news. This unease was further accentuated as the social justice movement gained momentum. Its advocates began to make it clear that they were not Luddites who were opposed to globalism; what they wanted was for the operations of globalization to be expanded to embrace the rights of ordinary citizens as well as the poor and disadvantaged and thus not be understood merely as the maximizing of global property rights. This message has long been advanced by influential individuals such as the financier George Soros and the political philosopher John Gray. Both argue that corporate globalization creates conflict and leads to the disenfranchisement of broader national communities because it has sought to globalize market relations while refusing to accept the need to globalize the social and political institutions that have been developed within nation states to 'civilize' market relations. As Prowse (2003, p. 9) has observed, what the social justice movement demands is not the end of globalization but an approach that will attend seriously to the question of 'how to create global institutions of governance that re-enfranchise the world's people: that is, institutions that allow people to choose the degree to which they want global capitalism to be subject to social controls'.

Similar concerns regarding social justice were registered in the institutional sector when leading figures such as Stiglitz lamented that 'We have no world government, accountable to the people of every country, to oversee the globalization process in a fashion comparable to the way national governments guided the nationalization process' (2002, p. 21), or when the IMF published critiques of the Washington Consensus, such as that of Moises Naim (1999), editor of *Foreign Policy Magazine*, who regarded this 'wonkish moniker' as obscuring 'profound disagreements among the experts in Washington and elsewhere' while failing to provide a self-reflexive account of the ways in which the Consensus kept adding 'new, more complex and more difficult goals to the list of requirements for an acceptable performance'.

But as a concerned global public began to reflect on the complexities of globalization that were being made visible by the often misnamed 'anti-globalization movement,' another chorus of voices began to express its own dissatisfaction with the view that old pathways to globalism could simply be modified at the edges. It did so, however, in terms entirely different from those of the global justice movement. Embodied in the form of the Bush administration in the US, these 'new' (or neo-conservative) critics of the old order insisted that henceforth the mode and pace of globalization should be determined by, as it were, a *true* Washington consensus, comprised of the US government and US corporations whose interests this administration represents. The view of this consensus was made public after the attacks on the World Trade Center on 11 September 2001. Since then, the Bush administration has become assertive about its intention to rewrite the rules of globalization in the national interest of the US and to ensure acceptance of this situation from other nations and regional coalitions through the deployment of its unrivalled economic and military power. This new challenge on the part of the Bush administration to the global economic status quo, has become an object of critical analysis in recent times.

Many critics, including several contributors to this volume (Nyland and Smyth; Wee; Wright-Neville), have raised concerns over the diminishing fortunes of effective multilateralism within the globalization process. The extent of the continuing divergence that exists amongst scholars and analysts is reflected in the differing understandings of globalization implicit in the different chapters of this volume. Many of the authors (Ballingal, Briggs and Smith; Desai; J. Lee; R. Lee; Mouer; Rice and Sulaiman; Tham) continue to accept that globalization is still best understood to mean the achievement of prosperity through the reduction of restraints on the movement of resources and people across national borders, guided by multilateral agencies working in tandem with national governments to determine the implementation of appropriate instruments of governance and development. Indeed Desai's contribution to this book he advances the view that global poverty can be effectively addressed only by 'match[ing] the free movement of capital with the free movement of labour'. Other contributors emphasize the negative impacts of such flows, especially when the free movement of capital is viewed in the context of the rise of Hindu fundamentalist nationalism in India, supported and funded by an enormous and growing Indian middle-class diaspora. This is a divisive and strident form of religious politics that has eroded the gains of Indian secularism and produced numerous acts of communal violence (Vicziany). Similarly, when the authoritarian Chinese party-state's active promotion of China's market economy is viewed against the new forms of corruption that have occurred with China's entry into globalization and the continued curtailed flow of free information, it is clear that capital flows vulnerable to mismanagement may increase (rather than reduce) socio-economic dislocation and poverty (Davies and Smyth). Some contributors are also concerned that the asymmetrical nature of globalization, and the 'old' rules that have favoured the rich over the poor, will be allowed to prevail, and that the introduction of 'new' alliances between the US government and its willing transnational corporate and foreign government partners may, in time, constitute an irresistible force that would overwhelm resistance from both the global justice movement and advocates of alternative Asian pathways to globalism that have proven relatively effective in nations such as Japan, Malaysia, and South Korea (Nyland and Smyth; Wee). These contributors fear, in short, that the regulatory structures governing globalism are being reconfigured in ways that may lead the US not only to exercise its hegemonic influence on the global economy (as it has done), but to arrogate to itself an imperial right to determine how globalization *should* proceed. In the rest of this introductory chapter we clarify what is distinctive about globalization and then discuss, in this context, recent ideas on hegemony and empire manifest in the emergent literature on globalization currently informing debate within governments, corporations and civil society.

CONCEPTIONS OF GLOBALIZATION

Questions relating to the origins of globalization, the means by which the process has evolved and diverged from its former course, and the positive and negative outcomes of the process and its complexity in holding together elements of the 'rich' and 'poor', 'haves' and 'have-nots' in a series of mutually dependent unequal relationships, have come to dominate much of intellectual and academic life in both Western and non-Western countries. The term 'globalization' has become so capacious that it constitutes a site of endless contestation in both specialist and general literature on the topic. In seeking to specify what is distinctive about globalization we borrow from the work of Jan Scholte (2000), who has sought to redress the ensuing state of confusion over globalization by discussing five broad definitions of the term and by explaining why only one of these really accounts for the dramatic technologically-enabled difference that constitutes contemporary globalization. All five definitions are related and overlapping but they also differ substantially in the emphases that they each place on globalization as a concept. The first of these conceives of globalization in terms of *internationalization*. Viewed from this perspective, 'global' is simply an adjective that describes economic relations *between* nations, and globalization refers, in this sense, to the growth of international exchange and economic interdependence between nations. Thus Hirst and Thompson

(1999) have identified globalization in terms of 'large and growing flows of trade and capital investment between countries', evidence of which is readily apparent in the form of unprecedented levels of the movement of capital, goods, ideas and, more recently, people between countries. A second and distinctly policy-oriented use of the term views globalization as *liberalization*, that is as the process of removing state-imposed restrictions on the movement of these same resources between nations in order to build an open and borderless world economy. Issues highlighted by advocates of this perspective are the widespread abolition of regulatory trade and investment structures, and the curtailment of restrictions on currency exchange and the issuing of visas. A third definition equates globalization with *universalization*, and this is where the concept begins to acquire a certain metaphysical shimmer. In this usage, 'global' suggests the worldwide diffusion of a common range of products, values and experiences to which people have access, wherever they are physically located. Those who embrace this understanding tend to stress the emergence of 'global products' such as Coca-Cola and Nike, but the notion can also apply to the establishment of uniform physical and social infrastructure (roads and educational, welfare and health facilities), as well as to a uniform set of work, social, cultural and religious practices at all points on the globe. A fourth policy-directed and also unavoidably metaphysical definition equates globalization with *Westernization* or *modernization*. According to this perspective, globalization is a 'dynamic whereby the social structures of modernity (capitalism, rationalism, industrialism, bureaucratism, etc) are spread the world over, normally destroying pre-existent cultures and local self-determination in the process' (Scholte 2000, p. 16). The fifth determines globalization in both phenomenological and critical terms as the spread of *supraterritoriality*. This interpretation accepts that globalization entails a reconfiguration of geography 'so that social space is no longer wholly mapped in terms of territorial places, territorial distances and territorial borders' (Scholte 2000, p. 16).

Scholte makes the invaluable point that the last of these conceptions is linked to a distinctly new phenomenon while the first four relate to issues and problems that have developed over a long period of time in human history and that became especially significant in the course of the twentieth century. In other words, the first four perspectives on globalization given above constitute ways of rethinking the *known* world that are, to a large extent, predicated on authoritative accounts of liberalization and modernization as social goods, within an institutionally entrenched language of modern ideas. By contrast, supraterritorial phenomena – in the sense of phenomena characterized by transworld simultaneity and instantaneity (such as the internet and global mass travel) – are a distinctly new feature of human social experience that terminology and concepts derived from older discourses on modernity cannot adequately represent without recourse to the use of new formulations and descriptions. Scholte develops, on this basis, a powerful analytical tool for understanding the nature of globalization as a process marked by the growth of supraterritorial spaces that does not, however, spell the end of territorial geography: rather, the two phenomena are seen to be complexly interrelated with the former constituting an often 'blind' or myopic mapping of the supraterritorial new against the 'old' geopolitical terrain. He also argues, along with many others, that though globalization has been with us for a long time, it was not until the mid 1960s that it developed into a 'trend' or force in its own right.[3] Those critics of globalization who assert that it has taken on certain juggernaut-like qualities in the contemporary moment often fail to acknowledge that the momentum of globalization is given to fluctuation depending on the events, as they arise, that impact on the global movement of people and resources. In this regard, the series of violent events that occurred on 11 September 2001, followed since then by ongoing threats and occurrences of terrorist attacks in both developed and developing countries, have had a decisive impact on the operations of the global economy. More recently, the initially uncontrolled eruption of the SARS virus in southern mainland China which spread rapidly to Hong Kong and then to different parts of the world has been *the* most significant cause of economic downturn in the Asian region in 2003. That this downturn resulted not from the actual incidence of SARS cases but from the curtailment of travel, relocation and investment plans brought about by fear and anxiety in the face of a disease for which no effective cure has yet been found provides a crucial instance of unpredictable flux within the intricate and highly vulnerable web of complexly interdependent economic relations that constitutes globalization. According to Neil Beck (2003),

> The Asian Development Bank has estimated that East Asia could lose nearly 28 billion dollars in income and output if SARS is not controlled by September. Under such a scenario, aggregate 2003 GDP growth in China, Hong Kong, South Korea, and Taiwan would be cut from 5.6 percent (pre-SARS) to 4.7 percent, while growth in Southeast Asia would drop from 4.0 percent to 2.5 percent.

Globalization at the level of the lived everyday has impacted differently on the well-being of individuals and communities, revealing the unevenness of the process, with most of the benefits accruing to the propertied professional classes in the world's key metropolitan sites while the adverse consequences have tended to be visited on the rural and urban poor. The process also commonly favours the younger, educated generations of any given population, who possess the necessary technological skills to participate in the global web of commercial activities spawned by the internet and other electronic modes of trade and communication. Since the causal dynamic of globalization is multifaceted, with rational knowledge, capitalist production, technological innovations and certain national and international regulatory measures taken as basic requirements for participation, it is not surprising that the process of globalization has also prompted important changes to these requirements as local economies and workers adjust to new market demands. Globalization has encouraged the growth of additional loci of governance besides the state and promoted the development of new forms of knowledge beyond those developed within the institutionally entrenched discipline-based paradigms of modern rationality. Important positive consequences have been generated with respect to the development of multicultural or culturally inclusive modes of social existence, the hyper-expansion of communicative possibilities via the internet, the decentralization of power, and the enhancement of economic efficiency and product availability, to list only the most obvious. At the same time, however, many negative consequences have also emerged. These include increased ecological and employment degradation, sustained poverty, disturbing and growing forms of ethnic and religious violence, increased inequality and a widening democratic deficit, with particular relevance post-September 2001 to the heightened state of security alertness on the part of governments everywhere.

Geographers such as Glenn Firebaugh and sociologists and anthropologists like Saskia Sassen (2001) and Arjun Appadurai (2001) have sought to provide nuanced critical perspectives on some of these positive and negative aspects of globalization in relation to supraterritoriality. For Firebaugh (2002; 2003), the oft-repeated cry that the world has become more sharply divided as a result of growing income inequality between rich and poor nations generally fails to take account of the difference between weighted trends (that consider different population sizes, economies of scale and income generation within a local context) and unweighted ones (that rely primarily on national income figures and currency exchange rates). He proposes instead a way of distinguishing between income inequality and income gaps using weighted trends, which has led him to provide a highly different picture of the *status quo* in contemporary globalization. He concludes that while income *inequality* (that is, weighted income growth ratios) across nations peaked around 1970 and has declined since then, income *gaps* (expressed in absolute numbers) have grown both across and within nations as a consequence of the accelerated income growth among elite sectors of advanced industrialized societies (Firebaugh 2002; 2003). Similarly, Sassen's work on the emergence of 'global cities' as strategic sites of globalization reintroduces the categories of place and production process into the analysis of globalization. She argues that these two categories, 'easily overlooked in accounts centred on the hypermobility of capital and the power of transnationals' do not negate the centrality of the latter but rather serve to foreground 'the fact that many of the resources necessary for global economic activities are not hypermobile and are, indeed, deeply embedded in place, notably places such as global cities and export processing zones' (Sassen 2001, p. 1). For Appadurai, the resurgence of ethnic and religious violence in recent times is symptomatic of the altered stakes of competition within contemporary globalization. As he sees it, there are 'deep histories of internal hate and suspicion waiting to be mobilized' when a nation's economy is in crisis. The minorities (including the enormous numbers of labour migrants and refugees worldwide who enter different national spaces, often to take up low-paying domestic and manual work) end up being the object of mob violence when deep histories of hate are deployed in the attempt to eliminate 'strangers' whose very presence evokes popular anxiety over the loss of nationhood and national cultural coherence within globalization (Appadurai 2001, pp. 6-7).

Our view, as represented in this introduction and in our design of this book, is that globalization is not inherently good or bad or even singular (that is the same thing for everyone). The manner of its evolution is greatly dependent on the policy alternatives chosen. In short, claims that there is only one best way or that there are no alternatives to a neoliberal, corporate agenda are inevitably ideological, though the political challenges blocking the attainment of any alternatives are vast and should not be underestimated. As Appadurai notes, the very newness of the experience of globalization for both 'haves' and 'have-nots' – the newness of what Scholte calls supraterritoriality – means that even our recourse to history, our most powerful tool to date for 'managing newness', will prove ultimately inadequate:

> We can do our best to see globalization as just a new phase (and face) of capitalism, or imperialism, or neo-colonialism, or modernization or developmentalism. And there is some force to this hunt for the analogy that will let us tame the beast of globalization in the prison-house (or zoo) of language. But this historicizing move (for all of its technical legitimacy) is doomed to fail precisely in accounting for the part of globalization that is unsettling in its newness (Appadurai 2001, p. 1).

Appadurai's comments clearly resonate with Scholte's understanding of globalization as a process entrenched in conventional modes of description and analysis that cannot properly account for the newness of supraterrioriality. We embrace this conceptualization of globalization as a supraterritorial phenomenon whose unprecedentedness cannot be glibly explained from any one given historicist perspective. Indeed the terms used and the conclusions and observations reached from any one such historicist perspective on, say, older forms of political and cultural imperialism would necessarily efface (rather than foreground) the supraterritorial reach of electronic communications in forging any number of common interests between individuals, groups and communities across national borders. The suddenness of gains and losses generated by electronic and borderless finance markets constitutes another marker of supraterritoriality that has yet to be adequately mapped.

The supraterritorial aspect of globalization is, to some extent, what this book foregrounds in the different accounts provided of the impacts and consequences of globalization in Asia. The book begins with three thematic and critical accounts of how different Asian societies have coped with and responded to the highly uneven economic arrangements within globalization, with specific reference to the altered role of the US government post-September 2001 (Wee), and the increased stakes of terrorism (Wright-Neville) and poverty (Desai). These are followed by nine country-specific studies of different aspects of globalization's impacts and consequences: a broad-ranging economic analysis of Malaysia that takes into account capital flows, international trade and labour flow implications (Tham); a survey of the increased vertical division of labour in global manufacturing and the growth of information communication technologies as these have impacted on Indonesia (Rice and Sulaiman); an analysis of the consequences of global economic and political integration as these have impacted upon India with specific reference to the rise of Hindu fundamentalist nationalism (Vicziany); an analysis of the shift from multilateralism to 'empire preference' in the Australian government's position on globalization, consequent upon both domestic and international events and crises (Nyland and Smyth); a report on New Zealand's performance within the global economy in relation to the movement of people, trade developments and the flow of ideas (Ballingal, Briggs and Smith); an analysis of the 'Japanese model' of corporate governance and practice, with specific reference to issues of divergence and convergence within the global economy and the changed nature of work that has accompanied Japan's economic recession in recent years (Mouer); and an analysis of China's performance since its entry into the global economy in the late 1970s, with particular reference to its recent accession to the WTO and the prospects for regional and global integration on the part of a nation – the world's most populous – which has remained under authoritarian one-party rule since 1949 (Davies and Smyth), based in part on a brief account of Foreign Direct Investment (FDI) into mainland China (R. Lee,) and a summary survey of the movement of people between China and Hong Kong (J. Lee).

The contributors to this book have each chosen to interpret the impacts and consequences of globalization in different ways, with most focusing on one or two issues as a means of providing elaboration on the range of capital, technological, cultural and labour flows in globalization; some others provide a more general account of how a given national economy has performed within globalization (notably Tham; Ballingall, Briggs and Smith); and three provide short surveys on key topics (Rice and Sulaiman; R. Lee, J. Lee,). This diversity reflects the book's origin as a joint venture between the Monash Institute for the Study of Global Movements, the Committee for the Economic Development of Australia (CEDA) and the Asian Region International Association of Co-operating Organisations (ARIACO). The first of these three bodies is an academic research unit based at Monash University in Melbourne, Australia. CEDA is a discussion and research organization established and funded by business as well as government and academic institutions in Australia, and ARIACO is a confederation of similar bodies from across the Asian region. Contributions for the book were sourced from these three participating organizations. As editors, we adopted an inclusive approach, welcoming critical analyses that queried assumptions of 'progress' within the current climate of globalization as well as practical surveys or empirical accounts that measure progress according to one or another existing set of economic performance criteria. In other words, some of our contributors problematize notions of 'growth' and 'progress' in globalization while others understand the process in precisely these terms. To reflect the experience of globalization as the sense of one's involvement in new, complexly interrelated and unpredictable movements – movements that resist totalization and that can only be mapped in fragments and from different perspectives, never definitively – one must accord space and attention to the discontinuities or incommensurabilities that result from different interpretations and understandings of globalization rather than attempt to smooth these over. As Shiv Visnavathan (2001) succinctly puts it, 'Any issue on globalization is a beginning, an invitation to a quarrel, a request to reinvent it further. But most of all, it is an attempt to locate [and to] *hybridize* the dreams of globalism and democracy' (our emphasis).

All chapters of this book (including this introduction) draw on the five definitions of globalization provided by Scholte, with particular reference to the implications of supraterritorial developments, whether these are elaborated as financial, trade, technological, and labour flows or as flows of knowledge, culture and religious ideas. Using a musical metaphor, the heterogeneity of this book – owing in part to the different idioms in which its contributors have written about diverse aspects of globalization – can be likened to variations on a common theme. Some of these variations are longer than others, especially when they recall the theme of globalization in self-reflexive and critical ways, while other variations articulate the same theme in the relatively neutral terms of economically driven processes that have made nations mutually dependent in complex ways. It should also be noted that this book covers some but not all Asian countries. Indeed a subsequent volume that deals with countries not discussed, including Cambodia, Myanmar, Laos, North and South Korea, Pakistan, the Philippines, Singapore, Taiwan, Thailand and Vietnam, is desirable. This book is focused to some extent on nations with the largest populations (China, India); the richest nation in the Asian region (Japan); nations that are identifiably 'Western' in the region (Australia and New Zealand); and nations with large Muslim populations (Indonesia and Malaysia). It also engages with questions of moment in globalization in the form of increased US military presence and terrorism. Some emphasis has also been placed on the relationship between China and Hong Kong in order to highlight problems that have emerged in that relationship since the handover of Hong Kong in 1997.

In several of its chapters, this book suggests that there is an urgent need for new and more equitable ways of thinking about globalization (notably Desai; Nyland and Smyth; Wee; Wright-Neville). In relation to this need, we wish to highlight an assumption in Scholte's work which as late as 2000 was common within the globalization literature but is now being widely contested. This assumption is most eloquently expressed by Hardt and Negri (2000) in their influential book *Empire* when they discuss contemporary economic power as the force that allows corporate globalizers to rule in an imperial manner, but with the signal difference that the 'empire' has no single political or economic centre since power has become so geographically and institutionally diffused within globalization. Scholte's focus on supra or trans-territoriality would suggest that he accepts this perspective on the diffused state of contemporary global power; but in the same year that his work first appeared, key members of the new Bush administration began to make it plain that as far as they were concerned, the United States constitutes a global empire that does have a centre located in sites of government and corporate power within the USA This is a critical claim on the part of the US leadership that, if achieved, would have grave implications for the future choices other nations and peoples can make when confronting the challenges of an already US-dominated globalization agenda. That a neo-conservative Republican administration would promote the 'right' of the US to rule the globe in a manner much more unilateral than had previously been the norm was public knowledge through the second half of the 1990s. But it was a development not appreciated by a great many, culminating in the 2003 war in Iraq when the Bush administration made it very public that in the defence of

US interests globally, it was prepared to weather the opposition of millions of anti-war protestors internationally and to put aside what had been a primary rule of the international relations game, namely mutual respect for national sovereignty. Indeed in the days leading up to and throughout the duration of the war on Iraq, the Bush administration stood firmly by its position of waging a pre-emptive strike and rejected the counsel of its critics. These developments have compelled the globalization debate to enter a new phase centred on whether the significant political shift in the US since September 2001 has transformed its approach to globalism and with it the prospects for progressive equitable globalization in the rest of the world. More specifically, what is being debated is whether the US is in the process of moving from being a hegemon to becoming an empire that will unilaterally determine the rules of globalization (for a small sample of the associated literature see: Anderson 2002; Schroeder 2003; Kolko 2003; Kruger 2003, Beste et al. 2003; Chomsky and Barsamian 2003; Ali 2003).

Three chapters of this book (Nyland and Smyth; Wee; Wright-Neville) discuss this question with particular reference to the formidable difficulties produced by the unilateral use of military force now favoured by the US government. As both Wee and Wright-Neville suggest, terrorism itself is a product of the globalization process, utilizing 'the tools and conditions given by globalization' (Wee) in ways that have led to a 'cohering [of] different elements of the Muslim community around political and religious agendas at odds with those of the prevailing political hierarchies', while 'simultaneously shattering old religious allegiances and loyalties' (Wright-Neville). With reference to the notion of power as diffused within globalization, one could argue that the widespread impact of terrorism functions in precisely this diffused manner, while the Bush administration has sought contrarily to make palpable the power of the US as *the* national terrain upon which all interlinkages of globalization are ultimately dependent. For the reasons given above, the significance of including discussions on US global power, terrorism and the war on Iraq in a book on globalization in the Asian region is obvious. Even in those chapters where the dominance of the United States in globalization has not been directly discussed, the implications of globalization as 'Americanization' for each of the Asian countries studied are also clear. Indeed, the numerous references to the US in different chapters of this book are indicative of the increasing synonymity between globalization and 'Americanization' in the minds of the concerned global public, a trend that is evidenced in the survey conducted by the multinational broadcasting event '*What does the World Think of America?*' which went to air on 19 June 2003 just as this book was going to press. Among other things, the eleven-nation survey showed that a majority disagreed with the notion that US economic policy should be copied in their own countries, while acknowledging the unrivalled status of US economic and military might and the likely effects of this power on their national and individual well-being (ABC TV 2003).

In concluding, we note that the military, economic and cultural power of the US has shaped the future of globalization in both direct and indirect ways. Perspectives that span the political spectrum of opinions on the role of the US in globalization, ranging from positions taken on the right such as Kruger's (2003), those in the 'middle' such as Schroeder's (2003), and those on the left such as Anderson's (2002) all concur with the view that the US constitutes a force that has direct impacts and consequences for the well-being and future development of justice and equitable and sustainable development within globalization, even though these authors are evidently divided on the positive and negative effects of US military operations and economic activities within the world scene. In championing the rise of a diverse and engaged global 'multitude' that resists the monopolization of power, thinkers on the left such as Hardt and Negri provide the basis for rethinking globalization in terms of push-pull factors that render the cyclopean power the Bush administration celebrates in the name of US-style democracy and freedom less absolute than it would appear. Indeed, even though increasing public reference is being made to the imperial power of the US, especially since the wars that it has recently waged on Afghanistan and Iraq with total disregard for the notion of national sovereignty, one must also take into account the mitigating factors of effective large-scale resistance and shows of protest – many of which are organized via the internet and email – and the growth of alternative media sources that have effectively prevented the monopolization of 'reality' by powerful transnational or official media sources. In this context, the influential independent Arabic television station *Al-Jazeera* and irreverent and critically effective online newspapers (like the Chinese-language *Renmin bao* and the bilingual *Malaysiakini*) have played a significant role in queering the pitch of any simplistic defence of either local authoritarianism or global unilateralism on the part of any one national government or political coalition. In relation to contemporary debate on the would-be imperial will of the Bush administration Gabriel Kolko (2003) has reminded us that since 1945 the US has consistently sought to develop and institutionalize its capacity to rule by decree and has failed on every occasion to fully attain this objective. But what should be hard to dismiss, in the wake of the dismissal of national sovereignty involved in the second Iraq war, is the idea that the concept of globalization and/or global movements has any great analytical value if the use of concentrated power is not a key and explicit element of the analysis.

We conclude, therefore, with the observation that we believe Scholte's notion of transterritoriality is of unique value to those wishing to study global movements.   But we add that when utilizing this notion it is not only imperative to remember that Scholte's perspective recognizes that globalization is a process that involves the interaction of the global and the territorial.   It is equally necessary to remember that a vital aspect of territorialism remains concentrated territorial power, and that those who would seek to use this power to rule Asia have never been able to foreclose on all options not to their liking.

REFERENCES

ABC TV (19 June 2003), 'What does the World Think of America?' Online at <http://www.abc.net.au/america/default.htm>.

Ali, Tariq (2003), 'Re-Colonizing Iraq', *New Left Review*, 21 May-June, online at <http://www.newlefreview.net/NLR25501.shtml>.

Anderson, Perry (2002), 'Force and Consent', *New Left Review,* 17 September-October, online at <http://www.newleftreview.net/NLR25101.shtml>.

Appadurai, A. (2001), 'New Logics of Violence' *Seminar* (No. 503), July 2001. online, at <http://www.india-seminar.com/2001/503/503%20arjun%20apadurai. htm>.

Beck, N.J. (2003), 'What does SARS Mean for China?' in *NBR Briefing* (The National Bureau of Asian Research), 9 May, online at <http://www.nbr.org/ publications/briefing/no.13-SARS/Beck.html>.

Bennis, Phyllis (2003), 'Going Global: Building a Movement Against Empire', Transnational Institute, 14 May, online at <http://www.zmag.org/content/ showarticle.cfm?SectionID=41&ItemID=3617>.

Beste, Ralf, Winfried Didzoleit, Hans Hoyng, Olaf Ihlau, Uwe Klubmann, Dirk Koch, Romain Leick, Andreas Lorenz and Gerhard Sporl (2003), 'The Masters of the World; The World Order of the Superpower', *The New York Times,* online at <http://www.nytimes.com/2003/04/21/international/europe/21SPIEGEL.html?ei=5 070>.

Braithwaite, John and Peter Drahos (2000), *Global Business Regulation,* Cambridge: Cambridge University Press.

Brecher, Jeremy (2003), 'Terminating the Bush Juggernaut', *Znet*, online at <http:// www.zmag.org/brecher jug.htm>.

Chomsky, Noam and David Barsamain (2003), 'Imperial Ambition', *Znet*, online at <http://www.zmag.org/content/print_article.cfm?itemID+3627&sectionID=40>.

Firebaugh, G. (2002), 'The Myth of Growing Global Income Inequality' 14 March, online at <http://www.nuff.ox.ac.uk/rc28/papers/Firebaugh.PDF>.

Firebaugh, G. (2003), *The New Geography of Global Income Inequality*, Cambridge, Mass.: Harvard University Press.

Hardt, M. and A. Negri (2000), *Empire*, Cambridge, Mass.: Harvard University Press.

Hirst, P. and G. Thompson (1999), *Globalization in Question: The International Economy and the Possibilities of Governance,* 2nd edn, Malden, Mass.: Polity Press.

Kolko, Gabriel (2003), 'The Perils of Pax Americana', *Counterpunch*, 15 January, online at <http://www.counterpunch.org/kolko01152003.html>.

Kruger, Daniel (2003), 'The War Must be Followed by Benevolent Colonialism', *New Spectator*, London, 15 March, online at <file:///H/Australia/THE West should not be afraid of Imperialism.htm>.

Naim, M. (1999), 'Fads and Fashion in Economic Reforms: Washington Consensus or Washington Confusion?' Working draft of a paper prepared for the IMF Conference on Second Generation Reforms, Washington, D.C., online at <http://www.imf.org/external/pubs/ft/seminar/1999/reforms/Naim.HTM#I>.

Prowse, Michael (2003), 'Globalisation is Not to Blame for the Unfairness of the World', *Financial Times*, 14 June, p. 9.

Sassen, S. (2001), 'The Global City: Strategic Site/New Frontier', *Seminar* (No. 503), July 2001, online at <http://www.india-seminar.com/2001/503/503%20saskia%20 sassen.htm>.

Scholte, Jan Aart (2000), *Globalization: A Critical Introduction*, London: Macmillan.

Schroeder, Paul (2003), 'The Best Deal In', *Centre for History*, online at <http://hnn.us/articles/1237.html>.

Stiglitz, J. (2002), *Globalization and its Discontents*, London: Penguin Books.

Visnavathan, S. (2001), 'The Problem' (An introduction to the special issue, *Globalization: A Symposium on the Challenges of Closer Global Integration*), *Seminar* (No. 503), July 2001, online at <http://www.india-seminar.com/2001/ 503/503%20the%20problem.htm>.

Williamson, John (1990), 'What Washington Means by Policy Reform', in John Williamson (ed.), *Latin American Adjustment: How Much has Happened?* Washington, D.C.: Institute for International Economics.

NOTES

1 It is worth noting that, in retaliating against this form of criticism, the Malaysian prime minister Mahathir Mohamad was reported to have said in a 2000 interview that 'Cronyism and corruption are more rampant in developed countries. The powerful countries use their influence on crony countries to get contracts for their companies. This is cronyism and corruption at the highest level' (in 'Why the West sucks', *The Globalist, 31* October 2000, online at <http://www.theglobalist.com/DBWeb/StoryId.aspx?StoryId=1303>).

2 For a general description of the global justice movement, see J. Cavanagh, and S. Anderson (January 2002), 'What is the Global Justice Movement? What does it want? Who is in it? What has it won?' published by the *Institute for Policy Studies*, online at <http://www.ips-dc.org/projects/global_econ/movement.pdf>. The movement maintains its own website at <http://www.globaljusticemovement.org/>.

3 See, for instance, the diverse range of accounts provided on the relatively comprehensive educational website on globalization, *Commanding Heights*, that echo Scholte's view; online at <http://www.pbs.org/wgbh/commandingheights/lo/index.html>.

1.   'Globalization' after 9/11 and the Iraq War: Implications for Asia and the Pacific

Vivienne Wee

RECOGNIZING THE MOMENT

The quantum leaps of global change may be indicated by how rapidly our discourses are overtaken by unanticipated events. I am reminded of an apocryphal anecdote of obsolete Sovietological writings marked with the letters 'OBE', meaning 'overtaken by events'. Two events frame this moment of writing:[1]

- 11 September 2001, when suicidal al-Qaeda jihadists killed an estimated 2795 people through the total destruction of New York's World Trade Center and 189 people died in a simultaneous attack on the Pentagon;
- the year-long prelude to a probable US-led war on Iraq – a prelude marked by divisions between states and massive anti-war resistance in cities worldwide.[2]

Have these events overtaken our discourses on 'globalization'? Or is it still business as usual? Or are these events manifestations of a 'new globalization'? And what do these different scenarios imply for the peoples and countries of the Asian-Pacific region?

WHAT IS 'GLOBALIZATION'?

Before exploring regional impacts of varied global scenarios, it is necessary for us to consider the scope and nature of 'globalization'. As the very term implies, 'globalization' is a global phenomenon. In considering the regional impacts of a global phenomenon, we implicitly locate the regional in the global, in a relationship of part to whole. Logically, changes that occur to the whole should also occur in the part; conversely, changes that occur in the part should also occur in the whole.

However, the conventional phrasing 'the impact of globalization on X' implies an agent-patient relationship, whereby globalization is a change that is initiated outside X, thereby impacting on X. One thus finds this phrasing articulated in relation to different regions and countries, women, indigenous communities, workers, the elderly, poverty, health, education, insecurity, labour, homelessness and so on. Perhaps one common characteristic of these categories is that they are social phenomena of lesser power.

However, there seems to be no articulation of the 'impact of globalization' on America and capitalism. This implies an opposition between the agency of that which globalizes and that which is being globalized and thereby impacted upon. There is an unspoken understanding of a global spread – a process whereby something originates in a particular site (which we may term 'core') and spreads to another site (which we may term 'periphery').[3]

What constitutes the originating site of 'globalization'? To answer this, let us consider how the term came about. Significantly, its coinage has been attributed to the business magazine *The American Banker* in its discussion of global capital flows (Laxer 2000). Indeed I found perhaps the first use of the term in the 7 February 1986 issue of this magazine in this context: the 'globalization of capital raising'.[4] Capital was thus the thing that was first seen as 'globalized'. The term 'globalization' then entered popular discourse, became fashionable after the end of the Cold War, and has since been used to label various phenomena that have potentially or actually spread to all parts of the world.

'Globalization', in its current usage, generally includes such trends as the following:

- the increasing integration of national economies within a global marketplace that is arbitrated by the World Trade Organisation (WTO);
- the declining power of nation-states, in inverse relation to the rise of transnational corporations, financial markets and the arbitrations of the WTO;
- the increasing volume of capital flows across national borders;
- the increasing flow of multiple types of information through electronic means; and
- increasing transnational labour migration.

The direction of these global changes may be understood as an attempt to reconstitute the whole world as a single market-driven economy, involving three inter-related processes: trade liberalization, the privatization of public services, and the marketization of society as a whole.

Is such 'globalization' a completely new phenomenon that has appeared only since the 1980s? Starrs (2002, p. 4) notes,

> Although the 'true globalization' that has evolved over the past few decades may be a genuinely new phenomenon both *in toto* and *in esse*, there are also undeniably elements of continuity between it and 'traditional' imperialism and colonialism.

What then are the elements of continuity and discontinuity in 'globalization'? The key elements of continuity are:

- Free-market capitalism, which first emerged in Europe in the sixteenth century (see, for example, Duplessis 1997);
- A transnational economic system that linked different parts of the world - a 'world system', to use Wallerstein's (1974) term - on the basis of an international division of labour, with some parts of the world benefiting more than others.

The key elements of discontinuity are:

- The universalization of this particular mode of economic organization, based on the claim that – to borrow the Thatcherite slogan – 'there is no alternative';[5]
- The post-Cold War decoupling of economic interests and military means, now that the 'battle for the world economy' has been won by capitalism.[6]

'Globalization' is thus a combination of old and new. What makes the new new is the comprehensive spread of the old, such that the existing capitalist world-system is now able to assert an encompassing universalism[7] that supposedly includes all parts of the world and everyone in it. Jeffrey Sachs (2000) calls this 'a capitalist revolution' whereby 'at the end of the 20th century, the market economy, the capitalist system, became the only model for the vast majority of the world'.[8] Significantly, this capitalist victory over the centrally planned economies of Communist countries was won in the marketplace and not on the battlefield.

Vietnam provides a telling example. In 1975, American troops were defeated and chased out of Vietnam by the Communists, after more than 90,000 American soldiers had died there.[9] However, after this military victory, the Communist government of Vietnam faced an economic crisis, marked by massive unemployment, food shortage, high foreign debt, an inefficient banking and finance system, lack of capital, and dependency on Soviet aid. When Soviet aid started drying up in the 1980s, the Vietnamese government introduced a new policy called *doi moi*, 'aimed at improving the standard of living of the people through relaxing macro-economic policy . . . reducing . . . government intervention in the market [and attracting] foreign direct investment (FDI)' (Ha Huong 1999, p. 2).

It is this non-military mode of capitalist penetration, coupled with its comprehensive spread, that has led to what Wang (2002, p. 226) calls the 'post-Cold War . . . note of triumphalism' marking 'a new mission to civilize the world'.   This 'note of triumphalism' was sounded by Lawrence Summers in 1996, when he was Deputy Secretary of the US Treasury: '[Our] ideology, capitalism, is in ascendance everywhere.'[10]   Such triumphalism reached an even more extreme expression with Fukuyama's assertion, first expressed in 1989, that with the end of the Cold War, history has ended:

> The triumph of the West, of the Western idea, is evident . . . in the total exhaustion of viable systematic alternatives to Western liberalism . . .   What we may be witnessing is not just the end of the Cold War, or the passing of a particular period of post-war history, but the *end of history* [emphasis added] as such: that is, the end point of mankind's ideological evolution and the universalization of Western liberal democracy as the final form of human government . . .   There are powerful reasons for believing that it is the ideal that will govern the material world in the long run.[11]

It is the non-military spread of capitalism all over the world that has enabled it to attain global hegemony in Antonio Gramsci's sense of the word, meaning 'rule by active consent'.[12]   Domination is thus achieved by claiming to include within its scope the views and concerns of those who are dominated.   As a result, not only is capitalism now found everywhere, but everyone is supposed to 'consent' to it, because it is supposed to benefit everyone.   There is hence a deeper sense of 'globalization' than just geographical spread.   As mentioned above, there is also the assertion of universalistic applicability for everyone, including all classes of society. This, in turn, implies a 'new capitalism' which claims to include and integrate all those on whom it impacts (such as developing countries, workers, women, the poor, indigenous communities, the elderly and so on).

However, this claim of universalistic inclusivity is hotly disputed.   An international anti-globalist movement has arisen almost simultaneously with the phenomenon of 'globalization'.   While a wide range of causes seems to be included in this movement – anti-capitalism, labour rights, opposition to multinationals, anti-Americanization, environmentalism, Third World debt, child labour and so on – these are nevertheless unified by a common theme: namely, opposition to 'neoliberalism' or what George Soros (1998) has called 'market fundamentalism'.

At the crux of 'globalization' is the prioritization given to market-led development over state-led development.   Indeed, what is now 'globalized' is a particular mode of economic organization, where the free market – not the state – is entrusted with the allocation of scarce resources. As noted by Clare Short (Britain's Secretary of State for International Development at the time), 'The move to globalization will be akin to the move from feudalism to capitalism . . . Globalization . . . is transforming what the nation-state can do' (*Suns Bulletin*, 25 March 1997). Indeed, governments have been increasingly seen by anti-globalists as facilitators of world trade, with greater accountability to transnational corporations than to their own citizens.

The anti-globalist movement has organized protests at the meetings of the WTO, the International Monetary Fund (IMF) and the World Bank, as well as other meetings of national leaders and businesses, such as the Summit of the Americas in Quebec and the World Economic Forum in Davos. The anti-globalist movement has managed, in several cases, to block or slow down the process of 'globalization'. For example, non-governmental organizations from different regions and countries worked together successfully to stop the Organisation for Economic Co-operation and Development (OECD)[13] from adopting a proposed 'Multilateral Agreement on Investment' (MAI), which would have led to the further integration of national economies in the global financial market, with a corresponding weakening of national sovereignty in favour of multinational investors. This international lobbying effort by the anti-globalist NGOs against the proposed MAI has been sustained from 1997 up to the present.[14]

Such successes have led proponents of 'globalization' – such as Mike Moore (February 2002), then Director-General of the WTO – to acknowledge the 'internet-linked NGOs' ability to influence the debate on the future direction of global trade and corporate responsibility'. This realization of the power of the anti-globalist movement has led Moore to 'reach out to civil society' in an integrative attempt to bring everyone under the umbrella of 'globalization'.

SEPTEMBER 11 AND ITS MILITARIZED AFTERMATH

September 11 demonstrated with tragic force that apart from the civil disobedience of anti-globalist protestors, there are others who are willing to die and kill to try and stop American-dominated 'globalization'. The irony of the situation is that – to use the words of Eisuke Sakakibara, former Japanese Finance Vice-Minister – 'those terrorists were acting globally [by] taking advantage of free flows of capital, free flows of people, and so on'.[15] Terrorism thus uses the tools and conditions given by globalization. Its impact is widespread as a result of the interlinkages of globalization. Inter-governmental attempts to stop terrorism are also dependent on the cooperative relations built up through globalization.

But the terrorist attacks and the attempts to stop terrorism, as well as armed conflicts between terrorists and anti-terrorists, are all inimical to globalization.   Risks in the entire global marketplace have multiplied, greatly increasing the costs of doing business and impacting with particular force on Asian economies.   The terrorist attacks exacerbated the decline of an already slowing US economy, resulting in falling consumer demand and increased unemployment, thereby accentuating already existing overcapacity. US fears of more terrorist attacks have led to higher insurance premiums (increasing as much as 60 per cent)[16] and increasing corporate expenditure on non-productive areas, especially security.   The likely outcome is a prolonged recession.   Since US GDP makes up almost one-third of the world's gross global output, the post-September 11 downturn of the US economy has brought about the following impact on Asia:

> Asian countries are reeling from a large drop in demand for consumer products and other related equipment.   Both Asian and European nations are experiencing rising unemployment rates.   Investors are virtually non-existent, hotels have empty rooms and airlines are cutting back as much as 20 percent.   Asian countries already in recession are Japan, Taiwan, and Singapore, with Hong Kong and Malaysia close behind.   Until the US, the European Union and Japan make significant recoveries, East Asia will not see any chance of improvement (Virgo 2001, p. 356).

Furthermore, the terrorism of September 11 has drawn attention to the failures and omissions of 'globalization', provoking questions even among mainstream proponents of 'globalization' who have been asserting its universalistic applicability.   The uneven impact of 'globalization' has been laid bare.   For example, three months after September 11, the World Bank's Chief Economist, Nicholas Stern, admitted: 'Globalization often has been a very powerful force for poverty reduction, but too many countries and people have been left out' (*BBC News*, 5 December 2001).[17]   The significance of this admission must be seen in relation to the hitherto consistent claim of the World Bank that 'globalization' universalistically eradicates poverty.[18]

In other words, the current mode of 'globalization' is now recognized as inadequate.   History is now perceived as not having 'ended'.   The future is not to be merely a serial replication of capitalist bliss.   At the World Economic Forum's East Asia Economic Summit 2001, the panel of invited experts agreed on the need to 'to tackle the root causes of terrorism and enduring poverty in developing countries' by discussing 'how to establish a *new development paradigm* [emphasis added] based on fair trade and equitable partnerships between developing countries and developed ones'.[19] This implies the current existence of unfair trade and unequal relationships between developing and developed countries.

What has also been laid bare is the uneven domination of the 'globalizers'. The claims of a neutral and universalistic 'globalization' have become less than plausible in a situation where US power has become naked. In an interview with *The Washington Post* (10 April 2002), the former CIA Director, Office of Regional and Political Analysis, William Christison, identified two global issues as root causes for terrorism: 'the US drive to spread its own hegemony and its own version of unregulated, free market globalization worldwide', and 'the very kind of war the US now wages'.

The US military response to September 11 – first in Afghanistan, in the Philippines and then in Iraq – has effectively ended the non-military spread of 'globalization'. Instead, economic interests and military means have now been visibly recoupled.

However, it is questionable whether there was any real decoupling in the first place. Friedman (2000, p. 373) pointed out the ineluctable linkage some time ago:

> The hidden hand of the market will never work without a hidden fist. McDonald's cannot flourish without McDonnell Douglas . . . And the hidden fist that keeps the world safe for Silicon Valley's technologies to flourish is called the U.S. Army, Air Force, Navy and Marine Corps.

Jayasuriya (2002, p. 131) argues that 'the motif of security and its associated antipolitical rationality which underpin the emerging transnational and domestic orders *predate* the WTC attacks' [emphasis added]. He traces this to the transformation of the state by 'globalization' into a law-and-order state to control and manage the free flows of capital, information, labour, people, goods, drugs, and so on (Jayasuriya 2002, pp. 140-141). However, I must point out that this process of 'securitization' does not occur evenly in all parts of the world. Countries that benefit more from 'globalization' have more at stake.

More than five decades ago, George Kennan, head of the US State Department policy planning staff, had written in a confidential government document:

> We have about 50% of the world's wealth, but only 6.3% of its population . . . In this situation we cannot fail to be the object of envy and resentment. Our real task in the coming period is to devise a pattern of relationships which will permit us to maintain this position of disparity . . . To do so, we will have to dispense with all sentimentality and day-dreaming; and our attention will have to be concentrated everywhere on our immediate national objectives. We should cease to talk about vague and . . . unreal objectives such as human rights, the raising of the [sic] living standards, and democratization. The day is not far off when we

are going to have to deal in straight power concepts. The less we are then hampered by idealistic slogans, the better.[20]

This world view was re-articulated in 1996 by the US Space Command in its *Vision 2020*, which stated that the 'globalization of the world economy will continue, with a widening between "haves" and "have-nots"'. So the mission of the US Space Command is: 'dominating the space dimension of military operations to protect US interests and investment'. The report explicitly compares the US effort to control space and the Earth below to how centuries ago, 'nations built navies to protect and enhance their commercial interests', thereby enabling the European colonial empires to rule the waves and thus the world.

In the wake of September 11, a conflict between two different agendas has emerged:

- Agenda 1: to seek greater fairness and equality, either by reforming 'globalization' or by creating a 'new development paradigm';
- Agenda 2: to retain the privileges of the 'haves' by keeping the 'have-nots' in line, by military means if necessary.

This conflict is being played out within and between countries. For example, in the US itself, those who have adopted Agenda 1 are exploring the 'root causes' of terrorism, including in their discussion such issues as the Israel-Palestine conflict, poverty and political marginalization. Those who have adopted Agenda 2, on the other hand, dispute the relevance of delving into 'root causes', preferring instead to use the non-negotiable discourse of 'evil' that has to be either eradicated or contained. For example, writing in *The Washington Post,* Krauthammer (2001, p. A37) opines: 'At a time like this, those who search for shades of evil, for root causes, for extenuations are . . . "too philosophical for decent company"'.[21]

In a seeming repeat of history, the articulation of Agenda 2 is coated with 'idealistic slogans', such as the claim that the US-led war against Iraq will bring democracy to that country.[22] Whether this actually happens, this claim marks a fundamental change in the discourse on 'globalization' – from non-militaristic voluntaristic acceptance to military coercion.

Furthermore, the issue of taking sides has come back, though the opposing sides are not the same as during the Cold War. Writing in the *International Herald Tribune*, Friedman (2003, p. 8) has proposed the following analysis of the current state of the world:

World War II gave birth to the United Nations, NATO, the IMF and the bipolar U.S.-Soviet power structure, which proved to be quite stable until the end of the Cold War. Now, Sept. 11 has set off World War III, and it, too, is defining a new international order.   The new world system is also bipolar, but instead of being divided between East and West it is divided between the World of Order and the World of Disorder.   The World of Order is built on four pillars: the United States, European Union-Russia, India and China, along with all the smaller powers around them.   The World of Disorder comprises failed states (such as Liberia), rogue states (Iraq and North Korea), messy states – states that are too big to fail but too messy to work (Pakistan, Columbia, Indonesia, many Arab and African states) – and finally the terrorist and mafia networks that feed off the World of Disorder.[23]

Such a polarizing world view is plausible only in the context of what Jayasuriya (2002, p. 131) has described as the 'new post-liberal politics of fear', where the true bipolarity is between security (that is zones of safety) and fear (that is zones of danger).   But is it still possible to have an integrated global marketplace if sizeable parts of the world are deemed too dangerous for certain countries to have anything to do with (except possibly via long-range missiles and aerial bombs)?

The bifurcation of the world into zones of safety and zones of danger (or, to use Friedman's terms, the World of Order and the World of Disorder) indicates a fragmentation of the global marketplace, but not along Cold War lines of market-driven versus centrally planned economies.   Instead, new alignments and divisions have emerged out of an ideological calculus of the relative safety or danger of regions, nations, ethnicities and religions.   Mere economic reckoning of profit and loss no longer suffices.   A logic of meta-economics has emerged: death makes profit impossible, while staying alive is profit enough.

Keohane and Nye (2001, p. 229) characterized 'globalization' as 'a state of the world involving networks of interdependence at multicontinental distances, linked through *flows of capital and goods, information and ideas, people and force*, as well as environmentally and biologically relevant substances' [emphasis added].   But these flows are now impeded by security concerns.

For example, under governmental pressure, thirty-two science journals in the US and UK have agreed to censor from publication data of potential use to terrorists (Bhattacharya 2003).   This action is tantamount to stopping the free flow of scientific information (*Public Library of Science Statement on Censorship,* 15 February 2003).   Such a move has completely shifted the debate about intellectual property.   In the context of the 'old globalization' focused on trade liberalization, developed countries (such as the US) were the ones previously advocating the free flow of information, while developing countries (such as India) were advocating the protection of their indigenous intellectual property.   The 'new globalization' is shaped, however, more by security concerns than by economic interests.

ASIA AND THE PACIFIC IN THE NEW GLOBAL ORDER-VS-DISORDER

Immediately after the al-Qaeda attack of 11 September 2001 in New York, the economies of Asia and the Pacific went into a steep decline. Stock markets fell to levels not seen for several years, regional airlines were severely affected and US-bound shipments from Korea, Taiwan, Singapore and Malaysia diminished by 20 per cent to 40 per cent (compared with the same period in the previous year) due to weak American demand (*The Economist*, 15 September 2001, p. 67; *Businessweek*, 8 October 2001, p. 54).

The regional economy worsened even more after the Bali bombing on 12 October 2002, when bombs set off in a tourist area of Bali killed 185 people from eighteen countries.[24]   Following this event, the US government issued a travel advisory to its citizens, advising them not to travel to Southeast Asia. The Australian government issued similar travel advice to its citizens, highlighting Indonesia as unsafe but also warning that Australians face security risks in six other Southeast Asian countries: Brunei, Cambodia, Laos, Malaysia, the Philippines and Singapore.   The governments of Britain, Canada and New Zealand gave similar advice to their respective citizens.

The Asia and Pacific region has thus been directly implicated in the global polarization of safe zones versus dangerous zones, with divisions emerging within the region.   It would seem that Australia and New Zealand perceive themselves as safe zones, while the countries of Southeast Asia are seen as dangerous zones.   The seriousness of this situation has led ASEAN leaders to criticize Western governments for 'their double standards in making travel advisories, issuing them when terrorist attacks hit developing countries, but not when they hit developed nations' (*Asia Times,* 15 November 2002):

> 'We call on the international community to avoid indiscriminately advising their citizens to refrain from visiting or otherwise dealing with our countries, in the absence of established evidence to substantiate rumours of possible terrorist attacks,' the leaders said in their statement.

The *International Herald Tribune* (12 November 2002) reported a conflict between the US Department of State and American ambassadors posted in Malaysia, Singapore and Thailand, over the issuance of advisories against these three countries, because in the ambassadors' opinion there was little risk of terrorism in these countries.   However, the State Department overruled these ambassadors and blacked out Southeast Asia as a whole.

Indeed, there is a clear difference in the responses of governments to al-Qaeda's attack in New York on September 11, 2001 and the attack in Bali on October 12, 2002.   This difference has been noted by certain European ambassadors to Southeast Asia, who have been reported to say:

> There are [al-Qaeda] cells in the United States, there are cells in Europe, and there are cells in Southeast Asia. Why then . . . was the travel warning only for the Third World nations of Southeast Asia? After the attacks on the World Trade Center and Pentagon, no European government advised its citizens not to travel to the United States (*International Herald Tribune*, 12 November 2002).

The difference is that while the Americans were treated sympathetically as victims of the 9/11 attack, in the case of the Bali bombing, as the Indonesian Minister for Culture and Tourism pointed out, the travel advisories implied that Indonesia as a whole was involved in terrorism (*Bali News*, 19 October 2002).

Revealingly, when the Australian Foreign Minister announced the government's travel advice to Australians to leave Indonesia, he said: 'The information we have relates more broadly to Westerners', not just Australians (*The Guardian*, 17 October 2002). This identification of Australians with 'Westerners' highlights an ethnicized bifurcation of the world, with the salient ethnic categories based on such criteria as religious identity, citizenship and physical appearance.

The zones of safety and danger are thus not universal but relative to specific ethnic categories. A complementary distribution of who is safe where seems to have emerged. There is, furthermore, a gender dimension in this process of categorization. Muslim men are now at risk of being barred from entry into the US, or else either detained or deported if they are there already.[25]

Twenty-five countries have been identified by the US State Department as 'terrorist-risk' countries.[26] Since December 2002, all men from these countries who are present in the US have had to register themselves at US immigration offices. The US government's fear of Muslim men extended to the Deputy Prime Minister of Malaysia, Abdullah Ahmad Badawi, who was made to take off his shoes and belt to be checked for hidden weapons when he entered the US, on a diplomatic passport, to address the United Nations general assembly in September 2002. This led the Malaysian Prime Minister, Mahathir Mohamad, to protest about the US labelling of all Muslims as potential terrorists (*BBC News*, 2 October 2002).

It is questionable whether this attempt by the US government to divide the world into safety and danger is really effective. Are Americans really safer in the US than in Southeast Asia? As American preparations for an attack on Iraq escalate, so too have their fears of impending terrorist attacks in the US. The US government has already twice placed the country on the second-highest level of security alert: 'Code Orange'.[27] The British government has already announced that Britain is almost certain to be the target of terrorist attacks (see, for example, *BBC News*, 14 February 2003).[28]

This bifurcation of the world into safe and unsafe has economic implications, regardless of whether or not it protects Western citizens effectively.   As shown above, the term 'globalization' was first used in the context of transnational capital flows.   But would one want to put money where one dares not even go?   Would one want to trade with people one fears? In other words, a process of market fragmentation is happening, with ethnicized markets emerging for ethnicized capital and products.

The categorization of Southeast Asia as dangerous has severely reduced the flow of foreign direct investments (FDI) to the region and has adversely affected the tourism industry, including the regional airlines and hotels. This has reversed incipient trends towards economic recovery after the Asian financial crisis of 1997.

For example, in 2001, US investors had occupied a lead position in Malaysia's FDI with US$900 million, followed by Japan, China and Singapore.   But after the al-Qaeda attack of September 11, Malaysia fell out of the top 25 countries for foreign direct investment that are tracked by the *FDI Confidence Index* of the Global Business Policy Council.   Among other reasons cited, the *FDI Confidence Index* (September 2002) specifically mentioned 'fears of terrorism' as a cause for the decline in Malaysia's 'investment attractiveness'.   As noted by the *Asia Times* (15 October 2002),

> If the perceptions of US security and immigration officials rub off on US investors interested in Southeast Asia, then the investment prospects for countries such as Malaysia are likely to look less than rosy.

I cite Malaysia in particular because, without any evidence whatsoever, allegations have been raised by a UN Security Council report that the ruling party is linked to al-Qaeda.   This has led the Malaysian government to lodge an official protest with the UN (*BBC News*, 18 October 2002).

This tarring of Malaysia as 'terrorist' has spurred Malaysian Muslims to boycott US and Western products, including Coca-Cola (*The Muslim News*, 12 December 2002).   Instead, like Muslims elsewhere, who are also boycotting Coca-Cola, they have started to import and drink Zam Zam Cola, made in Iran (*Newsmax Wires,* 14 October 2002).[29]   Religious identity has thus become a dimension of products, in much the same way as political ideology used to be during the Cold War.

Similarly, where tourism is concerned, as noted by the Malaysian Prime Minister, Mahathir Mohamed,

> As a result of the WTC (World Trade Center) attacks, Muslims are finding life in

Western countries and travelling there very difficult.   We don't have to expose
ourselves to this difficulty.   There are countries, Muslim and non-Muslim, where
there is no discrimination against us (*Middle East Times,* 12 October 2001).

As a result of Southeast Asia being categorized as 'terrorist' by the US and
other Western countries, intra-regional tourism has increased significantly.
An ASEAN pact to boost intra-regional tourism has even been proposed
(*Philippine Daily Inquirer,* 3 November 2002).

In this more and more fragmented market, China is being seen
increasingly by the US and Western countries as a safe haven.   Capital
flows are thus following the new fault-lines.   In addition to its cheap labour,
China is now drawing record levels of additional FDI because the country as
a whole has not been linked with al-Qaeda:[30]

Utilised foreign direct investment into China during the first nine months of 2002
totalled US$39.6bn, 22.5 percent higher than in the same period of last year,
according to [the] Ministry of Foreign Trade and Economic Cooperation figures
quoted by the *People's Daily* (*China Economic Review,* November 2002).

THE POTENTIAL IMPACT OF AN 'IRAQ WAR' ON 'GLOBALIZATION'

For more than a year, since February 2002, the US government has been
threatening to launch a pre-emptive war against Iraq, on the grounds that the
latter is alleged to possess weapons of mass destruction that may supposedly
pose a threat to the US.   As noted by US Senator Robert Byrd, speaking on
the Senate Floor (12 February 2003):

The doctrine of pre-emption – the idea that the United States or any other nation
can legitimately attack a nation that is not imminently threatening but may be
threatening in the future – is a radical new twist on the traditional idea of
self-defence.   It appears to be in contravention of international law and the UN
Charter.   And it is being tested at a time of world-wide terrorism, making many
countries around the globe wonder if they will soon be on our – or some other
nation's – hit list.[31]

This doctrine of pre-emption has already been adopted by the Australian
Prime Minister, John Howard, who has declared that he would be prepared to
launch a pre-emptive strike against terrorists in another country if he had
evidence that they were about to attack Australia (*Australian Broadcasting
Corporation,* 2 December 2002).   While this announcement aroused great
anger in Asian countries, Howard received the explicit backing of the US
President, George W. Bush, who said that 'the Howard position reflects US

policy' (*Australian Broadcasting Corporation*, 3 December 2002).
    As Senator Robert Byrd (2003) pointedly asked:

> What could be more destabilizing and unwise than this type of uncertainty,
> particularly in a world where globalism has tied the vital economic and security
> interests of many nations so closely together?

Is such destabilization merely a short-term disruption? Will the world
quickly and seamlessly revert to a 'globalized' normalcy?   In the wake of
the September 11 attack and even after the Bali bombing of 12 October 2002,
the general opinion was that such acts of random violence merely slowed
down the process of 'globalization' but did not lead to its reversal.[32]   But in
this moment of lull before the increasingly probable maelstrom of an 'Iraq
War', such complacency has become questionable.
    The eventual outcome may even be a process of economic
'de-globalization', as it becomes increasingly difficult to carry out business
as usual.   These uncertainties are hitting Asia with particular impact:

> As markets try to estimate the economic implications of war in Iraq, few regions
> have more to lose than Asia . . .   Asia is heavily dependent on oil imports, leaving
> its economies uniquely vulnerable to surging energy costs.   Its nations also rely
> on exports more than most industrialized countries, leaving Asians susceptible to
> weaker global growth . . .   The region imports between two and five times more
> oil than the world's three biggest economies, according to a Goldman Sachs
> report . . .   Southeast Asia's over-reliance on exports for growth is a key
> vulnerability. . .   Growth will not go very far without help from the United States,
> Europe and Japan.   Even if China's booming economy picks up some of the slack,
> it, too, depends more and more on selling goods overseas (*International Herald
> Tribune*, 25 February 2003).

Anxieties about the Iraq War and its potential disruption of oil supplies
from the Middle East have led China to stockpile crude oil, resulting in a
trade deficit for the first time in over six years, amounting to US$1.25 billion.
'"The country plans to stockpile 149 million barrels, enough to meet oil
demands for one month", said Song Chaoyi, a deputy director at the State
Department Planning Commission' (*International Herald Tribune*,
27 February 2003).   Despite China's large energy needs, it is relatively
industrialized Japan, South Korea and Taiwan that together account for
85 per cent of East Asia's oil imports.   Japan, in particular, has been
identified as 'Asia's most exposed economy to a possible U.S. war on Iraq
because of its high dependence on imported energy and exports'
(*CNN.com/business*, 11 September 2002).
    The US economy, in the meantime, is in the doldrums with capital
spending on technology at a standstill, 1.6 million jobs lost in the past two

years and consumer confidence at a nine-year low (*International Herald Tribune*, 25 February 2003).   Such vulnerabilities reveal the extent to which Asian economies are dependent on other regions – on the Middle East and Africa for oil imports and on the US, EU and Japan for export markets, as well as foreign direct investments.   At a deeper level, this has exposed the fragility of 'globalization' as a universalistic model of economic organization. The strategy of export-oriented growth as a panacea for developing countries is doomed without capital and markets.

A contrary process is under way: rather than trade, it is now fear that is being 'globalized'.   There are worldwide fears of the political and economic fallout of a potential 'Iraq War', not only in terms of oil and markets, but also of where, when and how any retaliatory attacks might occur next.   Such fears are aggravated by the sense that there is no end of such conflicts in sight. What will mark the end of this phase of terrorism and anti-terrorism – the end of Osama bin Laden?   The end of Saddam Hussein?   The end of al-Qaeda? The end of Palestine?   The end of Islamism?   What event is expected to end all potential acts of random violence against the US-dominated world order?

In this regard, we do well to remember how the Cold War ended.   It ended not with a bang, but with a whimper. Communism imploded.   It was not defeated on the battlefield.   The 'globalization' of capitalism came about by default, when Communism failed as a sustainable mode of economic organization.

Can capitalism score such a victory against the jihadist vision – not of material wealth, but salvation?   Can capitalism assuage the alienation and anomie it has globalized?[33]   The discourse of alienation and anomie is explicitly used by Muslim commentators to explain the emergence of jihadist terrorism.[34]

Ostry (2001, p. 12) attributes the emergence of current alienation and anomie to 'the disjuncture between the goals of free trade – rising living standards for all – and its distributional impact especially between rich and poor'.   In other words, it is the gap between the claims and the reality of 'globalization' that has engendered the opposition to it.   Only by closing this gap can there be a realistic hope of ending the current cycle of global violence.

Unfortunately, at this point in time, the world has become more unequal than ever before.   As shown in a recent World Bank study by Milanovic (2002, pp. 51-52),

World inequality has increased . . . from a Gini of 62.5 in 1988 to 66.0 in 1993[35] . . .   This is a very fast increase, faster than the increase experienced by the US and the UK in the decade of the 1980s . . .   The bottom 5 per cent of the world grew poorer, as their real incomes decreased by 1/4, while the richest quintile grew richer.   It gained 12 percent in real terms, that is its income grew more than twice as much as mean world income (5.7 per cent) . . .   The richest 1 per cent of people in the world receive as much as the bottom 57 per cent . . . The top ten per cent of the US population has an aggregate income equal to [the] income of the poorest 43 per cent of people in the world, or differently put, total income of the richest 25 million Americans is equal to total income of almost 2 billion people.   The ratio between average income of the world top 5 per cent and world bottom 5 per cent increased from 78 to 1 in 1988, to 114 to 1 in 1993.

The Asian and Pacific region has about 3.7 billion people, more than half the world's population.[36]   What proportion of the world's income do they have?   Will 'globalization' increase their share, given that world inequality has worsened in the context of 'globalization'?   These and other such questions require urgent and effective answers at this time of deepening global chaos.

REFERENCES

America's Wars (2001), Washington, D.C.: Department of Veterans' Affairs, at <http://www.va.gov/pressrel/amwars01.htm>.
American Banker (7 February 1986).
Asia after 11 September (2001), Davos: World Economic Forum, East Asia Economic Summit 2001, <http://www.weforum.org/site/knowledgenavigator.nsf/Content/Asia%20After%2011%20September>.
Asia Times (15 October 2002; 15 November 2002).
Australian Broadcasting Corporation (2 December 2002; 3 December 2002).
Bali News (19 October 2002).
BBC News (5 December 2001; 2 October 2002; 18 October 2002; 14 February 2003).
Bhattacharya, Shaoni (2003), 'Bioterrorist Fears Prompt Journal Paper Censorship', *New Scientist Online News,* 17 February 2003, <http://www.newscientist.com>.
Business Week Online (27 September 2001).
Business Week (8 October 2001).
Byrd, Robert (12 February 2003), 'Senate Remarks: We Stand Passively Mute', speech on the Senate floor, <http://byrd.senate.gov/byrd_newsroom/byrd_news_feb/news_2003_february/news_2003_february_9.html>.
Carroll, Mike (1986), 'Investment Banking Tasks Reorganized at First Boston Inc.', *American Banker*, 7 February 1986, p. 2.
Case study: Bosnia-Herzegovina, <http://www.gendercide.org/case_bosnia.html>.
CBSnews.com (24 September 2002), <http://www.cbsnews.com/stories/2002/09/24/attack/main 523095.shtml>.
China Economic Review (November 2002), <http://www.chinaeconomicreview.com/htm/n_20021102.487869.htm>.
Chomsky, Noam (19 March 1985), 'American Foreign Policy'.   Edited transcript of a talk given at Harvard University, <http://monkeyfist.com:8080/Chomsky Archive/talks/history_html>.
Choudhury, Masudul Alam (1 October 2001), 'Attack in the USA: Lessons to Learn',

Albalagh, <http://www.albalagh.net/current_affairs/attack_lessons.shtml>.

CNN.com/business (11 September 2002).

Deininger and Squire Data Set: A New Data Set Measuring Income Inequality (no date), Washington, D.C.: World Bank, Economic Growth Research, <http://www.worldbank.org/research/growth/dddeisqu.htm>.

Duplessis, Robert (1997), *Transitions to Capitalism in Early Modern Europe*, Cambridge: Cambridge University Press.

Durkheim, Emile (1966), *Suicide: A Study in Sociology* (trans. John A. Spaulding and George Simpson, ed. with introduction by George Simpson), New York: Free Press [originally published in French in 1897].

Durkheim, Emile (1984), *The Division of Labour*, (trans. W.D. Halls, with introduction by Lewis Coser), Basingstoke: Macmillan [originally published in French in 1893].

The Economist (15 September 2001).

FDI Confidence Index (September 2002), Alexandria, USA: Global Business Policy Council, A.T. Kearney, Inc., <http://www.atkearney.com/pdf/eng/FDI_Confidence_Sept2002_S.pdf>.

Fitzpatrick, Peter (2000), 'Globalization and the Humanity of Rights', *Law, Social Justice and Global Development (LGD)*, (1), <http://elj.warwick.ac.uk/global/issue/2000-1/fitzpatrick.html>.

Friedman, Thomas (2000), *The Lexus and the Olive Tree*, New York: Farrar, Straus and Giroux.

Friedman, Thomas (2003), 'Order vs Disorder', *International Herald Tribune*, 17 February 2003, p. 8.

Fukuyama, Francis (1989), 'The End of History?', *The National Interest*, 1989, Summer, <http://www.wku.edu/~sullib/history.htm>.

Fukuyama, Francis (1992), *The End of History and the Last Man*, New York: Free Press; Toronto: Maxwell Macmillan Canada.

Globalization, Growth and Poverty: Building an Inclusive World Economy (2001), Washington, D.C.: World Bank.

Gramsci, Antonio (1994), *Letters from Prison* (trans. Ray Rosenthal, ed. Frank Rosengarten), New York: Columbia University Press [originally published in Italian in 1947].

The Guardian (17 October 2002), <http://politics.guardian.co.uk/foreignaffairs/story/0,11538,813904,00.html>.

Ha Huong (1999), 'Vietnam: Economic Transition in the Perspectives of Public Policy in the Post Economic Crisis', paper presented at the *International conference on the challenges of globalization*, 21-22 October, Bangkok, Thammasat University, <http://econ.tu.ac.th/iccg/papers/hahuong-.doc>.

Halimi, Serge (2002), 'There is an Alternative: How Neo-liberalism Took Over the World', *Le Monde diplomatique*, January 2002, <http://mondediplo.com/2002/01/11alternative>.

Hussain, Tariq and Moin Uddin Ahmed (no date), 'The Miracle of Zam Zam Water', <http://www.themodernreligion.com/science/zamzam.html>.

International Herald Tribune (12 November 2002; 17 February 2003; 25 February 2003; 27 February 2003).

Jayasuriya, Kanishka (2002), 'September 11, Security and the New Postliberal Politics of Fear', in Eric Hershberg and Kevin W. Moore (eds), *Critical Views of*

September 11: Analyses from Around the World, New York: The New Press.
Joint Statement of Attorney General John Ashcroft and Secretary of Homeland Security Tom Ridge, <http://www.whitehouse.gov/news/releases/2003/02/20030227-3.html>.
Keohane, Robert O. and Joseph S. Nye (2001), *Power and Interdependence*, 3rd edn, New York: Addison Wesley Longman.
Krauthammer, Charles (2001), 'Voices of Moral Obtuseness', *The Washington Post*, 21 September 2001, p. A37.
Laxer, Gordon (2000), 'Parkland Researchers Win Major SSHRC Funding for Globalism Project', *Parkland Post* 4 (1), Winter, <http://www.ualberta.ca/~parkland/Post/Vol4_No1/laxer-globalism.html>.
Laxer, Gordon (2002), 'Challenging Corporate Rule and the American Empire: Protest to Make a Better World', presentation to the *Protest and Power* Conference, Calgary Institute for the Humanities, University of Calgary, 14 June 2002, <http://www.ualberta.ca/~parkland/Speeches/LaxerSpeechJune2002.html>.
Marx, Karl (1964), *Karl Marx: Early Writings*, trans. and ed. T.B. Bottomore, New York: McGraw-Hill.
Middle East Times (12 October 2001), <http://www.metimes.com/2K1/issue2001-41/reg/malaysias_premier_tells.htm>.
Milanovic, Branko (2002), 'True World Income Distribution, 1988 and 1993: First Calculation Based on Household Surveys Alone', *The Economic Journal* 112 (January), pp. 51-92, <http://econ.worldbank.org/files/978_wps2244.pdf>.
Moore, Mike (February 2002), 'Globalization: the Impact of the Doha Development Agenda on the Free Market Process', speech by the Director-General of the WTO to the US Chamber of Commerce, Florida, <http://www.wto.org/english/news_e/spmm_e/spmm77_e.htm>.
Mourning in Bali, <http://www.indo.com/bali121002/>.
The Muslim News (12 December 2002).
Newsmax Wires (14 October 2002), <http://www.newsmax.com/archives/articles/2002/10/13/130635.shtml>.
Ostry, Sylvia (25 October 2001), 'Why is Globalization a Bad Word?' *Alcoa-Intalco Works Distinguished Lecture*, Bellingham, Washington Western University.
Philippine Daily Inquirer (3 November 2002), <http://www.inq7.net/wnw/2002/nov/03/wnw_5-1.htm>.
Population and Development Indicators for Asia and the Pacific (1999), Bangkok: Economic and Social Commission for the Pacific, <http://www.unescap.org/pop/data_sheet/1999_tab1.htm>.
Public Library of Science Statement on Censorship (15 February 2003) <http://www.publiclibraryofscience.org/announce_censorship.htm>.
Sachs, Jeffrey (2000), Interview for the television programme *Commanding Heights: The Battle for the World Economy*, 15 June 2002; transcript at <http://www.pbs.org/wgbh/commandingheights/lo/story/index.html>.
Soros, George (1998), *The Crisis of Global Capitalism*, New York: Public Affairs.
Starrs, Roy (2002), 'Introduction', in Roy Starrs (ed.), *Nations under Seige: Globalization and Nationalism in Asia*, New York and Basingstoke: Palgrave.
*SunsBulletin (*25 March 1997), 3950, Geneva: Third World Network.
Terrorism: Q & A (2003), New York and Washington, D.C.: Council of Foreign Relations, in cooperation with the Markle Foundation.

Time magazine, Asia edition (23 September 2002), <http://www.time.com/time/asia/
magazine/article/0,13673,501020923-351276,00.html>.

US Space Command (1996), *Vision 2020,* Washington, D.C.: Pentagon.

Virgo, John M. (2001), 'Economic Impact of the Terrorist Attacks of September 11,
2001', *The Atlantic Economic Journal,* December 2001, 29(4), 353-357,
<http://www.iaes.org/journal/aej/dec_01/Virgo_pdf.pdf>.

Wallerstein, Immanuel (1974), *Capitalist Agriculture and the Origins of the European
World-System in the Sixteenth Century,* San Diego, California: Academic Press.

Wang, Gungwu (2002), 'State and Faith: Secular Values in Asia and the West', in
Eric Hershberg and Kevin W. Moore (eds), *Critical Views of September 11:
Analyses from Around the World,* New York: The New Press.

The Washington Post (31 May 2002; 10 April 2002).

Yergin, Daniel and Joseph Stanislaw (2002), *The Commanding Heights: The Battle
for the World Economy,* revised and updated edition, New York: Simon &
Schuster.   Also see <http://www.pbs.org/wgbh/commandingheights/lo/index.
html>.

NOTES

1   This chapter was completed on 3 March 2003.   I am grateful for the assistance given to me
    by Lin Chew and Amy Sim in the conceptualization and research done for this chapter.

2   The prelude to war on Iraq commenced on 29 January 2002 when US President George W.
    Bush named Iraq, Iran and North Korea as forming an 'axis of evil' in his State of the Union
    Address.

3   I have adapted these terms from the work of Immanuel Wallerstein (1974).

4   The paragraph in which the word first appears is in an article by Carroll (1986, p. 2):
    'Traditional underwriting activity that was the root of corporate finance has been turned on its
    head as deal-making became less relationship-oriented and far more transactional in nature.
    This change went hand-in-hand with the increasing globalization of capital raising and the
    growing sophistication of borrowers'.

5   'There is no alternative' is a sentence that was frequently used by Margaret Thatcher to defend
    the necessity of her neoliberal ideology; this became known by its acronym, TINA (Halimi
    2002).

6   The phrase 'battle for the world economy' is borrowed from Yergin and Stanislaw (2002).

7   See Fitzpatrick (2000).

8   Interview for the television program *Commanding Heights: The Battle for the World
    Economy.*

9   *America's Wars* (May 2001).

10 Cited from Laxer (2002).

11 Also see Fukuyama (1992).

12 See, for example, Gramsci (1994).

13 The OECD is made up of thirty member countries, including Australia, Japan and South
    Korea from the Asia-Pacific region. <http://www.oecd.org/oecd/pages/home/displaygeneral/
    0,3380, EN- countrylist-0-nodirectorate-no-no-159-0,00.html>.

14 <http://www.cepr.net/globalization/MAI/paris1pa.html>; <http://www.sunsonline.org/trade/
    process/followup/mai/02190198.htm>;   <http://www.oneworld.net/ips2/oct98/23_46_109.
    html>; <http://lists.essential.org/mai-intl/msg00160.html>.

15 *Business Week Online* (27 September 2001).

16 *The Washington Post* (31 May 2002).

17 <http://news.bbc.co.uk/1/hi/business/1694294.stm>.

18 In the World Bank's report *Globalization, Growth and Poverty: Building an Inclusive World Economy*, published in December 2001 (after the September 11 attack), the World Bank acknowledged that 'not all countries have integrated successfully into the global economy', including some 2 billion people in these countries – particularly in sub-Saharan Africa, the Middle East and the former Soviet Union.

19 *Asia After September 11* (29 October 2001).

20 Cited from Chomsky (1985).

21 *The Washington Post,* 21 September 2001.

22 As noted by Chomsky (1985), despite Kennan's advice in 1948 that the US should eschew 'idealistic slogans' so as not to be hampered in its maintenance of world power, these slogans have been 'constantly trumpeted by scholarship, the schools, the media, and the rest of the ideological system in order to pacify the domestic population' (<http://monkeyfist.com/ChomskyArchive/misc/grandarea_html>).

23 This conceptualization of the world order is reminiscent of an earlier conceptualization of the US government in 1939-1945 called the 'Grand Area' – that is 'a region that was to be subordinated to the needs of the American economy . . . (and) strategically necessary for world control'. The geopolitical analysis at that time included within the 'Grand Area' the Western Hemisphere, the Far East, and the former British Empire, which were then in the process of being dismantled (Chomsky 1985). The difference is that whereas the 'Grand Area' is an offensive strategy, Friedman's 'World of Order' is a defensive strategy that seeks to salvage an island of order in a sea of disorder.

24 *Mourning in Bali,* <http://www.indo.com/bali121002/>.

25 This singling out of Muslim men as potential terrorists is reminiscent of gender-selective practices in Bosnia-Herzegovina, Kosovo and Chechnya, which had even worse consequences – namely, death. However, the motivating fears are similar (see, for example, 'Case study: Bosnia-Herzegovina' at <http://www.gendercide.org/case_bosnia.html>).

26 The countries identified by the US State Department as dangerous are Afghanistan, Algeria, Bahrain, Djibouti, Egypt, Eritrea, Indonesia, Iran, Iraq, Jordan, Kuwait, Lebanon, Libya, Malaysia, Morocco, Oman, Pakistan, Qatar, Saudi Arabia, Somalia, Sudan, Syria, Tunisia, the United Arab Emirates and Yemen.

27 In the five-colour range of alerts yellow, the middle of the range, means a 'significant' risk and orange means a 'high' risk of terrorist attack. The US has been on Code Yellow as a norm since March 2002 when this colour-coded warning system was devised. The security alert was raised to Code Orange in September 2002, just before the one-year anniversary of September 11. After the anniversary passed without event, the alert reverted to Code Yellow. On 7 February 2003, the alert was again raised to Code Orange, in anticipation of terrorist attacks during the period of the haj to Mecca (beginning on 9 February 2003). When nothing happened, the alert was again reduced to Code Yellow (*Joint Statement of Attorney General John Ashcroft and Secretary of Homeland Security Tom Ridge*, <CBSnews.com>, 24 September 2002).

28 <http://news.bbc.co.uk/1/hi/uk/2487843.stm>.

29 Zam Zam Cola has reached new export levels and is now doubling its annual production of 2.5 billion cans (*Newsmax Wires*, 14 October 2002). The term 'Zam Zam' refers to water from a particular spring in Mecca, which apparently supplies millions of gallons of water to pilgrims every year (Tariq Hussain and Moin Uddin Ahmed, no date). Zam Zam Cola does not claim to use the water of this spring, even though it is named after it.

30 The US has not linked China to al-Qaeda or terrorism, even though it has agreed to add China's Uighur separatists to the UN list of international 'terrorists' (*Time* magazine, Asia edition, 23 September 2002).

31 Byrd (2003).

32 See, for example, *Terrorism: Q & A* (2003).

33 Marx used the term 'alienation' to refer to the condition whereby people come to feel dominated by forces of human origin that are beyond their control – for example workers are alienated by what they produce, from the process of production, and from their community.

Durkheim used the term 'anomie' to refer to a situation of social transition, when norms become confused, unclear or non-existent and people cease to know what to expect from one another (see Marx 1964; Durkheim 1984, 1966).

34   See, for example, Choudhury (2001).

35   The Gini Coefficient ranges from 0 to 1, with 0 representing perfect equality and 1 total inequality (see, for example, the World Bank's *Deininger and Squire Data Set: a New Data Set Measuring Income Inequality*).

36   *Population and Development Indicators for Asia and the Pacific* (1999)

2. Terrorism as a Global Phenomenon: The Southeast Asian Experience

David Wright-Neville

Almost two years after the September 11 terrorist attacks in New York and Washington, the political consequences continue to reverberate around the world. Many of these consequences result from a shift in the balance of power within the Bush administration, with the attacks boosting the influence of hawkish elements around Vice President Dick Cheney, the Secretary of Defence Donald Rumsfeld, and others now known collectively by the sobriquet 'neo-cons', or 'neo-conservatives'. Under the influence of this group, the US has thumbed its nose at international opinion, dealt a savage blow against the integrity of the United Nations, launched an offensive war against the Iraqi regime of Saddam Hussein, hinted at similar actions against Syria, Iran and North Korea, and signalled that further use of military force to pursue US national interests cannot be ruled out.

However, US-led victories in Afghanistan, Iraq and other places are likely to prove pyrrhic. Military successes against the Taliban in Afghanistan and the Saddam regime in Iraq are belied by a surge of anti-Americanism that threatens to undermine long-term US interests in several critical areas of the world. Most obviously, US-led actions in Iraq, and the prospect of an extended US military occupation to deal with the civil, communal and tribal conflicts unleashed by the toppling of Saddam, risk further undermining the legitimacy of those governments in the Middle East, such as those of Saudi Arabia, Jordan and Egypt, that are perceived by their constituents as pro-American.

It is a characteristic of the contemporary world, however, that such conflicts can be compartmentalized within the nation-state. Transnational coalitions based on religion, ethnicity, gender, sexuality or other cultural markers now help to internationalize conflicts. In recent times, this phenomenon has been evinced by the way the Soviet invasion of Afghanistan in 1979 rallied tens of thousands of Muslim volunteers from around the world, and also by the role global coalitions played in forcing the South African regime to release Nelson Mandela and then dismantle its system of apartheid.

Yet anger with the United States government over its invasion of Iraq is not confined to the Middle East. It is probably true that in many instances this anger will prove transitory and will pass quickly. However, this is less likely to occur in those parts of the world where anger with the US, and the West more generally, evinces a cumulative character. Southeast Asia, especially its Muslim components, is one such region.

OMINOUS SIGNS?

Despite popular perceptions to the contrary, Southeast Asia has until recently been relatively free of the internecine hatreds that have fed the murderous rampages in places like Chechnya, Rwanda, and the former Yugoslavia. Although the region has its fair share of unrest, against a background of extraordinary cultural and ethnic diversity, Southeast Asia today is a long way from the internecine conflicts that beset the region in the immediate postcolonial decade of the 1960s. Moreover, those intra-state conflicts that have persisted over time, such as the Muslim insurgencies in the Southern Philippines and Muslim-Christian violence in Indonesia, have differed from religiously inspired conflicts in many other parts of the world in that Southeast Asian protagonists have relied much less on a civilizational rhetoric that implicates the US or other Western countries in the repression they are occasionally subjected to by their secular leaders. In other words, until recently intra-mural conflicts in Southeast Asia have not reflected the international dimension evident in similar conflicts in many other parts of the world.

However, there are signs that this is changing. Intra-mural conflicts in Southeast Asia are assuming a civilizational dimension in that a growing number of protagonists are identifying the US in particular, but the West in general, as a target of their anger. Often this reflected hostility stems from disapproval of US foreign policy per se, especially with regard to the Muslim world. But to an important degree it also reflects a belief that the US and its allies support a belligerent disregard for Islamic opposition voices by regional governments. This is especially so in the post-September 11 environment wherein a number of states have gambled (successfully) that they can move to silence their domestic critics and avoid Western censure by branding these critics as 'terrorists'. It is against the background of Western governments refusing to criticize the recent surge of repressive political repression that many Southeast Asians (Muslims and non-Muslims alike) have come to judge the US actions in Iraq as part of a general campaign against the Muslim world (Rashid 2003).

SIMILARITIES AND DIFFERENCES

At a deeper level, these developments reflect the reality that Southeast Asia is not immune from the worldwide rise of identity politics, a phenomenon that has, in the words of Nancy Fraser, reflected a shift in political attention from 'economic harms' to 'cultural harms' (Fraser 2001).

This sense of 'cultural harm' provides the backdrop against which many conflicts in Southeast Asia are increasingly being waged. The insurgency in the Southern Philippines spearheaded by the Moro Islamic Liberation Front, along with a range of smaller groups, the resistance movement in the Indonesian province of Aceh led by the *Gerakan Aceh Merdeka* (GAM – Free Aceh Movement), the insurgency at the other end of the Indonesian archipelago led by the *Organisasi Papua Merdeka* (OPM – Free Papua Movement), and similar unresolved and simmering disputes in southern Thailand and different parts of Myanmar, are all cases in point. Moreover, in many of these cases, but not all, existing cultural grievances have been intensified by a belief that the US in particular is an accessory to the subjugation of dissident Islamist voices regardless of whether these voices have any connection to terrorists.

It is wrong, however, to overgeneralize the Islamist resurgence. While it is true that Islam in Southeast Asia is changing, it is not doing so in a uniform direction. Indeed, the rise of Islamist political organizations has resulted in a highly pluralist movement marked more by disagreement than agreement in several key areas, including political strategy. For instance, in Malaysia the spectrum of Islamist politics encompasses the non-violent activism of organized political parties like the *Parti Islam SeMalaysia* (PAS), the militancy of groups like the *Kumpulan Militan Malaysia*, and the violent terrorism of regionally active groups like the *Jemaah Islamiyah*. The range of groups and Islamist perspectives is much larger in Indonesia where more than 50 Islamic political parties are expected to contest national elections scheduled for mid-2004.

For the most part activist and militant groups confine their politics to the domestic realm, using non-violent political strategies designed to infuse local politics with a stronger Islamic flavour. The only indigenous Southeast Asian terrorist organization currently identified, the *Jemaah Islamiyah* (JI), differs from activist and militant groups in two important respects. Firstly, the JI is clearly committed to pursuing a violent strategy for change. Secondly, the JI refuses to be bound by a traditional conception of the nation-state, seeing it as a largely Western construct that artificially segregates the Southeast Asian *ummah*.

However, despite the differences in scriptural interpretation and political strategies, a common thread continues to bind activists, militants and terrorists. This thread is a shared sense that the overwhelmingly secular and capitalist orientation of the postcolonial Southeast Asian state is responsible for inflicting significant cultural damage on Muslim communities across the region. This common perspective provides the basis for a discursive link between activist, militant and terrorist groups and as such it is not unusual to sometimes find individuals from across the Islamist spectrum speaking on the same platform and with the same types of political messages. However, this shared sense of cultural angst does not mean that activists or militants support the wider aims of terrorist groups or their violent methods.

This shared perspective of cultural anxiety not only links disparate groups across the political spectrum in Southeast Asia, but also provides the basis for deepening contacts with similar movements in other parts of the Muslim world. Indeed the rejuvenation of Islamic politics in Southeast Asia can be understood only within a larger global context. To be sure, Islamist groups within Southeast Asia often reflect their own particularistic characteristics; traits deeply rooted in the respective histories and cultures concerned. But at a deeper level, regional Islamist groups also reflect important empirical and symbolic connections to the Islamic world more generally.

THE ORIGINS OF ANGER

From the perspective of understanding why some of these individuals and groups have embraced terrorism as a mode of political agency, there is a need for researchers to untangle a complex mixture of existential and material factors, a task that lies beyond the ambit of this particular chapter. However, for the sake of brevity, two causal factors of global significance seem especially important.

The first is a loss of faith in the secular state and its embrace of capitalist modernization. As Saskia Sassen has pointed out, at a material level 'the growth of debt and unemployment, the decline of traditional economic sectors, and other similar trends in the global south are feeding multiple forms of extreme reactions, including political violence and an exploding illegal trade in people, largely directed to the rich countries' (Sassen 2002, p.108).

However, the argument that there is a correlation between poverty and terrorism is far from clear. Critics of the view that there is a direct correlation point to the middle-class backgrounds of most of the September 11 hijackers as well as the privileged upbringings of senior terrorist personnel such as Osama bin Laden and his deputy Ayman al-Zawahiri. However, it is naive to assume that poverty and global economic inequalities more generally can be ignored altogether. Rather, the importance of poverty seems to lie more in its ability to fuse with other social phenomena, such as a sense of political and cultural disempowerment, to form a highly combustible social milieu within which terrorism can germinate. Michael Mann hints at the systemic significance of poverty when he argues that it is the combination of economic failure and religious conflict that is critical. Drawing on the work of Singer and Wildavsky (1993), Mann notes how these two factors combine to undermine regime legitimacy and foment an environment which yields 'desperate extremists, roving teenage paramilitaries, civil wars and anarchy. They create turbulence within states, and conflict between them' (Mann 2001, p. 63).

In the Southeast Asian context, Mann's perspective helps explain the surge in support for militant and extremist Islamist groups in the wake of the regional economic crisis that occurred in 1997. However, it also needs to be acknowledged that many of these movements, such as the *Jemaah Islamiyah*, have their genesis during the more prosperous 1980s (International Crisis Group 2002), an historical truism that suggests the parallel importance of other causal factors. To this end, a survey of the political rhetoric of key players in the *Jemaah Islamiyah*, and other militant groups such as the *Front Pembela Islam* and the *Hizb ut-Tahrir*, suggests that a growing sense of anomie and cultural disorientation caused by the encroachment of Western cultures and norms has been a pivotal factor in the rise of such groups. This theme is captured in an open letter prepared for Indonesian Ulema by the Middle Eastern-based *Hizb ut-Tahrir*, which currently claims to have around 100,000 Indonesian members (Dhume 2003, p. 19). Published in early 2002, the letter reads in part, 'O pious and noble Ulema: The time has come to take the opportunity to save your Ummah from the control of the Kuffar, and from being disgraced before them, and *from the tyranny of their thoughts, rules and systems implemented over you*' (emphasis added) (Hizb ut-Tahrir 2002, p. 6).

Hizb ut-Tahrir's open letter encapsulates both the existential angst generated by the perceived Westernization of society, and also the reactive construction of an idealized Islamic cultural rampart both to defend society from further attacks and to claw back what has already been lost to the predatory encroachment of an alien and threatening culture.

However, the phenomenon is not particular to Islam: cultural and religious revivalisms the world over rest on idealized and exaggerated notions of the past. As such these revivalisms are inherently connected to global modernity itself. This is especially clear in the way that many Islamist groups construct and promote their political agenda as a palliative to the negative cultural, economic, and political costs generated by Western modernity. But rather than being a rejection of modernity per se, these agendas reflect the utopian belief that modernity can be disaggregated into distinct spheres, in other words that a system based on *shari'a* law can maintain the material benefits generated by the global economy but quarantine Muslims from its deleterious social and cultural consequences. In many respects these Islamist agendas can be regarded as a variety of what Chatterjee (1986) has called 'derivative discourses', in that their outward anti-modern character is belied by an instrumental logic that is both deeply modern and global in character, two qualities integral to the Western project they seek to displace.

The global character of derivative discourses is especially clear at the attitudinal level. In an empirical sense it is evident in the growing influence of conservative Middle Eastern clerics in shaping the evolution of Islamic beliefs in countries such as those of Southeast Asia. It is also evident in the growing number of Southeast Asian Muslims studying at Islamic institutions in the Middle East and in the speed and intensity with which tragedies that befall fellow Muslims in other parts of the world can motivate Southeast Asian co-religionists to protest, raise money, and agitate on their behalf. Finally, the power of a transnational sense of identity is also evident in the willingness of a small but growing number of disillusioned young Southeast Asian Muslims to rally behind the violent global agendas of demagogues like Osama bin Laden (Abuza 2002).

This brings us to a second causal dynamic behind the rise of Islamist politics in Southeast Asia, a phenomenon encapsulated in Zygmunt Bauman's (2001) concept of 'great wars of recognition'. Running throughout Bauman's recent work is the notion that 'solid modernity', along with its associated categories of national identity, has been displaced by 'liquid modernity' wherein the ability to 'dis-engage' from established modes of political and social representation plays an increasingly important role in shaping politics. Moreover, individuals' ability to 'dis-engage' is enhanced by their ability to reshape their identities and then demand recognition by tapping into wider global currents. Indeed at the level of identity, it is the crumbling effectiveness of traditional borders and national spaces and the corresponding emergence of an era of 'global space' that lies at the heart of the disintegrative power of liquid identity. Bauman writes,

> . . . (t)he sacrosanct division between *dedans* and *dehors*, that chartered the realm of existential security and set the bridgeheads and targets for future transcendence, has all but been obliterated . . . We are all 'inside', with nothing left outside. Or, rather, what used to be 'outside' has entered the 'inside' – without knocking; and settled there – without asking permission. The bluff of local solutions to planetary problems has been called, the sham of territorial isolation has been exposed (Bauman 2002, pp. 83-4).

In this passage Bauman refers specifically to a critical lesson drawn from the terror attacks of September 11, namely, the failure of national borders to quarantine societies from the intrusions by symbolic and material forces capable of inducing serious cachectic effects. But the organic metaphors used to elucidate the complex global dynamics at work also offer a useful vehicle for understanding why postcolonial elites in Southeast Asia have responded so negatively to outside cultures and ideas, especially those associated with so-called 'Western individualism'.

THE POLITICS OF RESISTANCE

The rise of cultural politics, especially that centring on religious identities, has been a cause for particular concern to Southeast Asian states. This is particularly so in the majority Muslim countries of Indonesia and Malaysia, but also in the Philippines, Singapore and Thailand, where the rise of a conservative Islamic consciousness has initiated a potentially explosive dynamic that could, over time, radically redraw the political topography of these countries.

The source of much of this concern is the tendency for new cultural and religiously based movements to compete against the postcolonial state for the loyalty of a growing body of the citizenry. Applied to the Muslim world more generally, Bassam Tibi draws on the work of Benedict Anderson and Norbert Elias to point to an emerging international 'imagined community' of Muslims, a romanticized idea of the *Ummah*, within which a growing number of believers define themselves as a 'we-group' juxtaposed against a 'they-group', the 'they' being 'the West' and those locals who uphold the primacy of Western modernity (Tibi 2002, p. 118). At its core, Islamic revivalism is therefore both inherently modern *and* inherently political, its agenda defined by the general notion of the de-Westernization of Muslim societies.

But as mentioned briefly above, consistent with the paradoxical nature of globalization itself – a dynamic constellation of forces that simultaneously draw in and drive apart – new patterns of transnational Islamic identity are matched by parallel schisms between Muslims within Southeast Asian nations. Notwithstanding the surface-level consensus on the undesirability of certain aspects of Western cultures, the surge in Islamist politics in Southeast Asia is accompanied by a widening gulf of interpretative and prescriptive religious views. As Robert Hefner has observed, the 'decisive battle is taking place *within* Muslim civilization, where ultraconservatives compete against moderates and democrats for the soul of Islam' (Hefner 2002, p. 146).

But for many in the West and political elites in Southeast Asia itself, the plural character of Islamist politics is usually overlooked. Southeast Asia's postcolonial elites in particular are concerned not so much by religious resurgence per se, but by its potential to undermine old categories of privilege and power. In this sense, the explosive characteristics of identity politics in contemporary Southeast Asia are not embedded in the resurgent religious identities themselves, but are contained in the dialectical process that is generated when the state denies the recognition demands they make.

At risk, it is argued, is the integrity of the nation-state itself. With regard to Islamic identities Hefner observes that the Southeast Asian state's

> capacity to shape public affairs and intervene in the most intimate domains of private life has presented Southeast Asian Muslims with a historically unprecedented challenge. It has reduced the territorial fragmentation long characteristic of this region, undercut the autonomy of Muslim social organisations, and at times, deployed its forces to hunt down and eliminate Muslim rebels (Hefner 1997, pp. 5-6).

Hence any individuals eager to transfer their Islamic ideals to the political sphere have typically been regarded as a danger to the established order, especially when their activism centres on calls for greater administrative and political accountability and transparency. In many cases these individuals are singled out for harsh treatment, feeding political frustrations and in some instances driving a few towards more extremist ends of the Islamist movement.

SAME OLD MISTAKES

To deflect criticism from within, several regimes in the region (notably that of Mahathir in Malaysia and the former Indonesian administration of Suharto) camouflaged the repression of Islamist dissidents by enveloping themselves in their own Islamic veneer. This became especially evident in the 1980s when political elites sensed a sea change in public opinion and began to infuse their own rhetoric with a more Islamic and occasional anti-Western flavour. This strategy ultimately contributed to a discursive process within which governments and oppositions tried to out-Islamize each other, a phenomenon known colloquially in Malaysia as 'Kafir-Mengafir'. This dynamic was not particular to Southeast Asia. Throughout the 1970s and 1980s secular nationalist leaders across the Muslim world moved to shore up their authority and ward off growing calls for greater democracy and accountability by appropriating the trappings of Islamic government. The selectivity of this process, the bending of small portions of Islamic scripture to suit their goal of self-preservation, reflected a wider global tendency towards the instrumentalization of religion (Roy 1996; Mernissi 2002).

In Southeast Asia attempts to recast the postcolonial imaginary in a religious guise not only failed to ward off the challenge posed by Islamist oppositions, but it also had the effect of turning Islam into an object over which governments and oppositions now battle. As this struggle has developed, the parameters of what constituted 'appropriate' Islamic behaviour shifted to the conservative end of the spectrum. But attempts to confine these dynamics within a carefully demarcated private sphere and out of the public and political realms were always going to fail. The nature of resurgent Islam, like its Christian counterpart, impels its adherents to drive their piety to the public domain, and it is in this regard that the recognition demands of Islamist groups in many parts of Southeast Asia appear to have exhausted political elites. In other words, belligerently secular state authorities feel they have made enough concessions to the demands of Islamist groups and since September 11 there have been signs, especially in Malaysia, the Philippines and Singapore, that they are now prepared to roll back many of these concessions and reassert their secular authority.

Pursued with more success in Singapore, Malaysia and the Philippines (on behalf of Muslim communities in the South), this strategy is hardly surprising. Although the flowering of alternative patterns of Islamic identity has been evident for several decades, it is only recently that the dynamic has gathered sufficient force to worry secular elites. Despite the privileged power of the state's narrative on 'real' Asian culture and the use of an array of subtle and not so subtle forms of cultural policing, Southeast Asian states have been singularly unsuccessful in achieving the cultural and behavioural uniformity they crave. Indeed, not only have alternative identities and associated patterns of political behaviour continued to deny elites the absolute authority they long for, but dissident identities and cultures have flourished, contributing to a vibrant cultural milieu that has pricked conservatives into an increasingly shrill defence of the prevailing order.

A HIGH RISK STRATEGY

The crackdown against Islamist dissidents in Southeast Asia in the wake of the September 11 attacks has taken on an indiscriminate character that carries significant political risk. In particular, the deliberate blurring of the distinction between violent and non-violent Islamist groups and the targeting of peaceful oppositionists under the guise of counter-terrorism risks adding to the frustrations and anger of religious oppositions.

History suggests that ignoring the distinction between moderates and extremists, extremists and terrorists is a strategy that is fraught with danger. This is because people rarely embrace terrorism easily. Rather, active support for terrorism is usually the result of a socialization process within which alienation, a pervasive sense of powerlessness, and violence combine to produce a state of mind that dehumanizes society and reduces it to an existential evil impervious to all but the most extreme forms of political agency. To this end, counter-terrorism strategies that target activists and militants for repression and pre-emptive violence carry a significant risk of producing the types of existential hostility upon which terrorism thrives. In his excellent review of a recent wave of new books on the Algerian war of independence, Adam Shatz (2002) highlights how the decision by French magistrates to allow 'murderous sweeps through Arab neighbourhoods and permit executions of Arab prisoners' not only failed to stop terrorist attacks by the pro-independence *Front de Libération Nationale* (FLN), but had the reverse effect.

> Torture not only failed to repress the yearnings for independence among Algerians; it increased popular support for the FLN, contributing to the transformation of a small vanguard into a revolutionary party with mass support, and rendering impossible the emergence of the *interlocuteur valable* with which the French government claimed to be seeking a dialogue. Indeed, France's tactics helped the FLN to win over Algerian moderates (Shatz 2002, p. 57).

In attempting to offer a more nuanced account of Islamic politics in the Middle East, Najib Ghadbian (2002) draws a distinction between moderate and extremist groups that is also applicable to the Southeast Asian scene. He defines moderate movements as those that pursue change through 'gradual and peaceful means', whereas extremists are those 'ready to use all means necessary to implement their vision of Islam' (2002, p. 92). While it may seem an obvious distinction, Ghadbian is right when he suggests that it is one that is too often ignored. This is especially so in the post-September 11 environment when, in their panic to round up as many 'terrorists' as possible, Western governments have accepted at face value claims by regional governments that their attempts to reassert the integrity of the postcolonial imaginary constitutes an exercise in counter-terrorism. Hence, under the pretext of counter-terrorism, elements of the Indonesian armed forces have set about destroying a fragile cease-fire in the province of Aceh; Kuala Lumpur continues to hold without charge or trial over sixty alleged 'extremists'; Singapore has moved to further increase surveillance and intimidation of any members of the minority Malay population whose views depart from those expounded by the ruling People's Action Party; and Manila has deliberately escalated tensions with Muslim and Communist insurgents at a time when workable peace talks seemed a distinct possibility.

While it is true that terrorist networks in Southeast Asia lack the moral imperative that boosted support for anti-colonial movements like the FLN and their Southeast Asian counterparts, the lessons of the past are far from moot. Indeed, to the extent that several insurgent and terrorist groups in Southeast Asia have recently embraced more fully the language of anti-colonialism, seeing their struggle as one of resistance against Western political and cultural imperialism, important parallels with the past seem increasingly apparent.

A growing embrace of the idea among Muslims that the struggle of Southeast Asian Islam cannot be divorced from that of co-religionists in other parts of the world poses a significant challenge for the West. The ability to abrogate involvement has been effectively denied by this development that has also produced the view, rightly or wrongly, that the denial of a cultural and political space for pious Islam by regional governments cannot be divorced from a larger Western agenda to consolidate the global primacy of non-Islamic values. In other words, the increased repression since 11 September is viewed as consistent with the interests of the US and its allies, and as such many Muslims see Washington, London and Canberra as accomplices to their repression.

In this sense, the repression of alternative identities, especially Muslim identities, by Southeast Asian governments cannot be conceived as a purely domestic matter. It is inevitable that such repression will feed into an existential angst that is universally evident and grounded in the sense that pious Muslims are perennially on the losing side of any effort to carve out a larger and more autonomous political space.

In this way, the festering of Muslim anger builds on a widely held image of the United States as the main prop to an international system that denies Muslims their cultural, economic and political rights. At a practical level it is irrelevant that this view might be naively simplistic or that its prevalence often results from deliberate disinformation spread by the political elites in these countries as a way of deflecting critical attention away from themselves. What matters is that *the myth is believed* and that, in so being, it is for many a reality.

As the Turkish author Orhan Pamuk has put it, rather than increasing understanding of the anger felt by the West at the 11 September attacks and other atrocities such as the Bali bombings and the murder of a dozen French engineers in Pakistan, US-led military operations in the name of combating terrorism only widen misunderstandings and add to the 'overwhelming feeling of humiliation experienced by most of the world's population' (Pamuk 2002, p. 64). This is true in the case of large-scale military operations such as those used to dislodge the Taliban from power in

Afghanistan and the war to remove Saddam Hussein from power, and it is also true of the smaller-scale operational or material support for the armed forces of 'front-line' countries, such as Indonesia, the Philippines and the former Soviet Central Asian Republics.

CONCLUSION

It is difficult for an outsider to judge with any degree of confidence the positive or negative impact of globalization in Southeast Asia. Such an assessment is bound to be highly subjective and dependent on where one stands within the respective national and regional hierarchies. While most Chinese Singaporeans are likely to concede that the island state's immersion into the global economic milieu has had substantial material benefits for the country, this same view is unlikely to be shared by a similar majority of the numerically smaller Malay community. The rest of the region reflects similar divisions both between and within different communities.

What can be said with confidence is that the dynamics of globalization are the same in Southeast Asia as in other parts of the world, simultaneously cohering and disaggregating different elements of the community. While it is cohering different elements of the Muslim community around political and religious agendas at odds with those of the prevailing political hierarchies, it is simultaneously shattering old religious allegiances and loyalties. Or, to paraphrase Urry, globalization generates economic, political and cultural dynamics that are never complete but are inherently disordered, paradoxical, complex and irreversible (Urry 2002, p. 58).

Under such circumstances terrorism cannot be defeated. Rather, it is a tragic consequence of our turbulent times, or, as Colin Powell has put it, 'terrorism is the dark side of globalization' (Urry 2002, p. 57). The best that can be hoped for is a strategy that effectively minimizes and manages the terrorist threat. Such a strategy needs to address the deep existential anger generated by the economic and cultural inequities of our time. Or, to put it slightly differently, it must reflect an attempt to address in some way the recognition claims of new and sometimes challenging patterns of identity and belonging.

This is not the route that Southeast Asian states are taking. On the contrary, steps taken in the name of counter-terrorism in the wake of the September 11 attacks in New York and Washington, and after the similarly tragic attacks in Bali in October 2002, are designed more to reconsolidate the integrity of a postcolonial state apparatus that is increasingly out of sync with global dynamics. To this end, Southeast Asian states are replicating mistakes that are even more glaringly evident in Western countries, especially the

United States and Australia, which have responded to the terrorist challenge through strategies based on the unilateral use of violence (Iraq) and the suspension of basic civil liberties for *alleged* or *possible* terrorist sympathizers.

In our globalizing world, the weapons of economic power and warfare are no longer the monopoly of states, and any counter-terrorism strategies that are predicated solely on force without a corresponding effort to understand the grievances of the disenfranchised will do nothing to roll back the growing tide of existential anger that feeds terrorism. On the contrary, there is a very real risk that counter-terrorism strategies predicated only on military force and political repression will only exacerbate the problem. The violent religious fantasies of groups like al-Qaeda and *Jemaah Islamiyah* are a product of sustained brutalization and misery, hence we should not be surprised when similar deprivations not only fail to dissuade their members from further attacks, but swell their numbers even more.

REFERENCES

Abuza, Z. (2002), 'Tentacles of Terror: Al Qaeda's Southeast Asian Network' *Contemporary Southeast Asia*, **24** (3), 427-465.

Bauman, Z. (2001) 'The Great War of Recognition', *Theory, Culture and Society,* **18** (2-3), 137-150.

Bauman, Z. (2002), 'Reconnaissance Wars of the Planetary Frontierland', *Theory, Culture and Society,* **19** (4), 81-90.

Chatterjee, P. (1986), *Nationalist Thought and the Colonial World: A Derivative Discourse?* London: Zed Books.

Dhume, S. (2003), 'Radical Appeal', *Far Eastern Economic Review*, April 3, p. 19.

Esposito, J.L. and J.O. Voll (2001), *Makers of Contemporary Islam*, Oxford: Oxford University Press.

Fraser, N. (2001), 'Recognition Without Ethics?' *Theory, Culture and Society,* **18** (2-3), pp. 21-42.

Ghadbian, N. (2002), 'Political Islam: Inclusion or Violence?' in K. Worcester, S. Avery Bermanzohn and M. Ungar (eds), *Violence and Politics: Globalization's Paradox*, New York: Routledge, pp. 90-106.

Hefner, R.W. (1997), 'Islam in an Era of Nation-States: Politics and Religious Renewal in Muslim Southeast Asia', in R.W. Hefner and P. Horvatich (eds), *Islam in an Era of Nation-States: Politics and Religious Renewal in Muslim Southeast Asia*, Honolulu: University of Hawaii Press, pp. 3-40.

Hefner, R.W. (2000), *Civil Islam: Muslims and Democratisation in Indonesia*, Princeton: Princeton University Press.

Hefner, R.W (2002), '11 September and the Struggle for Islam', *Ethnicities,* **2** (2), pp. 144-146.

Hizb ut-Tahrir (2002), 'Open Letter to the Ulema from Hizb ut-Tahrir – Indonesia', Khilafah.com March 17, <*http://www.khilafah.com/home/category.php?/*>.

International Crisis Group (2002), 'Al Qaeda in Southeast Asia: The Case of the "Ngruki Network" in Indonesia', *Indonesia Briefing*, Jakarta/Brussels, August 8.

Mann, M. (2001), 'Globalization and September 11', *New Left Review*, **12**, November-December, pp. 51-72.

Mernissi, F. (2002), *Islam and Democracy: Fear of the Modern World* (2nd edn), Cambridge: Perseus Publishing.

Muzaffar, C. (1987), *Islamic Resurgence in Malaysia*, Petaling Jaya: Fajar Bakti.

Pamuk, O. (2002), 'The Anger of the Damned' in R.B. Silvers and B. Epstein (eds) *Striking Terror: America's New War*, New York: New York Review Books, pp. 59-66.

Rashid, A. (2003), 'What Do You Think of America Now?' *Far Eastern Economic Review*, April 3, pp. 12-14.

Roy, O. (1996), *The Failure of Political Islam* (trans. by Carol Volk), Cambridge, Mass.: Harvard University Press.

Sassen, S. (2002), 'Governance Hotspots: Challenges We Must Confront in the Post-September 11 World' in E. Hershberg and K.W. Moore (eds), *Critical Views of September 11: Analyses From Around the World*, New York: The New Press, p. 108.

Shatz, A.C. (2002), 'The Torture of Algiers', *New York Review of Books*, November 21, pp. 53-57.

Singer, M. and A. Wildavsky (1993), *The Real World Order: Zones of Peace/Zones of Turmoil*, New Jersey: Chatham.

Tibi, B. (2002), *The Challenge of Fundamentalism: Political Islam and the New World Disorder* (updated edn), Berkeley: University of California Press.

Urry, J. (2002), 'The Global Complexities of September 11th', *Theory, Culture and Society*, **19** (4), pp. 57-69.

3. Globalization and Poverty[1]

Vi Meghnad Desai

INTRODUCTION

Globalization may be the only way that mass poverty will be cured; no better way has yet been found. Paul Baran (1960) and Andre Gunder Frank (1965) have suggested that if developing countries depended on capitalism, they would never get rid of poverty because monopoly capital hinders development of the 'Third World'. As a result, the only way the 'Third World' could develop would be by rejecting capitalism and taking on socialism. The argument from Baran's book *The Political Economy of the South* was based on his pessimism about the possibility of growth in developing countries because he and others believed that developed countries would suffer from secular stagnation, and that if they suffered from secular stagnation, the forces of monopoly capitalism would then not allow rivals to exist and to come into world markets. Markets would be restricted and competition would be deleterious, and so developed countries would keep developing countries out of the market.

It is interesting to note that it was not only economists who were pessimistic. Politicians have also been pessimistic about developing countries ever getting out of poverty. Henry Kissinger commented that if only China and India could get rid of the problem of food supplies we could then proceed to tackle other problems. No one in the 1960s would have believed that China or India would have developed as they have today. My argument is not only that the Baran thesis is wrong in hindsight, but that he was in fact already wrong in his own day because in the late 1950s secular stagnation was not the story in the capitalist countries. Rather, sustained growth was the story.

What happened in the second half of the 20th century was the defeat of the Leninist model as an alternative path of development for all developing countries. This model was unsuccessful, although the Leninist political programme survives in China, Cuba and North Korea. But the story of China is a quite remarkable example of first having tried the Leninist economic model, then abandoning it in the late 1970s and latching onto a different path and achieving success. Asia has had spectacular success, and it is a profound fact that East Asia and Southeast Asia have achieved such remarkable growth. I am old enough to remember when people had not seen 5 per cent growth rates. Growth rates of 8 or 9 per cent are now not uncommon. First Japan then South Korea achieved these growth rates in the 1970s. Various commentators suggested that this was due to American defence aid and would all collapse, yet it continued. Asia has demonstrated that, contrary to a Weberian model of Protestantism, capitalism has no cultural restrictions. Thus it has become pointless to think within a cultural paradigm which assumes that capitalism is an exclusively Western ideal. The success of Asia has defied that Eurocentric logic – the first example being the astonishing development of Japan (I deal with this issue in *Marx's Revenge*, Desai 2002).

One of the most remarkable things about the 20th century was the defeat of fascism in Italy and Germany. It must be recalled that fascism was the first system under which planning was attempted. Unfortunately, the bad press received by these fascist regimes has led us to dismiss their efforts at planning. The Germans developed five-year plans for both private and state enterprises. The defeat of fascism was a consequence of the Second World War. In the post-war era, communism was defeated. Thus, by the end of the 20th century only one mode of production was left standing, and that was capitalism. There may be different varieties of capitalism, but there is still only the one capitalist mode of production.

ASIA'S ACHIEVEMENTS

Another remarkable thing about the history of Asia, especially from 1970 onwards, is the extraordinary reduction of mass poverty. The figures for China, Taiwan, Korea, Thailand, Malaysia and Sri Lanka all show real success stories. The stories in the Philippines, Indonesia and India are not so good. Given that much of the world lives in Asia, the reduction of poverty in Asia in absolute numbers must be the largest reduction in human history. From the mid 1970s onwards, a number of Asian countries acknowledged the need for an open economy policy. This is not necessarily related to the concepts of free markets or free trade. What is relevant is that it is about pursuing policies that are profit-friendly and not profit-reducing. The contrast between India and Korea is not that the state did not intervene. It interfered in both countries; but in Korea, the state embraced the market and encouraged industries and firms that were competitive. These received subsidies but were monitored to ensure competitive performance. The only point of competitive performance was to produce for export. In contrast, India was not export-oriented. It catered for the home market, and foreign trade pessimism remained.

All of the Eastern European economies during the 1945-1989 period were involved in substantial investments.   The reports of the Economic Commission of Europe showed that every year Eastern Europe was growing healthily and all the GDP calculations showed impressive growth.   What occurred in Eastern Europe was the production of output which did not sell abroad.   Producers did not have to satisfy what Marx called the law of value. As a result, many economic activities (such as producing concrete and steel buildings) ignored the markets.   No economic value was being generated. Economic value is not a matter of engineering.   What occurred in the German Democratic Republic (GDR) was a system without economic value.   As a result, when Germany was unified, the entire capital stock of the GDR could not be sold.   It is possible to pursue policies, as India has, merely to generate output and create little value.

The open economy context in East and Southeast Asia was different.   The concept of globalization was advanced when capital movements became possible across countries in a reasonably unregulated fashion.   Capitalist firms understood that if they were going to realize adequate profits they had to relocate their companies.   The relocation of industries from the industrial North to the developing South began in the 1970s and accelerated in the 1980s and 1990s to the extent that the manufacturing industry has been redefined.   The developed countries are witnessing a decline in the share of manufacturing in terms of output and employment.   Manufacturing is no longer the leading sector in many developed countries and manufacturing employment is increasing, particularly in the developing countries.

GLOBALIZATION AND INDUSTRIALIZATION OF THE SOUTH

In the late 1960s there was a conference of the United Nations Industrial Development Organisation in Santiago, Chile.   They had set a target that by 2000 the South's share of manufacturing export should be 25 per cent.   At the time, this proposal was considered impossible.   In the 1980s many people remained pessimistic about this.   Now there is a remarkable resurgence of manufacturing exports from the South.   This did not occur by South-South cooperation, as was considered fashionable.   South-South cooperation was not effective.   Rather, developing countries were able to access the markets of developed countries.   East and Southeast Asia reduced their poverty by gaining access to the markets of the West and selling items that the West could not make itself at prices that people were able to afford.   This has been the case for many mature industrial products that have migrated to the South from the North.   Northern capital and Southern labour are creating a whole new manufacturing industry in the South, and this is linked to globalization. It has been made possible by other aspects of globalization such as the IT and communications revolution, satellite technologies, cheaper transport and the more efficient movement of money.

Globalization has made possible the relocation of production processes. At the same time it has also made possible the fragmentation of the production process so that an entire product is not made in the same location. Much of the success of the 1950s and 1960s, particularly the Japanese success story, was to do with recognizing this principle. In the 1950s and 1960s people believed in economies of scale. Steel factories were integrated and attempts were made for independent ownership of mines and steel marketing. For example, the former powerful corporation US Steel survived President Kennedy's attempts to regulate its price fixing powers. Currently, however, there is no steel manufactured by US Steel in the USA, because Japanese companies discovered the irrelevance of economies of scale and vertical integration: that not all stages of production need to be located in the same place. There are just-in-time inventories and completely displaced branches which allow the assembly of different manufacturing components. In no single location in Europe is a car made; parts of cars are made in different locations and then put together. What this achieves is that it retains the high value-added, high knowledge-intensive parts of the production process (design and engineering) in the West, and the more routine part of the production processes in the South. Only 10 per cent of the price of a pair of Nike shoes is due to labour costs; much of the rest of the cost is due to the design, promotion and so on. Consumers pay for the small holes on the Nike shoe through which one's feet can breathe and suchlike, and for the Michael Jordan image because Michael Jordan is endorsing the product. What is bought is a dream: an abstract commodity. What globalization has made possible is the production of a significant quantity of abstract commodities in which, to some extent, the North has an advantage but what is also required is routine production of the kind that takes place in the South.

POVERTY AND THE WELFARE STATE

The idea of globalization seemed impossible in the 1950s and 1960s. There was no likelihood that this kind of industrialization could be realized during this time. It is also noteworthy that in the West poverty was reduced significantly only after the Second World War. The living conditions of poorer people in the inter-war years were astonishing. In the North poverty was tackled under the Keynesian regime. There was sustained full employment and sound growth. Yet during this period participation in the labour force was quite limited. Core poverty was addressed through the state. What resulted was that in the North, state action was regarded as the way of addressing poverty by creating a welfare state. Through the state, people who were unemployed received part of the surplus via government taxation.

Two things have occurred since then. Such a strategy cannot work in a developing country that cannot afford to establish a welfare state. Moreover, those who are living in poverty cannot afford to be unemployed. In a developing country, anti-poverty strategies need to be implemented that depend on creating work and creating skills for that work. Developed countries are also realizing after the Keynesian boom that they cannot afford the welfare state that existed previously. They cannot afford it partly because their own employment structures have been transformed by globalization. Their unskilled workers no longer have the lifetime employment that was provided in manufacturing, because those manufacturing jobs have ceased. Their workers are having episodic employment experiences, and do not have continuity of employment. At the same time, they are living longer. Previously, the welfare state took a person's own income and redistributed it over their lifetime. What the welfare state did not do, at least in Britain, is take from the rich and give to the poor. British studies show that the welfare state took from the poor while they were young and working and then gave back to them when they retired, or in between during periods of unemployment (which were very infrequent).

Today that model is breaking down because people are living longer after retirement, and the savings they are setting aside during their working lives will not be sufficient to finance their retirement. Ageing thus becomes a problem, and all welfare states are facing this crisis of how to tackle poverty and retirement. They have responded in exactly the manner of developing countries: a work-related poverty reduction strategy. Poverty reduction cannot be achieved as a result of state help detached from work. If the UK government is to help people out of poverty, this means that people have to find work and be given subsidies and tax cuts in order to enhance their take-home pay. They will get their tax payments back in some form or another, as long as they stay in work. Across the world, the strategies for poverty reduction have become identical because of globalization and increased longevity. Even in the heyday of the Keynesian policy, people argued that poverty was not being addressed properly. What is noticeable about poverty reduction is that it is very difficult to design large redistributive programmes that can effectively counter poverty in any meaningful sense. Alternative strategies need to be implemented, even in developed countries; this is because, while they remain capitalist, the nature of capitalism has changed. The developed countries are more subject to global competition than ever before.

MIGRATION AND STABILIZATION

It may be seen as a paramount duty of developed countries not to obstruct the process of globalization and not to adopt restrictive trade policies. The abolition of all agricultural subsidies in Europe and in the USA would be one possible solution. Each cow in Europe has a subsidy of US$2.25 cents per day. This is above the poverty line that the World Bank applies to the poor in developing countries (in other words, the poor are defined as those that live below $2 per day per capita). According to this definition, the European cow is above the global poverty index. The smallest American cotton farmer receives US$100,000 for an industry which should not exist at all; why does America need to grow cotton when there is perfectly good cotton grown in the Third World? The European Common Agricultural Policy, by dumping abroad, is a serious cost to Third World agriculture. (There is no point in Lionel Jospin, the former Prime Minister of France, talking about Tobin taxes when if he really does want to redistribute wealth he should stop his own agricultural subsidies. Many anti-globalizing movements should really be marching in the streets against agricultural subsidies. I have been quoted as saying that the Common Agricultural Policy is a crime against humanity and I stand by that.)

The same applies to industrial products. There has to be continuous liberalization of trade. Some of the events that took place in Seattle at the WTO meeting were a protectionist backlash against the growth of trade. The American Trade Union Movement opposed the admission of China into the WTO because they could see that this would mean the displacement of their jobs. Developed countries need to be prepared for the restructuring of manufacturing towards more research and development intensive, more knowledge-intensive manufacturing and service activities that are more value adding.

These are the two primary problems that developed countries need to address. In addition to removing agricultural subsidies and expanding markets for manufacturing, there is a third aspect which is increasingly important. This is the more controversial question of the movement of people. With globalization there comes an acceptance that one of its distinguishing marks is the freer movement of capital across the world. This does not mean complete freedom of movement for capital. Many restrictions remain; but by and large all the OECD countries have completely liberalized capital markets. There are an increasing number of countries of the Second and Third World that have capital liberalization policies (I have nothing against this, and am very sure that the volatility that goes with such capital movements is something that can be lived with).

The movement of capital, however, is not the only movement to be discussed. It is quite remarkable that in the 19th century when we had the phenomenon of globalization, there was also a great deal of movement of people. Today we have forgotten that between 1914 and 1945 the world became de-globalized and we started thinking within the boundaries of the territorial state. Today we think of economics within the territorial state, and we think of welfare as taking place within the territorial state. We have forgotten that that was not the way the world normally functioned. The territorial state was a very short, peculiar period in European history. During the 19th century people moved across international boundaries quite significantly; one third of the population of Europe moved to North America and Australia. The notion of one third being displaced suggests that there have been fundamental changes to the prospects for poverty reduction. Clearly people moved across state boundaries because they knew their conditions would improve. They endured a horrible passage across, and when they arrived they had no entitlements. They had no welfare payments; they had to work their way up; practically nothing was given except admission to the USA. The second generation achieved a remarkable living standard that would not have been possible had they stayed in Europe. It is also pertinent that poverty reduction occurred by means of people moving away from where they were based.

In the 19th century it was quite possible for the poor to go somewhere with better job prospects. There is a lot of movement within countries now, but in the 19th century there was a lot of movement across countries. Many people from the Indian subcontinent moved to Malaysia, to the Caribbean and to Africa. Many Chinese moved to Southeast Asia, to the west coast of America and to Australia until the beginning of the 20th century when Asian immigration in Australia was curtailed.

In this new phase of globalization, migration will be an important topic in the next 10 to 15 years. People have taken the initiative on their own to travel across state boundaries; they are taking enormous risks to move to where there is prosperity. As a result, country after country has to address immigration problems. Developed countries are not responding well. Decisions have been made that economic refugees will not be admitted, on the assumption that they are dirty people who want to make themselves better off. The contention is not necessarily to give them foreign aid but not to include them. This is the situation even in countries already full of economic refugees.

Another consequence of globalization is the issues surrounding asylum seekers. Some, but not all, asylum seekers are included; restrictions have been placed on the number of asylum seekers admitted. Nigel Harris commented in *The New Untouchables* that when the welfare state was created during the First World War it guaranteed that it would look after the welfare of its citizens. The emergence of the welfare state coincided with the emergence of the territorial state. By creating a category of citizen, it also created a category of foreigners that had not existed in the 19th century. Today's state will look after its citizens but not foreigners. The nation-state was invented to stop the movement of people. The nation-state also had aspirations to stop people leaving. The issue is that welfare does not come packaged with the territorial state; it travels with people. We have to understand that there is going to be a need to match the free movement of capital with the free movement of labour. There is little reason why people who accept the free movement of capital should not accept the free movement of people.

Many arguments have been used to consider welfare in terms of territorial states. The 'good people' or progressives in the territorial state (NGOs, bishops and so on) have a view that they should only admit people to whom they can give the full welfare entitlements. There is great resistance to diluting the conditions of citizenship. Many countries are attempting to restrict the access of asylum seekers that they are, by treaty, bound to admit. A whole range of arguments is deployed – for example, 'you are not a genuine asylum seeker and you are an economic refugee'. The 19th century approach was very different. The 19th century said, 'You can come in if you want to, but you need to go through an intermediate stage until you get full citizenship'. It was a bit like the Green Card system today: you are welcome to come and live in America but you are not a citizen; you pay tax but you do not get a full entitlement to welfare. You only get a full welfare entitlement when you become a citizen.

I suggest that countries should adopt 'Green Card' strategies. Some people would argue that the conditions are harsh but they are actually more reasonable than the strategies we are adopting now. There should be full child benefits but adults should not get any benefits. Adults know what is right for them; they have chosen to come to a new country. After perhaps five or ten years they would get full citizenship rights.

Even with this strategy, there are all sorts of cultural problems, but the economic problems are also interesting. The major economic problem is that if these people are going to work and they have been asked to work, some labour market structures are very exclusionary and will be undermined by an influx of people. Most particularly, minimum wage legislation will be affected. Ronald Dworkin, a distinguished advocate of human rights, provided the example of a case in a New York bakery with an employee working 16 hours a day. He asked the opinion of the audience. They were all horrified. In effect, the immigrant could not obtain employment in most regulated industries; he could only find work in an unregulated industry. He could only get a job where he had to work for 16 hours. For him this was the only humane passage out of poverty into work, owing to the regulations and restrictions on people coming in and getting jobs.

We do have to think very seriously about the nature of the labour market structures we adopted for a certain era of capitalism when we thought only about the territorial state in which there was privileged membership for citizens and no membership for outsiders. Clearly we want to make many more people better off, and one way we can do this is to have an intergenerational shift in benefits by saying, 'You can come into this country to work and your children will be better off but you won't be entitled to benefits'.

A majority of the developed world, having come through a development process, is now essentially taking away the ladder for other people who have come later. One reason is that the age structures in developed countries are already such that they cannot afford their pension system or their welfare state, and the clear demographic projections in Britain and Europe and possibly Australia show a dependency ratio of aged people that is already of such proportions that all the needed welfare cannot be financed by the welfare state.

There are obviously some other solutions whereby one's working life is extended and pension entitlements are diluted, but another solution is to import people. Calculations have been made about this for the European Union. It has been estimated that the EU needs to import some 100 million people over the next 15 years in order to keep up its current economic output. The EU was so alarmed by this study (conducted by the UN Department of Social and Economic Affairs) that member countries refused to have the report circulated. They were worried about the impending demographic crisis. It can be shown that there are certain cruel but kind ways of dealing with immigration that are mutually beneficial – not in the immediate short term but in the intermediate and long term. There has been no political leadership that has been able to explain this to the citizens of the developed countries; nor have the people who have argued for mass poverty reduction in the World Bank and UNDP taken this option. There is an assertion that countries are separate little blocs and can only deal with poverty by the relief of money but not the movement of people.

The argument that people have been the most immobile factor of production and that everything else can move is a flawed one. World history suggests that people do move. Different countries will solve this problem in different ways. The USA has an interesting strategy of getting skilled people into the country in generous quantities. They also get unskilled workers illegally across the Mexican border. The American population figures demonstrate that the country has a growing population both in terms of internal reproduction rates and net migration – unlike Europe, which has a stagnant or declining population and severe restrictions on immigration. Europe will have to respond accordingly, perhaps adopting a strategy similar to that of the USA. Strategies will differ according to the relative economic strengths and weaknesses of the economies concerned.

This issue requires a global examination of some kind through the WTO or ILO; the world will have to reach a decision of some sort over the next 50 years to address the mass movement of people. In principle, asylum seekers are temporary stayers. There is some evidence in the UK with Kosovo and Afghanistan that asylum seekers came only temporarily and many returned. One can be generous to them, knowing that they wish to return, and one might admit them on the basis of temporary migration only. In relation to the admission of economic refugees, however, there is little scope for generosity. These people will bear the costs of migration and there will be no costs bearing on the citizens. Of course citizens will carry the indirect cost of such economic refugees, but in return they will also have some benefits from that migration in terms of a more youthful age profile and increased economic productivity.

Globalization has provided a remarkable opportunity for tackling mass poverty, but there is one exception to this: Africa as a continent has not benefited as much as Asia. In part, this has to do with commodity prices. Another feature of modern industry is that commodities have become 'weightless' – they use less raw material and are lighter, and artificially manufactured materials are used. As a result, primary commodity prices have been on a secular decline through the last 25 years. Another problem has been the failure to create nation-states and coherent political societies or governance. This is a major contrast between Asia and Africa. It is not a problem to do with corruption or authoritarian versus democratic systems; rather, it is a question of the difference between a responsive state and an unresponsive state. The Asian state in a variety of forms has always responded and provided its citizens with some of the fruits of development. That connection between the state and the people is evident in the case of Malaysia and China. In both Malaysia and China the ruling parties have been in touch with the grass roots and have been able to deliver some development. This has not been the case in Africa. Except for the first few years after independence there has been an extraordinary failure of the rulers to respond to the citizens. Why this is true is very complex, but I believe one thing to be certain: it has nothing to do with globalization. Globalization has ignored Africa rather than ruined it, whereas globalization has helped Asia because Asia was able to create successful polities. We must now consider how Africa can be introduced into globalization.

REFERENCES

Baran, Paul (1960), *The Political Economy of the South*, New York: Monthly Review Press.

Desai, Meghnad (2002), *Marx's Revenge: The Resurgence of Capitalism and the Death of Statist Socialism*, London: Verso.

Frank, Andre Gunder (1965), *Capitalism and Underdevelopment*, New York: Monthly Review Press.

Harris, Nigel (1997), *The New Untouchables*, London: I.B. Taurus.

NOTE

1   This is the revised text of a speech delivered by Lord Desai in a public lecture in Melbourne (Australia) on 11 December 2002. The lecture was hosted by the Monash Asia Institute, the Monash Institute for the Study of Global Movements and the Productivity Commission. Lord Desai's visit to Australia was made possible by the Australian South Asia Research Centre at the Australian National University, Canberra.

4. The Impact of Globalization on Malaysia

Tham Siew-Yean

INTRODUCTION

Since the crisis and the imposition of capital controls in September 1998, Malaysia has often been perceived to be anti-globalization. This perception is certainly incorrect as Malaysia tapped heavily into the economic drivers of globalization in order to develop the country. At the same time, it does not mean that Malaysia embraced globalization without any reservations, as the government did not utilize strictly 'market-friendly' policies for developing the economy. Rather the government pursued 'open' policies in certain sectors while protecting others, sometimes temporarily, for the sake of national interest.

The roots of this dual approach in economic development can be traced to the promulgation of the New Economic Policy (NEP) in 1970. The twin objectives of the NEP are growth with equity or the eradication of poverty and the restructuring of society to redress the economic imbalances between the different ethnic groups in Malaysia. In order to achieve growth, a concerted effort was made to develop the manufacturing sector by utilizing 'open' policies such as export and Foreign Direct Investment (FDI) promotion. On the other hand, the redistribution goal led, for example, to restrictions on foreign equity ownership in all sectors. Specifically, wealth and employment in Malaysia were targeted for restructuring so that the proportion of corporate wealth and employment accruing to indigenous Malaysians *(bumiputera)* other Malaysians and overseas investors would achieve a '30:40:30' percentage respectively by 1990.

This dual objective led to a gradual and selective approach towards opening the economy. Hence, restrictions were occasionally relaxed or reinstated in response to the developments, as in the case of the capital controls that were administered in 1994 and 1998.

Consequently it would be more accurate to describe Malaysia's approach toward globalization as one that sought not 'close' but selective integration with the world economy. In other words, Malaysia integrated up to the point where it was useful for the country to do so, as in the case of FDI and trade (Singh 1999). What is the impact on Malaysia of such a selective approach towards globalization? The main objective of this chapter is to answer this question.   Specifically, the chapter aims to analyse the impact of globalization on Malaysia and its policy implications for the country.

IMPACT OF GLOBALIZATION ON MALAYSIA

Globalization, as defined by the widening and deepening of international economic relations (Braunstein and Epstein 1999), has accelerated the integration of developing countries into the world economy. Two dimensions of economic globalization in particular, namely long-term capital and trade flows, contributed to the spectacular economic growth in Malaysia before the outbreak of the Asian financial crisis (AFC) in 1997. Speculative short-term capital inflows contributed, in part, to this crisis. Apart from these flows, Malaysia has also tapped into international labour flows in order to maintain its cost competitiveness, especially in the 1990s. The impact of these flows on Malaysia will be examined in the following section.

LONG-TERM CAPITAL FLOWS

Both 'pull' and 'push' factors can be used to explain the outflow of long-term capital from source countries, as multinationals (MNCs) seek to maximize the expected returns on their investment by adopting a global production strategy. In developing this strategy, MNCs have chosen to 'slice up the value-added chain' by locating separate activities in different countries (Reinicke 1998). In turn, developing countries in need of foreign capital, technology, and marketing channels have utilized various policies to attract MNCs into their countries.

In the case of Malaysia, the switch from a public sector-led to a private sector-led growth strategy due to the twin deficits and economic recession in 1985 gave impetus to the provision of a more congenial investment climate for FDI.   For example, the Promotion of Investments Act of 1986 was enacted to stimulate the expansion of private investment through tax and other incentives. FDI was actively courted as foreign equity ownership was liberalized subject to export conditions. Institutional changes such as the provision of one-stop agency for the processing of investment approvals were also undertaken in order to enhance the other prevailing locational advantages of the time (Tham 1998).

As shown in Table 1, net inflows of corporate investment into the long-term capital account increased steadily from 1987 to 1992. Subsequently, the onset of the global slow-down in the developed economies checked the outflow of capital from these countries. As a result net inflows of corporate investment fell in 1993-95 before picking up again in 1996 and 1997. The AFC has clearly affected corporate investment in Malaysia as net inflows fell dramatically from RM14.5 billion to RM8.5 billion in 1998.Gross inflows of FDI are mainly concentrated in the manufacturing sector. This is not surprising given the aggressive promotion of this sector in the government's pursuit of rapid industrialization and the need for foreign technical knowledge and marketing channels. Within the manufacturing sector, the electrical and electronics sub-sector has received the largest share of total FDI in this sector since 1989.

In terms of source countries, Singapore was one of the two primary suppliers of foreign capital to Malaysia owing to its historical and geographical proximity (Tham 1999). Japan was the other major investor, outstripping the contribution of the United States and the United Kingdom before the crisis in 1997. Over time, Taiwanese investment gained in importance as its contribution to total FDI in the manufacturing sector rose sharply from 0.5 per cent in 1986 to 14.7 per cent in 1997. The share of South Korean investment also increased steadily from 0.1 per cent to 1.3 per cent in 1997 for the same duration.

The clear dominance of East Asian investment during this period resulted from several 'push' factors that were at work in tandem with the 'pull' factors outlined above. The realignment of exchange rates after the Plaza Accord of 1985 was one of the contributing 'push' factors. At the same time, the increase in production costs in East Asian countries as well as the withdrawal of privileges under the Generalized System of Preferences (GSP) from the Newly Industrialized Economies (NIEs) encouraged the outflows of capital from these countries. Apart from Malaysia, other Southeast Asian countries also benefited from these outflows with the liberalization of trade and investment policies within the region as a whole. In fact in 1993 the ASEAN-Four (Singapore, Malaysia, Indonesia and Thailand) were listed among the 10 largest host economies for both FDI flows and stock as a result of both the 'pull' and 'push' factors (Tham 1998).

Although net inflows have recovered in Malaysia post-crisis, they have yet to return to pre-crisis levels, owing to increasing competition from other countries such as China, regional instability and the dismal economic performance in Japan that has adversely affected outflows of Japanese Direct Investment (Anuwar and Tham 2002). The importance of Japan as a source country has also declined as approved investment post-crisis has shown the increasing importance of American investment (MIDA 2000).

Table 1. Net captial inflows to Malaysia, 1985-1999 (in RM million)

Year	Official long-term capital				Corpor-ate invest-ment	Balance on long-term capital	Private short-term capital			Errors and commissions
	Federal Govern-ment	NFPEs	Others	Total			Commercial banks	Others	Total	
1985	1339	962	203	2504	1725	4229	-164	1034	870	-168
1986	1611	20	493	2124	1262	3386	-1050	1003	-47	1322
1987	-2438	7	-39	-2470	1065	-1405	-2320	171	-2149	147
1988	-3094	-1984	-24	-5102	1884	-3218	-2498	-416	-2914	289
1989	-1038	-1631	853	-1816	4518	2702	1137	425	1562	358
1990	-787	-2064	15	-2836	6309	3473	2286	-930	1356	3015
1991	106	-740	-31	-665	10996	10331	3605	1530	5135	-395
1992	-3170	389	-95	-2876	13204	10328	9249	2708	11957	81
1993	-3134	4277	-164	979	12885	13864	10875	3056	13931	9370
1994	-4764	5761	-136	861	11394	11659	-13306	4821	-8485	3333
1995	-1633	7768	12	6147	10347	16611	229	2183	2529	-1896
1996	-2179	2844	83	748	12777	13525	8562	2639	10317	-6371
1997	-1683	6366	-38	4645	14450	19095	n.a	n.a	-12913	-1254
1998	1819	361	-43	2137	8490	10627	n.a	n.a	-20633	13513
1999	n.a.	n.a.	n.a.	5300	6170	11470	n.a.	n.a.	-22000	-5400

Notes: * = estimates; n.a. = not available.
Source: 1980-1996: Extracted from Nayaranan et al. (1999); 1997-1998: Central Bank, Annual Report 1999; 1999-2002: Economic Report 2002/2003.

The influx of FDI into the manufacturing sector before the crisis enabled the sector's share in the total Gross Domestic Product (GDP) of the country to increase steadily from 13.9 per cent in 1970 to a peak of 35.7 per cent in 1997 (Table 2). Its contribution to total employment also increased in tandem with the increasing importance of this sector, rising from 8.7 per cent in 1970 to 27.1 per cent in 1997. Although the crisis in 1997 adversely affected the performance of the manufacturing sector, it recovered in 1999 and continues to be the main engine of growth for the economy.

Table 2. Manufacturing's share of gross domestic product (GDP), employment, and exports, 1970-2001

Year	Manufacturing value added as % of total GDP*	Manufac- turing employment ('000)	Manufac- turing employment as % of total employment	Manufac- turing exports as % of total exports
1970	13.9	290	8.7	11.9
1975	17.4	398	10.1	21.9
1980	19.6	802	15.8	22.4
1985	19.1	836	15.1	32.8
1990	27.0	1290	19.5	62.8
1995	33.1(27.1)**	2027	25.7	79.6
1996	34.2(29.1)**	2230	26.4	80.5
1997	35.7(29.9)**	2375	27.1	81.0
1998	34.4(27.9)**	2277	27.0	82.9
1999	(29.9)**	2343	26.4	85.5
2000	(33.4)**	2558	27.6	86.6
2001ᵉ	(32.8)	2574	27.3***	86.4
2002ᶠ	(33.2)	n.a	n.a	n.a

Notes: * In 1978 constant prices; estimate; forecast by Ministry of Finance.
              ** In 1987 constant prices or numbers in parentheses.
              *** January-August.
              n.a. - not available.
Source: Anuwar and Tham (2002); Malaysia 2002.

SHORT-TERM CAPITAL FLOWS

As in the case of long-term flows, short-term flows are also guided by the expected return to investment and the variability of the rate of return over the life of the investment. According to Bercuson and Koenig (1993), movements in interest rate differentials and expected exchange rate changes were found to be highly correlated to movements in short-term flows for Thailand, Malaysia and Indonesia between 1986 and 1991.

For Malaysia, therefore, the unfavourable domestic interest rates relative to foreign rates as well as the expectation of a depreciation in the exchange rate caused a net outflow of short-term capital between 1986 and 1988 (Narayanan et al. 1999).

Conversely, the surge in net inflows between 1991 and 1993 (Table 1) was due to the shift in interest rate differential in Malaysia's favour and the expectation of the appreciation of the Ringgit (Central Bank 1995). The surge in net inflows reached a peak in 1993 when net inflows of short-term capital exceeded the net inflow of corporate investment for the same year. Further, the Central Bank's Annual Report of 1994 noted that a significant portion of these funds was for portfolio investment in the stock market.

The Central Bank intervened with various measures that were designed to curb these speculative inflows, since large inflows of short-term capital could cause the Ringgit to appreciate, and the corresponding deterioration in Malaysia's export competitiveness could worsen the current account. Besides intervening in the foreign exchange market in order to maintain stable exchange rates, attempts were also made to sterilize the impact of foreign exchange intervention to offset its impact on liquidity (Central Bank 1995). However since sterilization is costly, the Central Bank also utilized short-term administrative capital controls to deal directly with the inflows and to reduce the need for sterilization operations. Subsequently, the downward drift in the domestic interest rate together with these capital controls reversed the inflow of short-term capital in 1994 (Table 1). But net inflows grew rapidly after 1994, particularly in 1996 just before the emergence of the AFC.

The crisis in 1997 created an unanticipated shock as the Ringgit depreciated by over 35 per cent against the US dollar between 2 July and December 1997. The currency crisis in turn swiftly affected the financial sector as a severe contraction was experienced, with the Kuala Lumpur Stock Exchange losing half of its market capitalization while non-performing loans (NPLs) in the banking system rapidly increased with rising corporate insolvency. Hence the crisis triggered a net outflow in 1997 as capital moved out in search of better returns elsewhere. Ong (1999) contended that more than RM25 billion left Malaysia for Singapore owing to the higher deposit rates offered by the foreign banks there at that time.

As the crisis progressed, the domestic economy contracted sharply as domestic demand shrank owing to the negative wealth effects from the decline in share prices and increasing unemployment as a result of corporate failures and retrenchments. The initial response was to tighten fiscal and monetary policies in accordance with the orthodox International Monetary Fund (IMF) prescriptions. This, however, further aggravated the weakening domestic demand while external demand also contracted as the regional financial crisis worsened. Consequently, real output declined progressively throughout 1998 with the largest contraction in the third quarter of that year. For the year as a whole, real output fell to -7.4 per cent, far exceeding the contraction that was experienced in the last recession in 1985.

Uncertainty over the health of the financial system and economy of Malaysia as well as the region as a whole led to large outflows of portfolio investment, especially in the second and third quarters of that year (Central Bank 1999). As a result the net outflow of short-term capital was substantially larger (RM20.6 billion) in 1998 than that recorded for the previous year (RM12.9 billion, Table 1).

In order to counter the recession-deflation spiral, the government reversed the fiscal and monetary policy stance in 1998. Nevertheless, by the end of August 1998, the Ringgit had depreciated by 40 per cent against the US dollar from the pre-crisis level while the stock market fell by 72 per cent for the same period (Central Bank 1999). Hence on 1 September 1998 the government introduced more stringent measures in the form of selective capital controls. For example, the Ringgit was pegged at RM3.80:US$1 while portfolio investment was subjected to a one-year holding period. Monetary policy was further relaxed and interest rates were reduced to stimulate lending and to ensure funds were available for viable businesses.

Based on recommendations of the National Economic Action Council (NEAC) that was set up to oversee the recovery of the economy, reforms were also implemented to rehabilitate the banking sector with the establishment of Danaharta, an asset management company, to deal with the NPLs in that sector. At the same time a special-purpose vehicle, Danamodal Nasional Bhd., was also established to facilitate the re-capitalization of the banking institutions while the Corporate Debt Restructuring Committee was formed to assist the restructuring of troubled Malaysian companies.

In February 1999, in view of the increase in external reserves, the one-year holding period for portfolio funds was replaced with a two-tier exit levy. Under this system, profit made and repatriated within the space of a year incurred a 30 per cent levy while a 10 per cent levy was imposed on profit repatriated after a year. The two-tier system was administratively cumbersome, however, and was therefore replaced in September 1999 with a simpler flat exit levy of 10 per cent for the repatriation of profit made on portfolio investment. According to Thillainathan (1999), the perception that the exchange rate is undervalued and that the capital controls are temporary have not led to any serious capital flight as feared. Instead, net outflows of short-term capital increased by 6.6 per cent between 1998 and 1999 as compared to the 60 per cent increment between 1997 and 1998 (Table 1). By 2001, the capital controls that had been imposed on foreign portfolio investments had all been removed. Post-crisis, however, even those

Malaysians without any domestic borrowings have been required to obtain the approval of the Central Bank for investments abroad.

INTERNATIONAL TRADE

The structure and pattern of trade in Malaysia clearly reflects the increasing emphasis on the manufacturing sector as well as the influence of MNC production. According to Tham (1999), primary commodities was still an important component in total exports in 1985 as reflected by its relatively higher share in total exports compared with that of manufactured exports. But by 1998 this pattern had reversed, as the share of manufactured exports grew progressively until its share escalated to 83 per cent in 1998, while the share of primary commodities declined sharply to a mere 15.2 per cent. By 2000, manufactured exports accounted for 85.5 per cent of total exports (Table 2).

The increasing importance of manufactured exports can also be seen in the changing pattern of comparative advantage in Malaysia. Tham (1999) demonstrated that the revealed comparative advantage (RCA) of agricultural raw commodities, as measured by the trade balance coefficient, declined from 0.89 in 1988 to 0.44 in 1998. The RCA for manufactures, on the other hand, improved from -0.13 to 0.09. The change in comparative advantage for manufactured goods is tied to globalization and the progressive restructuring of international trade around the operations of global corporations and inter-firm arrangements for production and supply. In seeking to harness internationally the benefits of product differentiation and economies of scale, MNCs have disaggregated the production process into a number of stages. The different stages of production are located in countries that are most advantageous to that stage of production in order to maximize profits. Therefore, international sourcing of intermediate inputs as well as intra-firm trade have increasingly dominated the trade pattern of host economies to MNC production.

In the case of Malaysia, the strong presence of MNCs in the electronics and electrical sub-sector since the establishment of Free-Trade Zones (FTZs) in the early 1970s has affected both the export and import structure for manufactured goods. This in turn has had repercussions on the merchandise balance and the composition as well as the form of trade in Malaysia. For example, the share of exports of electronics and electrical appliances in total manufactured exports was not only the largest but increased from 52 per cent in 1985 to 68 per cent in 1998. Post-crisis, its share in total manufactured exports had further increased to 72.5 per cent in 2000 (Malaysia 2001).

The production of electronics and electrical products in the FTZs and Licensed Manufacturing Warehouses (LMWs) in the early days did not encourage the utilization of domestic inputs. This was a result of the removal of import duties on raw materials, component parts and machinery that are required directly in the manufacturing process for firms operating in the FTZs and LMWs. Customs formalities were also kept to a minimum. Moreover, domestic sourcing in the non resource-based sector was in general hindered by the low technological competence at that time as input requirements could not be met at the level of quality needed by the MNCs. Thus the imports of investment goods (31.1 per cent) and intermediate goods (47.7 per cent) constituted the bulk of imports in 1985. Besides the import of intermediate goods, investment goods were the largest for the manufacturing sector relative to the other sectors shown.

Nonetheless the strong growth in manufacturing exports generated an increasing surplus for the merchandise account until 1988. Subsequently growth in imports accelerated such that the deficit in the merchandise balance for all manufactures more than doubled from RM7,263 million to RM15,758 million from 1988 to 1990 (Piei and Khalifah 1996). Given the importance of manufacturing exports to total exports, any worsening in the deficit for manufactured products in the merchandise balance has been accompanied by a shrinking overall surplus in the merchandise balance. Therefore the overall surplus in Malaysia declined by almost half from 1988 to 1990 (Table 3).

Table 3. Balance of payments, RM million

	Merch-andise Account balance	Exports (f.o.b.)	Imports (f.o.b.)	Services Account balance	Balance on goods and services	Trans-fers (net)	Balance on Current Account
1985	8883	37576	28693	-10391	-1508	-14	-1522
1986	8378	34970	26592	-8790	-412	96	-316
1987	14703	44733	30030	-8409	6294	348	6642
1988	14524	54607	40083	-10180	4344	395	4739
1989	11871	66727	54856	-11392	479	219	698
1990	7093	77458	70365	-9723	-2630	147	-2483
1991	1449	92220	90771	-13195	-11746	102	-11644
1992	8609	100910	92301	-14568	-5959	337	-5622
1993	8231	118383	110152	-16670	-8439	513	-7926
1994	4460	148506	144046	-17005	-12545	-2225	-14770
1995	97	179491	179394	-19229	-19132	-2515	-21647
1996	10088	193363	182275	-18371	-8283	-2943	-11226
1997	10273	217712	207439	-22748	-12475	-3345	-15820
1998	69008	281947	212939	-22338	46670	-9876	36794
1999	86535	318946	232411	-32164	49004	-6499	47902

Note: Data cannot be updated beyond 1999 as the Balance of Payments has been reformatted and direct comparison with the previous years is not possible.

Source: Tham 1999; 1997-98 extracted from Malaysia, 2002.

The high import content in the manufacturing sector also implied a greater importance of intra-industry trade for manufactures as opposed to net trade or one-way trade that is based on endowment differences. Tham (1999) has shown that more than 50 per cent of the trade in manufactures was in the form of intra-industry trade for the years 1988-90, and that this has continued to increase over time.

Although an increase in domestic sourcing was reported for the electrical and electronics sub-sector in the late 1980s and 1990s due to the need for proximate suppliers with the introduction of flexible production techniques, imports of investment and intermediate goods nevertheless continued to register high growth rates (Rasiah 1995). This resulted from the rapid rate of expansion in the manufacturing sector as well as imports of lumpy items such as aircraft, ships and oil and gas exploration equipment (Central Bank 1996). At the same time, growth in manufacturing exports declined from 33.9 per cent in 1994 to 22.9 per cent in 1995. Despite improvements in the rate of growth for primary commodities due to the strong performance in rubber and palm oil, total export growth fell from 26.8 per cent in 1994 to 20.2 per cent in 1995. Consequently the surplus in the merchandise balance hit an all-time low in 1995 for the period shown in Table 3.

Growth in manufacturing exports further slowed down in 1996 due to the sharp fall in the rate of growth in the exports of electronics and electrical products from 38.4 per cent in 1994 to 7.6 per cent in 1996. This slow-down in export growth continued for the first half of 1997 while the decline in import growth was less for the same time period (Central Bank 1998).

The advent of the crisis in the second half of 1997 and the subsequent depreciation of the Ringgit enabled merchandise exports to achieve a growth rate of 23.3 per cent for the second half of that year in Ringgit terms. However, discounting the valuation gains due to the depreciation of the Ringgit, export growth rate in dollar terms was only 0.7 per cent for the whole year. As reported by the Central Bank's Annual Report for 1997, this was attributed to the fact that increases in export volume were offset by decreases in prices due to competitive pressures as the currencies of other countries from within the region also depreciated against the US dollar.

Despite valuation gains and stable export volumes, the deepening of the crisis in 1998 caused overall exports to decline by 6.9 per cent in that year as the fall in US dollar export prices exceeded the marginal gains in export volume (Central Bank 1999). The poor performance of exports can be attributed to the progressive fall in manufacturing exports throughout the first three quarters of 1998, before this turned around to register positive growth in the last quarter of that year. Therefore overall contraction for that year moderated to 4.6 per cent, in US dollar terms. This was owing to the fall in external demand from the Asia-Pacific region that was partially compensated by an increase in exports to the United States. Nonetheless severe price competition and excess capacity among the crisis-stricken countries caused a decline in export prices in US dollar terms that continued to pull down the export value despite improvements in export volume.

The crisis also impacted on gross imports, which shrank by 26.2 per cent in US dollar terms as import volume contracted sharply as a result of the fall in domestic demand, the fall in demand for input from the manufacturing sector, and the postponement of non-critical infrastructure and other large-scale projects. As a result, the surplus in the merchandise balance continued to improve from 1996 to 1998 (Table 3). Post-crisis, the merchandise balance continued to improve, achieving a positive net balance of RM79,247 million in 2000 (Malaysia 2002).

FOREIGN LABOUR

While Malaysia has imported foreign labour since colonial times, data on the stock and inflows of labour remain fragmented and uncertain. Even the Immigration Department was reported to have no estimates of the number and the distribution of immigrant workers in the early 1990s (World Bank 1995). This has been attributed to poor data management by the relevant authorities and the apparent lack of coordination between them as matters relating to immigration and labour are administered separately by the three major states of Malaysia: Peninsular, Sabah and Sarawak (Azizah 2001).

The lack of reliable data is in turn compounded by the presence of illegal workers and the fluidity of their status, as legally recruited workers become illegal overnight when they default on their job contracts. Conversely, illegal workers can be legalized through any of the regularization exercises that are conducted periodically. Officially, the number of foreign workers in Malaysia was estimated to be about 1 million in 1992/93 (Malaysia 1993) and to have grown to 1.7 million by July 1997 (Malaysia 1997). However, as Azizah (1998) has reported, the number of illegal workers can be substantial: the number identified by the authorities in Peninsular Malaysia alone between 1991 and 1996 amounted to 1.2 million.

In Malaysia, foreign workers are permitted to work in four main sectors – plantation, construction, manufacturing and services (primarily as domestic helpers). In terms of their distribution among these sectors, in 1993, 37.6 per cent worked in plantations, followed by 34.6 per cent in construction and 20.1 per cent in domestic households, while manufacturing accounted for only 6.3 per cent of the total (Azizah 2001). However, the sharp contraction of the construction industry as a result of the financial crisis in 1997 shifted the employment pattern. The manufacturing sector became the largest employer of foreign labour in 2001 (32 per cent), followed by plantation (21 per cent) and construction (16.7 per cent), while the share of domestic employment fell to 19.6 per cent.

The rapid growth of the manufacturing sector reduced unemployment from 6.9 per cent in 1985 to 2.8 per cent in 1995 – well below the natural rate of unemployment (Lee 1998). Malaysia thus moved from a labour surplus environment to one of labour shortage between 1985 and 1995. Consequently, the real monthly wage rate rose at an average of about 3.7 per cent per annum over the period 1991-93, thereby pushing up labour costs and reducing Malaysia's geographical advantage for labour-intensive manufacturing. The manufacturing sector took recourse to importing unskilled and semi-skilled foreign workers, legally and illegally, from neighbouring countries in an effort to overcome labour shortages.

The most acute shortage of labour, based on the number of unfilled vacancies between 1992 and 1996, was found in the category of production workers (Shamsulbahriah Ku 1998). This category of workers alone accounted for 68 per cent of the labour shortage in 1996. Furthermore, unskilled workers formed the largest percentage of unfilled vacancies by occupational category, averaging 81 per cent, between 1994 and 1996. Therefore it is not surprising that the occupational categories of legal foreign labour in Malaysian manufacturing show an increasing concentration of foreign workers in semi-skilled and unskilled jobs (Table 4).

Table Four also clearly shows the phenomenal growth in legal foreign workers in these two categories of workers for both direct and contract employment. For example, the percentage of foreign workers in the semi-skilled category grew from 2.5 per cent to 16.7 per cent between 1988 and 1996 for directly employed production workers while it grew from 8.6 per cent to 78.6 per cent in the case of contractual production workers. In the case of unskilled workers, this percentage grew from 1.5 per cent to 24.2 per cent between 1988 and 1996 for directly employed production workers, while it grew from 5.4 per cent to 37.9 per cent for contractual workers. Thus not only are foreign workers concentrated in the semi-skilled and unskilled categories, they also registered significant increases between 1988 and 1996.

According to manufacturing employers, foreign workers are hired because local workers cannot be found for these jobs. Nevertheless, it is possible that discriminatory wages may have contributed to the preference for foreign workers. Although legally foreign workers have been accorded the same status, wages and benefits as local workers since the revision in immigration policies in October 1991, employers may not necessarily abide by these regulations owing to poor enforcement.

Table 4. Percentage of foreign to total employed in the manufacturing sector, 1988-1996

Industry	1988	1989	1990	1991	1992	1993	1994	1995	1996
Electrical & Electronic Products	0.318	0.654	0.480	0.544	0.868	3.238	5.388	7.257	10.630
Textiles & Clothing	0.330	0.600	0.342	0.354	1.180	3.898	7.628	10.313	16.447
Chemicals & Chemical Products	0.676	0.918	0.573	0.552	0.930	4.322	7.400	9.553	13.338
Machinery, Appliances & Parts	1.348	1.566	1.623	1.906	1.590	2.411	4.844	6.673	13.763
Wood Products	3.830	4.341	2.003	7.665	13.640	22.595	27.110	28.089	33.320
Manufactures of Metal	1.823	2.167	2.004	2.227	3.400	4.352	6.480	9.360	13.167
Transport Equipment	1.367	2.536	0.975	1.141	1.490	2.253	4.253	7.931	8.982
Optical & Scientific Equipment	0.538	0.696	0.715	0.716	0.840	2.553	5.111	8.514	13.348
Food	2.410	2.877	2.341	2.630	2.680	3.903	5.455	6.810	10.440
Non-metallic Mineral Products	1.980	2.369	2.957	3.363	3.310	4.837	8.680	9.023	13.086
Iron & Steel Products	0.731	1.130	0.568	0.680	1.530	4.836	6.164	8.248	11.277
Rubber Products	0.450	0.586	0.492	0.525	2.480	6.509	9.978	11.634	17.847
Paper & Pulp Products	1.638	1.924	0.474	0.500	1.020	2.568	5.213	5.836	11.000
Beverages & Tobacco	0.482	0.811	0.450	0.454	0.610	1.097	1.126	1.697	2.456
Petroleum Products	3.827	8.545	3.800	4.250	2.980	3.602	2.965	5.877	4.492
Other Manufactures	0.146	0.400	0.330	0.476	2.980	2.888	5.095	4.407	5.564
All manufacturing	1.719	2.110	1.979	2.171	3.252	6.259	8.843	10.397	14.311

Source: Unpublished Data from the Department of Statistics.

In contrast to production workers, it can be observed that the change in the percentage of foreign workers is smallest for the managerial and professional category, growing from 9 per cent in 1988 to a peak of 12.6 per cent in 1991 before falling to around 11 to 11.7 per cent between 1994 and 1996 (Table 4). In the case of technical and supervisory workers, although the percentage of foreign workers grew steadily from 0.6 per cent in 1998 to 1.5 per cent in 1996, it nevertheless remains a rather small percentage. Comparing across the different categories of workers, it can be concluded that the utilization of legal foreign labour in manufacturing is relatively higher for semi-skilled and unskilled workers.

Moreover, the constant vacillation in government policy on foreign workers due to revisions in policies in response to employers' protests, has not been effective in reducing the dependency on foreign labour to meet the excess demand for semi-skilled and unskilled labour in this sector (World Bank 1995; Pillai 1998). Thus while total labour in the manufacturing sector registered an average annual rate of growth of 10.1 per cent between 1991 and 1996, the average annual rate of growth of foreign labour grew five times faster, at 53.2 per cent for the same duration (Tham and Liew 2002).

While recourse to foreign workers may have helped to keep the cost of unskilled labour down, it also encouraged continued investment in less skill-intensive industries, thereby delaying the restructuring of Malaysian industries into skill-intensive and higher value-added industries (World Bank 1995).

POLICY IMPLICATIONS

Globalization in the form of FDI flows has affected the pattern, structure and form of trade in Malaysia as well as economic growth, especially the growth of the manufacturing sector. The current challenge is to continue to grow in the midst of declining inflows of FDI and at the same time to move up the value-added chain of production of the MNCs and to reduce the dependence on semi-skilled and unskilled labour in the manufacturing sector. Clearly, the government has also identified this need, as seen in the increasing emphasis on skill-intensive and technology-intensive FDI in line with the industrial objective of moving up the value-added chain.

Creating FDI-friendly policies to induce the required increase in high-technology FDI requires going beyond incentives per se and must instead address improving Malaysia's overall geographical advantages. Given the policy preference for moving into higher value-added manufactured goods and the human capital requirements of this type of production, there is an urgent need to complement FDI policies with a suitable human capital formation policy. Producing workers who can think, adapt and innovate should be of the utmost importance if Malaysia is to succeed in attracting high-technology FDI.   This of course has significant implications for education policy in the country, and not only at tertiary level, as the love of learning and creative thinking should be instilled at the formative stages of the education process.   Rapid changes in technology will also require Malaysia to shift towards implementing the life-long learning paradigm in its education policy.

In addition, given the high rate of domestic savings and the positive resource gap in the country, domestic investment has to be harnessed for development in order to reduce the dependence on FDI.   Concurrently indigenous research and development capabilities have to be fostered in order to move Malaysia up the technology ladder.   Given the government's considerable investment in research facilities of rubber and palm oil, there needs to be a greater effort to promote the growth of these two sub-sectors, especially in the downstream segments of these industries.

Increasing competition for FDI also points to the need for regional cooperation in this area, as this can help to substitute for declining individual geographical advantages or compensate for individual geographical disadvantages in the region.   Modalities for cooperation can take the form of improving the implementation of the ASEAN Free Trade Area (AFTA), deepening economic integration beyond AFTA, joint promotion of FDI, improving transport and communication networks in the region, accelerating plans for the proposed ASEAN investment area and harmonizing investment regulation among member countries (Tham 1998).

Regional cooperation is even more important when speculative flows are considered.   As a small country, it is unlikely that Malaysia will be able to achieve the necessary safeguards in the international environment to contain excessive speculative activities on currencies on its own.   Hence it is important to be able to negotiate for these changes at a regional level, particularly among developing countries that have been affected by the same crisis.   The urgency for regional cooperation is underscored by the fact that there has been little progress in building a consensus for implementing reforms in the international financial system despite international recognition of the need for a global solution (Central Bank 1999).

CONCLUSION

Malaysia has industrialized rapidly by tapping into the main economic drivers of globalization such as long-term capital, trade, and labour flows. However, this rapid growth was curtailed by the massive outflow of short-term capital during the financial crisis in 1997, thereby demonstrating the negative impact of these flows.   Post-crisis developments indicate that

Malaysia is still dependent on the very same drivers of globalization that spurred its development before the crisis, as demonstrated by the contribution to the recovery in 1999 made by the revival of exports. Economic growth since then has continued to oscillate with the fluctuations in global growth.

The challenge, therefore, is to continue to sustain the development and industrialization of the country by utilizing these same drivers of globalization while at the same time encouraging domestic investment and increasing domestic research and development capabilities. In this regard, the development of human resources in Malaysia as well as regional cooperation, especially at the ASEAN level, will enhance Malaysia's capabilities to meet this challenge.

REFERENCES

Anuwar, Ali and S.Y. Tham (2002), 'Malaysia's Industrialisation in a Globalised World', paper presented at the 20th Anniversary Tun Abdul Razak Chair Conference, *Malaysia in the Twenty-First Century*, Ohio University, 2-3 April.

Azizah, Kassim (1998), 'Profile of Foreign Migrant Workers in Malaysia: Towards Compiling Reliable Statistics', paper presented at Conference on Migrant Workers and the Malaysian Economy, 19-20 May, Kuala Lumpur.

Azizah, Kassim (2001), 'Recent Trends in International Migration in Malaysia', paper presented at the First National Population Forum of the Millennium, 11 July, Faculty of Economics and Administration (FEA), University of Malaya, Kuala Lumpur.

Bercuson, K.B. and L.M. Koenig (1993), 'The Recent Surge in Capital Inflows to Three ASEAN Countries: Causes and Macroeconomic Impact', Occasional Papers No. 15, Kuala Lumpur: SEACEN.

Braunstein, E. and G. Epstein (1999), 'Creating International Credit Rules and the Multilateral Agreement on Investment: What are the Alternatives?', in Michie, J. and J.G. Smith (eds), *Global Instability*, London: Routledge.

Central Bank (1995), *Annual Report,* Kuala Lumpur: Central Bank.

Central Bank (1996), *Annual Report*, Kuala Lumpur: Central Bank.

Central Bank (1997), *Annual Report*, Kuala Lumpur: Central Bank.

Central Bank (1998), *Annual Report*, Kuala Lumpur: Central Bank.

Central Bank (1999), *Annual Report*, Kuala Lumpur: Central Bank.

Department of Statistics (2002), Unpublished Data on the Manufacturing Sector.

Lee, Kiong Hock (1998), 'Labour Market Issues: Skills, Training and Labour Productivity', in Soon, Lee Ying and Nagaraj Shyamala (eds), *The Seventh Malaysia Plan: Productivity for Sustainable Development*, Kuala Lumpur: University of Malaya Press.

Malaysia (1993), *Mid-Term Review of the Sixth Malaysia Plan*, Kuala Lumpur: National Printing Department.

Malaysia (1997), *Economic Report*, 1997/98, Kuala Lumpur: National Printing Department.

Malaysia (2001), *Eighth Malaysia Plan, 2001-2005*, Kuala Lumpur: Malaysian National Printing Corporation.

Malaysia (2002), *Economic Report*, 2002/2003, Kuala Lumpur: Malaysian National

Printing Corporation.

MIDA (Malaysian Industrial Development Authority) (2000), 'Statistics on the Manufacturing Sector', Unpublished paper.

Narayanan, S. et al. (1999), 'The East Asian Economic Crisis: Why was Malaysia Vulnerable?', *Malaysian Journal of Economic Studies*, **34** (1 & 2), June/December, 93-112.

Ong, H.C. (1999), 'Evolution of the Malaysian Financial System Beyond the Financial Crisis', in Masuyama, S., D. Vandenbrink and S.Y. Chia (eds), *East Asia's Financial Systems: Evolution and Crisis,* Singapore: Nomura Research Institute and Institute of Southeast Asian Studies.

Piei, M.H. and N. Khalifah (1996), 'Enhancing Competitiveness in a Dynamic Global Economy: Moving from Comparative Advantage to Competitive Advantage', paper presented at the MIER 1996 National Outlook Conference, 3-4 December, Kuala Lumpur.

Pillai, P. (1998), 'Managing Foreign Labour', in Ishak, Y. and A. Ghafar (eds), *Malaysian Industrialisation: Governance and Technical Change*, Bangi: Penerbit UKM.

Rasiah, R. (1995), *Foreign Capital and Industrialization in Malaysia*, London: St Martins Press.

Reinicke, W.H. (1998), *Global Public Policy*, Washington, D.C.: Brookings Institution Press.

Shamsulbahriah Ku Ahmad (1998), 'The Political Economy of Intra-ASEAN Labour Movements: An Overview of Issues and Implications', paper presented at Conference on Migrant Workers and the Malaysian Economy, 19-20 May, Kuala Lumpur.

Singh, A. (1999), '"Asian Capitalism" and the Financial Crisis' in Michie, J. and J.G. Smith (eds), *Global Instability*, London: Routledge.

Tham, Siew-Yean (1998), 'Competition and Cooperation for Foreign Direct Investment: an ASEAN Perspective', *Asia-Pacific Development Journal*, **5** (1), June, 9-36.

Tham, Siew-Yean (1999), 'Trade, Investment and Financial Flows Post-Crisis: the Case of Malaysia', paper presented at 24th Annual Conference of the Federation of ASEAN Economic Association on 'Markets, Governance and Comprehensive Developments: Recapturing the Pacific Century', Manila.

Tham, S.Y. and C.S. Liew (2002), 'Foreign Labour in Malaysian Manufacturing: Enhancing Malaysian Competitiveness', paper presented at International Conference on Globalisation, Culture and Inequalities: In Honour of the Work of the Late Prof. Dr. Ishak Shari (1948-2001), 19-21 August, Bangi, Malaysia.

Thillainathan, R. (1999), 'Malaysia's Exchange Control: The Case for a Review', *Newsletter of the Malaysian Economic Association,* **11** (4), October, 2-3.

World Bank (1995), *Malaysia: Meeting Labor Needs: More Workers and Better Skills*, Washington, D.C.: The World Bank.

5. (Case Study 1) Globalization and the Indonesian Economy: Unrealized Potential

Robert C. Rice and Idris F. Sulaiman

INTRODUCTION

Globalization has both caused difficulties and created opportunities for the Indonesian people. The openness of the economy proved to be a major problem when the Asian economic crisis struck in 1997. Indeed Indonesia was the country hardest hit, a fact that suggests that local issues had rendered the economy particularly vulnerable and that local regulatory agencies were far from adequate. This was not so much because of economic weaknesses as because of a growing expectation that the Suharto government might fall, given its worsening performance (especially in terms of governance) in the early 1990s and also given serious concerns about Suharto's health.

The crisis badly damaged the economy. The growth rate of real GDP fell from an average annual rate of 7.3 per cent from 1992-1996 to 4.7 per cent in 1997 and -13.0 per cent in 1998. It recovered slightly in 1999 at 0.3 per cent, and since then has been growing around 4 per cent per annum. This substantially slower post-crisis growth rate is not large enough to lower the massive disguised unemployment and underemployment rates. The rates of growth of the manufacturing and construction sectors were similarly adversely affected by the crisis, with a minus 11.4 per cent growth rate from 1997 to 1998. On 14 August 1997 Bank Indonesia allowed the rupiah to float freely, resulting in it depreciating from Rp 2,650 per US$ to around Rp 3,600 at the beginning of October 1997. It then weakened to Rp 9,500 per dollar in the first week of January 1998, and on 22 January 1998 reached its lowest level at Rp 16,000 per dollar. By the end of March it had appreciated back to Rp 8,325 (Bank Indonesia: *Report for the 1997/98 Fiscal Year*, pp. 75-78). This depreciation from Rp 2,650 to Rp 8,325 would eventually lead to the rupiah price of imports increasing 214 per cent. The flow-on effect resulted in the Indonesian inflation rate increasing from 6.5 per cent in 1996 to 11.1 per cent in 1997 and 77.6 per cent in 1998.

The crisis in 1997 'forced' Indonesia to request assistance from the International Monetary Fund.   The IMF recommended its usual tight money/high interest rate policies for fighting inflation and large capital outflows, which made the situation resulting from the crisis even more difficult for the highly indebted Indonesian private enterprises.   It also required the Indonesian government to undertake many actions that were reflected in the 17 Letters of Intent (LOI) from the Indonesian Government to the IMF starting with the LOI of October 31, 1997 and ending with March 18, 2003.[1] In general the IMF has strongly supported policies favourable to globalization. These include: ongoing convertibility of the rupiah for both current and capital account transactions; shortening the list of areas closed to foreign direct investment; lowering import and export taxes and removing quantitative restrictions on imports and exports; privatization of government enterprises; and policies to encourage competition, including in the information and communications technology area.   These measures strengthen manufacturers' competitiveness in export markets.   In spite of these pressures, the state-owned PT Telkom continues to inhibit competition in ICT activities (as discussed below).

Although IMF influences on the Indonesian government have favoured foreign direct investment and international trade, domestic factors have adversely affected the investment climate and stymied foreign direct investment (as discussed below).   Normally a large rupiah depreciation would increase the export competitiveness of manufacturers using imported component parts to produce for export.   The crisis affected Indonesia's international credit rating so adversely, however, that Indonesian letters of credit were no longer accepted overseas. This caused great difficulties for these manufacturers, including firms producing component parts for export. Fortunately with IMF support this problem has now been solved.

Indonesia is now extricating itself from the crisis and has entered a phase of development that, if well managed, will enable the society to optimize the benefits and opportunities made available by globalization. Unfortunately, Indonesia has far from realized the steps needed to exploit these opportunities. In this chapter we seek to assist rectification of this situation by highlighting two areas we believe are critical to the nation's development effort and by stressing the need for the government to take appropriate steps to ensure that an appropriate regulatory framework is in place. These are the opportunities made possible by the global vertical specialization of labour and the growth and diffusion of information and communication technologies.

GLOBALIZATION AND THE INCREASED VERTICAL DIVISION OF LABOUR IN MANUFACTURING

One potential benefit from globalization available to Indonesia is increased foreign direct investment, which can bring with it job creation, tax revenues, technology transfer, information about opportunities in export markets, and managerial know-how. From 1985 to 1997 foreign direct investment approvals increased from $1.06 billion to $33.82 billion, peaking in 1995 at 39.89 billion.[2] However, only a small percentage of the approved investment was actually realized (estimated at between 6 per cent and 17 per cent through 1997-2000). This was often owing to the fact that the country did not have the institutional and regulatory structures in place that could ensure realization of these opportunities (Gianie 2002, p. 96). After 1997, both approved and realized FDI further decreased (see Table 1) as the investment situation deteriorated owing to a decaying law and order environment and other adverse developments including an increase in the minimum wage (see SMERU Research Institute on the effects of minimum wage rates).

Table 1. Foreign direct investment in Indonesia

Year	Approvals ($ bill.)	Realized net private direct investment ($ mill.)
1985	1.06	
1995	39.89	4346
1996	29.94	6193
1997	33.82	4677
1998	13.59	-356
1999	10.89	-2754
2000	15.43	-4451
2001	15.06	-5877

Source: Bank Indonesia Website <http://www.bi.go.id/bank_indonesia2/utama/data_statistik/data.asp?head=71>, and Badan Koordinasi Penanaman Modal (December 2002).

As can be seen from Table 1, the capital inflow that has been approved is now on the increase, but as of 2001 the situation in relation to realized investment remained dire. We suggest that this situation can be turned around if opportunities made possible by the global division of labour in the automobile, motorcycle, electric and electronic equipment industries are capitalized upon and if a regulatory framework suitable to a globalizing economy is cemented in place and adequately managed. In short, if Indonesia does adopt the needed reforms it can capitalize on the decreased transportation and communications costs associated with globalization and on the increased vertical division of labour in manufacturing between countries in accordance with their comparative advantages made possible by globalization. It is this process that has increased the imported component content of finished manufactures in six of the largest developed countries from an unweighted average in 1950 of 5.3 per cent to 26.3 per cent in 1985 (Perraton et al. 2000, p. 145). In the case of Indonesia this vertical division of labour can result in producers of final goods in other countries electing to source labour-intensive intermediate inputs either through the establishment of new factories or by subcontracting to existing factories. This has happened already to a considerable degree in Malaysia (Rasiah 2001; Edgington and Hayter 2001).

What makes the situation especially opportune is the fact that Indonesia has already undertaken substantial infrastructure development designed to support the automobile and motorcycle industries and to a lesser extent the agricultural machinery and bicycle industries.[3] Vertical division of labour has already resulted in the growth of exports of some 'parts and accessories not elsewhere stated of motor vehicles' (Standard International Trade Classification (SITC) 784). This has happened for several types of parts and accessories, although for the whole category from 1988 to 2002 the value of net exports (exports minus imports) was negative, decreasing from minus $375 million in 1988 to minus 889 million in 2000, and then becoming less negative.[4] Two items showing large increases were road wheels and parts (SITC 784391), and radiators (SITC 784394) with net exports of $32.3 million and $36.5 million respectively in 2000, up from -$4.4 million and -$2.0 million in 1990 and $10.7 and 24.2 million in 1994. There appears to be good potential for further exports of automotive parts and components (JICA 2000, p. 4-86 to 4-88).

The motorcycle industry in Indonesia is generally considered to be more internationally competitive than the motor vehicle industry and a higher percentage of its component parts is produced in Indonesia. This resulted in rapid growth between 1988 and 1994 in exports of SITC group 785 (motorcycles, motor scooters and other cycles motorized and non MT), but the industry then declined. Exports in millions of US dollars in 1988, 1992, 1994, 2000, and 2001 were 16, 110, 243, 227, and 170 respectively. Net exports, however, have always been negative except in 1999, mainly because of the large net imports (imports minus exports) of SITC 78535910 (parts and accessories of vehicle for assembly purposes) and SITC 78535990 (other parts of motorcycles), which were $66 million and $150 million respectively in 2000. There has been little export of motorcycle component parts except those embodied in the motorcycles exported (net exports of $48 million in 1996, 60 million in 1998, and 38 million in 2000). Net exports of other bicycle parts increased from $2 million in 1992 to $92 million in 1994 and to $91 million in 1997, then decreased to $60 million in 1998 and stayed about the same thereafter. Indonesia has good potential for the production for export of some motorcycle and bicycle component parts because its large domestic market enables the realization of economies of scale, an important development given that the ASEAN Free Trade Area (AFTA) is to commence in 2003.

Other export areas that have high promise exist in the electrical and electronic equipment industries. These are SITC 75 (office machines and automatic data-processing), SITC 76 (telecommunications and sound-recording and reproducing apparatus and equipment), and SITC 77 (electrical machinery, apparatus and appliances, n.e.s., and electrical parts thereof – including non-electrical counterparts, n.e.s., of electrical household-type equipment). As these industries require many components for their manufacture there were good possibilities for realizing substantial gains from the global division of labour. For all three of these product groups there has been substantial progress in increasing exports, especially since 1994 (Thee 1996, p. 24). Respectively, the net export values are large at $2.9 billion (SITC 75), $3.0 billion (SITC 76) and $1.3 billion (SITC 77) in 2000 and $1.9, $3.1 and $1.6 billion in 2001. By way of comparison, the largest manufacturing industry in terms of net exports in 2000 and 2001 was clothing (SITC 84), at $4.7 and $4.5 billion respectively.

The rapid growth of Indonesian exports from the electric and electronic components industries in the 1990s is very encouraging. Foreign direct investors, especially from Asia, have played a leading role in increasing production and exports, mainly in the greater Jakarta and Batam island areas. The electrical and electronics components industry is dominated by Japanese enterprises (JICA 2000, pp. 3-28). It is important that the Indonesian government should continue to improve the investment climate for both local and foreign producers. Critical here is the need to permit 100 per cent foreign capitalization as it did in 1994. In the longer term these industries also need to be developed because they have the capacity to act as a vehicle enabling Indonesia to source higher technology exports.

INFORMATION COMMUNICATION TECHNOLOGIES

There is little doubt that Indonesia has the potential to accelerate and realize the benefits of information communication technology (ICT) and the knowledge-based economy. Here we argue that thus far the diffusion of the Internet and other ICT products and services has not been optimized primarily because of the inadequate regulatory system. This is part of a broader problem which we highlight by focusing on the ICT area. The lack of commitment to ICT regulatory reform by the government, coupled with the lack of compliance on the part of the telecommunications incumbent, has resulted in the less than impressive outcome of low e-readiness and other measurements of ICT diffusion. The section is divided into three parts. First, we detail Indonesia's e-readiness relative to other APEC member economies. We then provide an overview of the diffusion of ICTs in Indonesia and we identify some key policy impediments that have hampered the growth of ICTs. We close with some key recommendations that could put Indonesia on an open market path and enable ICTs to become instruments that empower and improve people's quality of life.

GLOBALIZATION AND E-READINESS

ICT is not a goal in itself but an instrument for development. A country's ICT diffusion can be measured by the e-readiness measurement. A recent study by APECTEL (2002) on e-commerce readiness in 10 East Asian APEC economies ranked Indonesia last.[5] While East Asia as a whole (average ranking of 3.00) needs to catch up with the ranking of leading nations (the US at 4.36, G7 at 3.92), there is a clear gap between rich and poor economies. By contrast Indonesia, with a score of 2.17, is not far behind Vietnam (2.28) and China (2.33). McConnell International's second e-readiness report (May 2001) assessed 53 countries that represent over two-thirds of the world's population and the greatest potential markets. The countries are rated on a scale of blue, amber and red. Indonesia ranked poorly, achieving the last ranking of 'red status'.[6] Worse, in none of the five categories of attributes was there any indication of improvement being made through 'public-private partnerships that are achieving E-Readiness impact' (McConnell International 2001, p. 13).

The e-readiness assessment of 60 countries by the London-based Economist Intelligence Unit (EIU 2003) is based on the extent to which a country's business environment is conducive to Internet-based commercial opportunities. Indonesia ranked 53rd in this survey. One of the conclusions of the EIU survey was that the Asian countries that gained high e-readiness rankings typically have adequate IT infrastructure, high per capita income, a significantly deregulated telecommunications sector, decreasing transaction costs, a pro-active government, a good education system and an openness towards trade and new ideas. In addition to creating an enabling environment, the countries that ranked highly (such as South Korea, Singapore and Hong Kong) have also introduced many 'online' government services using the Internet through e-government programs. Some of the difficulties in diffusing ICTs can be attributed to the recent economic crisis and its aftermath. There is little doubt that these events can be linked with Indonesia's low e-readiness ranking. However, it can be argued that Indonesia's poor ranking is in fact a direct result of the strength of the monopoly power of its telecommunications operators. The telecommunications sector represents the 'upstream' part of the ICT industries value chain continuum. As a result, cost structures in this segment of ICT directly affect the speed and spread of the diffusion of the Internet which, in Indonesia, principally runs on the telecommunications 'backbone' network of the main incumbent, PT Telkom. Efforts to deregulate this sector have slowed since August 2002. However, before detailing these developments, we provide some evidence of the existing diffusion and tremendous potential in Indonesia's telecommunications regime.

ICT-INTERNET DIFFUSION AND THEIR CATEGORIES

This section provides survey data on the characteristics of Internet use in the general urban population and more specifically amongst small and medium enterprises (SMEs). The survey was undertaken by the Indonesian Internet Industry (IIBC 2001) and examined 1,500 respondents in 10 large cities. It was found that most connections to the Internet were made by 26-35 year olds (38 per cent), followed by 14-25 year olds (32 per cent) and 36-55 year olds (30 per cent). The largest group of users had a bachelor's degree (39.6 per cent), followed by high school students (34.5 per cent), undergraduates (20.1 per cent) and post-graduate students (5.7 per cent). Occupationally, the largest users were private companies (43 per cent), followed by civil servants (11 per cent). The remaining users were entrepreneurs (10 per cent), professionals (3 per cent), housewives (1 per cent), students (25 per cent) and miscellaneous (6 per cent).

The existence of Internet kiosks or Warnet in Indonesia is of significance to SME exporters. The section below describes the current usage pattern of e-commerce by SMEs and the nature of the benefits derived. We also identify barriers to greater use of Internet and e-commerce by SMEs. In a survey of 227 companies – 50:50 small (5-25 employees) and medium (26-3000 employees) – conducted by the Asia Foundation and Castle Asia Group (2002), 153 companies (or 67 per cent) were found to have used the Internet. Most (41 per cent) had started within one to two years prior to the survey and were maintaining strong growth, with 20 per cent having joined in the last year.[7] Internet access was slow, with 93 per cent of users using dial-up connections because other connections were not available or were too expensive. Of companies surveyed, 86 per cent used the Internet to access e-mail (90 per cent with buyers and 48 per cent with suppliers).

The technical implementation of the Telecommunication Law No. 39/1999 began in August 2002 when the two incumbents, PT Telkom and PT Indosat, were allowed to compete in both the domestic and international communications markets.   PT Telkom commenced with an enormous advantage as it controlled almost all the telephone lines in the country and is the largest player in the ISP market. Given this situation, it is critical that the government as regulator ensures the two incumbents do not dominate the ISP market at the expense of retail customers and SMEs. This can be done by applying the Anti-Competition Law (1999) to state-owned companies such as PT Telkom or else by regulating competition through an independent telecommunications body. The Government should also open the market for global access so that charges on international bandwidth are reduced to the benefit of retail customers and SMEs.

PT Telkom has a particularly advantageous position in the ISP market and is gaining an ever greater market share (more than half as at January 2003) as it is able to offer combined ISP billing with its telephone service. With its 'TelkomNet Instan' service, it can offer combined Internet/telephone pulse rate without a monthly subscription fee at a cost cheaper than other ISPs for low volume users who access the Internet for less than 15 hours a month. These services have placed an enormous competitive pressure on other ISPs and have created an environment in which the industry is becoming monopolized and will continue to do so unless the government takes the steps needed to introduce and enforce a globally oriented competition policy.

In Indonesia, ISPs play a pivotal role in the diffusion of the Internet and in raising public awareness of the potential of ICTs, particularly in regional cities and towns. In January 2003, according to the ISP Association (APJII), the estimated number of Internet users reached 4.5 million and registered ISP subscribers reached 583,861. Of the total number of subscribers, 544,272 (93 per cent) were domestic subscribers while the remaining 39,583 (or 7 per cent) were from the corporate sector. According to the ISP Association, the estimated number of Internet ISP subscribers stood at 583,861 at the end of 2002.   Of the total number of subscribers, 544,272 (93 per cent) were domestic and other subscribers, while the remaining 39,583 (or 7 per cent) were from the corporate sector. While the total number of fixed telephone lines owned by both categories has reached 7.807 million lines (see Table 3), future growth will come mainly from the new fixed wireless CDMA technology rather than from PSTN telephones. Nevertheless, it is curious that the data from PT Telkom show that the projected growth will decline after 2003.

CONCLUSION

As noted at the outset, while Indonesia is the country that was hardest hit by the Asian economic crisis, it has now entered a phase of development that, if well managed, will enable the society to optimize the opportunities made available by globalization. We have sought to highlight some of the opportunities made possible by the vertical specialization of labour by focusing on the diffusion and development of information and communication technologies. We have argued that the infrastructure provided by the state has created significant opportunities in specific areas of manufacturing that can be realized. And by focusing on the diffusion of the Internet and other ICT products and services in Indonesia we have highlighted the fact that the government has not paid adequate attention to the need to shape the regulatory framework to a form appropriate to globalization. In short, the promise made possible by the reduction in transportation and communication costs, and the breaking down of barriers to the flow of goods, services, capital and knowledge is still not forthcoming as a result of an unimpressive regulatory regime.

Notwithstanding the limited diffusion of ICTs, various sections of the society, particularly small and medium enterprises and people from middle and upper income groups have benefited from ICT products and services. The main factors hindering the realization of this potential are related to PT Telkom's rent-seeking venture. Rather than functioning as a defender of the public interest to ensure that the monopoly acts as if it were competitive, the government has allowed PT Telkom to raise price caps under the guise that the rise was necessary to allow Telkom to expand the number of connections in Indonesia. Given this situation, it is doubtful that there will be any great increase in ICT diffusion until the government comes clean on its dealings with Telkom. Little can be expected from the current administration, which is already preoccupied with the coming elections of 2004. Future governments, however, can realize Indonesia's potential by taking steps to rectify the prevailing situation by establishing an independent telecommunications regulatory body (IRB) to monitor the competitive behaviour of the telecommunication sector. Also required is the full implementation of the 1999 telecommunication law in a spirit of open and fair competition. This can only be achieved when a truly 'modern licensing' system is implemented by the IRB to provide private independent operators in a fair and transparent manner.

In conclusion we reiterate our key point, this being that the opportunities for increased beneficial foreign direct investment have failed to be adequately capitalized on since the 1997 crisis, mainly because of adverse domestic factors – most notably the failure to establish a regulatory structure appropriate to globalization. Some of the potential for increased benefits from the production of component parts for export to the global market is being realized, but much more could be done.

REFERENCES

Asia Foundation (2002), 'SMEs and E-Commerce', unpublished report.

Asia-Pacific Economic Cooperation Telecommunications and Information Working Group (APECTEL) (2002), 'E-Commerce Readiness in East Asian APEC Economies: A Precursor to Determine HRD Requirements and Capacity Building', Bangkok: National Electronics and Computer Technology Center, National Science and Technology Development Agency, December.

Badan Koordinasi Penanaman Modal Republik Indonesia (Republic of Indonesia Investment Coordination Board) (2002), *Perkembangan Persetujuan Penanaman Modal* (Trend of Investment Approvals), Jakarta: Badan Koordinasi Penanaman Modal Republik Indonesia.

Badan Pusat Statistik (2002a), *Statistik Perdagangan Luar Negeri Indonesia: Ekspor 2001* (Indonesian Foreign Trade Statistics: Exports 2001), Jakarta.

Badan Pusat Statistik (2002b), *Statistik Perdagangan Luar Negeri Indonesia: Impor 2001* (Indonesian Foreign Trade Statistics: Imports 2001), Jakarta.

Booz, Allen and Hamilton (by consultants to the World Bank's Information Infrastructure Development Project) (2002), *Technical Assistance to Facilitate the Deployment of Government Online in Indonesia, Final Report Revised*, Ministry of Culture and Tourism: Jakarta, 22 March.

Economist Intelligence Unit (2003), 'E-Readiness Rankings 2001', online at <http://www.ebusinessforum.com/>.

Edgington, David and Roger Hayter (2001), 'Japanese electronics firms in Malaysia: after the financial crisis', in Chris Nyland, Wendy Smith, Russell Smyth and Antonia Marika Vicziany (eds), *Malaysian Business in the New Era*, Cheltenham, UK: Edward Elgar.

Feridhanusetyawan, Tubagus (2002), 'Kebijakan Ekonomi Makro Dalam Ekonomi Terbuka' (Macro-economic Policy in an Open Economy), in Indra J. Piliang, Edy Prasetyono and Hadi Soesastro (eds), *Merumuskan Kembali Kebangsaan Indonesia* (Reformulate the Indonesian Nation), Jakarta: Centre for Strategic and International Studies.

Gianie (2002), 'Penananam Modal: Kerja Keras Meyakinkan Investor' (Investment: Working Hard to Assure Investors), in Salomo Simanungkalit (ed.), *Indonesia Dalam Krisis 1997-2002* (Indonesia in Crisis 1997-2002), Jakarta: Penerbit Buku Kompas.

IIBC (Indonesia Internet Business Community and Internet Service Provider Association of Indonesia) (2001), 'Indonesia Cyber Industry and Market', Jakarta: PT Elex Media Komputindo.

International Telecommunications Union (2002), 'Kretek Internet: Indonesia Case Study', Geneva, January, <http://www.itu.int/ITU-D/ict/cs/)>.

Japan International Cooperation Agency (JICA) (2000), *Study on Inter-Firm Linkages and Financial Needs for the Development of Small- and Medium Scale*

Manufacturing Industry in Indonesia, Final Report March 2000, Jakarta: Japan International Cooperation Agency.

Japan Research Institute, Limited, and Yachiyo Engineering Co., Ltd. (1999), *The Follow-up Study on the Development of Supporting Industries in the Republic of Indonesia: Main Report.* Jakarta: Japan International Cooperation Agency and The Ministry of Industry and Trade, Republic of Indonesia.

McConnell International (2001), 'Ready? Net. Go! Partnerships Leading the Global Economy', <www.mcconnellinternational.com> in collaboration with <www.witsa.org>.

McLeod, Ross H. (1998), 'Indonesia', in Ross H. McLeod and Ross Garnaut (eds), *East Asia in Crisis: From Being a Miracle to Needing One?,* London: Routledge.

Morrissey, Oliver, and Michael Tribe (eds) (2001), *Economic Policy and Manufacturing Performance in Developing Countries,* Cheltenham, UK: Edward Elgar.

Owen, D., I.F. Sulaiman, S. Baldia and S. Mintz, 'Republic of Indonesia: Information Communications Technology Assessment', USAID-NEA Bureau, Washington, D.C., Indonesia Mission, Jakarta, February 2001, <http://www.pegasus.or.id/Reports/>.

Partnership for Economic Growth Project (2001), 'Survey on Uses of Information and Communications Technology by Indonesian SME Exporters and Regional Autonomy in Indonesia', unpublished report, <http://www.pegasus.or.id/Reports/>.

Perraton, Jonathan, David Goldblatt, David Held and Anthony McGrew (2000), 'The Globalisation of Economic Activity', in Richard Higgott and Anthony Payne (eds), *The New Political Economy of Globalisation,* Vol. 1, Cheltenham, UK: Edward Elgar.

Rasiah, Rajah (2001), 'The Importance of Size in the Growth and Performance of the Electrical Industrial Machinery and Apparatus Industry in Malaysia,' in Chris Nyland, Wendy Smith, Russell Smyth, and Antonia Marika Vicziany (eds), *Malaysian Business in the New Era,* Cheltenham, UK: Edward Elgar.

SMERU Research Institute (2001), 'Wage and Employment Effects of Minimum Wage Policy in the Indonesian Urban Labor Market', Jakarta: Partnership for Economic Growth Project, <http://www.pegasus.or.id/Reports/65)%20Minimum Wage.pdf>.

Thee, Kian Wie (1996), 'Pengembangan Daya Saing Industri Kecil dan Menengah' (Development of the Competitiveness of Small and Medium Industries), *Jurnal Analisis Social* (Social Analysis Journal), February, pp. 19-37.

Thoha, Mahmud (2001), *Globalisasi, Krisis Ekonomi dan Kebangkitan Ekonomi Kerakyatan* (Globalization, Economic Crisis and the Rising Up of the People's Economy), Jakarta: Pusat Penelitian Ekonomi, Lembaga Ilmu Pengetahuan.

Vietor, Richard H.K. and Robert E. Kennedy (2001), *Globalisation and Growth: Case Studies in National Economic Strategies,* Fort Worth, Texas: Harcourt.

World Bank (2003), *Global Development Finance 2003: Striving for Stability in Development Finance,* Washington, D.C.: World Bank.

World Bank (2002), *Globalisation, Growth, and Poverty: Building an Inclusive World Economy,* Washington, D.C.: World Bank.

Yusuf, Shahid (2001), *Globalisation and the Challenge for Developing Countries,* Washington, D.C.: World Bank.

NOTES

1   These are available on the IMF website, <http://www.imf.org/>.
2   Investment approval values are the sum of new projects, expansion of projects, and change of status of projects. Not included are foreign investments in oil and gas, banking, non-bank financial institutions, insurance and leasing.
3   This report is the second of two reports funded and published by the Japanese International Cooperative Agency as part of their technical assistance to Indonesia. Both reports dealt with the machinery parts and components, automotive parts and components, and electric and electronic parts and components industries. The first one was completed in March 1997.
4   All export and import data are taken from Badan Pusat Statistik export and import yearbooks.
5   E-readiness can be defined as 'the aptitude of an economy to use Internet-based computers and information technologies to migrate traditional businesses into the new economy, an economy that is characterized by the ability to perform business transactions in real-time — any form, anywhere, anytime, at any price. E-readiness reaches its optimal level when the economy is able to create new business opportunities that could not be done otherwise'. The framework used in ranking covers both macro and microeconomic factors that mirror the ability of an economy to compete in the new economy, and the eight measurable sets of variables considered in the ranking are: Knowledgeable Citizens, Macro Economy, Industry Competitiveness, Ability and Willingness to Invest, Access to Skilled Workforce (Supply Skills), Digital Infrastructure, Culture, Cost of Living and Pricing (APECTEL 2002).
6   The McConnell 'Global E-Readiness Summary' has three rankings representing various conditions necessary to support e-business and e-government. The ifve categories of ranking include infrastructure and access ('connectivity'), government policies ('e-leadership' and 'information security'), ICT education ('human capital'), and 'e-business climate'. There are three to five criteria to be measured in each category (McConnell International 2001).
7   The Asia Foundation study is based on a survey in 12 cities on Java, Sumatra, Sulawesi, Kalimantan and West Nusa Tenggara (Bali and Lombok) conducted between August and November 2001.

6. Globalization and *Hindutva*: India's Experience with Global Economic and Political Integration[1]

Marika Vicziany

This chapter examines the extent and nature of globalization and its impact on India. It is argued that the current degree of economic and technological integration is small and that more globalization rather than less would be to India's benefit. The obstacles to more integration are both internal and external. Policy makers in India continue to struggle with the meaning of market discipline and so economic reform has been slow. External forces have been even more restrictive. Economic subsidies continue to advantage European and American agriculture over Indian agriculture. What happens to Indian agriculture remains critical because so much of India's population will continue to rely on rural employment even when India's urbanization passes the halfway mark in the next ten or twenty years. Ironically, the developed nations that have been pushing hardest for more globalization are also the very countries most resistant to allowing a globalized world to emerge. Globalization, however, is not only a matter of economics. The most palpable evidence for globalization in India today is to be found in foreign funding to a virulently right-wing Hindu nationalism that has gripped the country in the last ten years. The consequences of the *hindutva* (Hindu nationalism) campaign were seen in the state of Gujarat that suffered from mass anti-Muslim killings in 2002. The chapter concludes that economic globalization or integration has yet to happen for India and that when it does, it could be enormously beneficial to India. Political and cultural integration, however, has been more intense with highly damaging consequences for Indian democracy and secularism.

HOW GLOBALIZED IS INDIA?

The proliferation of 'western' consumer goods in contemporary India is not a good index of India's globalization. In the capital cities there are more and more McDonald's, Coca-Cola, Barista coffee shops, Spanish-made designer clothing and cable TV. This showy presence of familiar, global products marks a change in the urban landscape since the opening up of the Indian economy after 1991. But it is a superficial presence. India remains at the margins of globalization by some key indices. In the words of Bimal Jalan, the Governor of the Reserve Bank of India, India is 'off the map' when globalization is measured as a percentage share of either world trade or foreign direct capital inflows: India's share is only 0.7 per cent and 0.4 per cent respectively (Jalan 2002, p. 2) and these figures have not been weighted against the reality of the Indian population representing about a fifth of the world's population. Taking population into account, India is even less integrated into the global economy. When globalization is defined as the growing integration of the processes of production and distribution, India's score rises in certain sectors. In the provision of customized software, for example, India is a world leader with Indian companies providing a large number of multinationals with specialized services in dedicated software development centres located in Indian cities (Vicziany 2001). This Indian success story does not enter most measures of 'globalization' because typically these do not include measures of services. However, success in one sector would not be sufficient to lift the total Indian experience to a point where one could say that 'globalization' was a major consideration in India's performance. As Figure 1 shows, beyond the isolated enclaves of technical excellence in cities like Bangalore, Mumbai, Chennai, Delhi and Hyderabad, India's IT and telecommunications infrastructure, relative to that of a comparable country like China, remains unimpressive. Most of the Indian indicators in Figure 1 fall far short of being equal to even 12 per cent of China's connectivity. With low technological connectivity, it is impossible to imagine how globalization in India can accelerate.

According to the 13 indicators used in the *Foreign Policy* globalization ranking of 62 countries representing some 85 per cent of the world's population, India's overall rank is 56 compared to 51, 45, 21, 18, and 4 for China, Russia, Australia, Malaysia and Singapore (Table 1). In 2003, Ireland was ranked as the world's most globalized country. The *Foreign Policy* indicators are based on four groups of variables: economic integration, personal integration, political integration and technical integration. While India's overall ranking is low, using the criterion of 'political integration' India's score is very high and exceeds those of Malaysia and Singapore: 14, 32 and 53 respectively. India's score of 14 even exceeds that of Ireland (22) which was, as noted, ranked as the world's most globalized country according to the overall index (Table 1). This political integration is measured by the following variables: the number of foreign embassies in the country; the number of Indian representatives in international organizations; and Indian participation in UN Security Council missions.

Figure 1. India's telecommunications infrastructure compared with China 2002

India as a % of China (India/China*100)

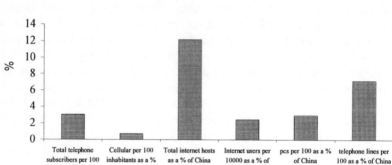

Source: International Telecommunications Union, 'Free statistics', <http://www.itu.org/>.

But India's political integration is far deeper than these indices suggest. One measure of this is the extensive political and financial connections between the Hindu fundamentalist parties in India and abroad. India's *sangh parivar*, the name given to a number of related Hindu fundamentalist organizations described in Figure 2, has developed parallel organs in America and Britain with the main objective of recruiting people and funds for the Hindu movement in India. Millions of dollars have been raised by these parallel organizations for Indian election campaigns and social programs designed to develop a mass support base for *hindutva*. In particular, the *sangh parivar* has evolved literacy programmes for tribal people who until now have remained at the margins of Indian political mobilization. During the first four decades after Indian independence in 1947, the *adivasis* (tribal people) voted for the Indian National Congress Party, but the decline of Congress dominance saw the *adivasi* vote being gradually weaned away from secular parties to communal parties such as the Bharatiya Janata Party (BJP). The mass electoral vote by the *adivasis* for the BJP in the Gujarat elections of December 2002 is only one sign of the effectiveness of the communal campaigns of the *sangh parivar*. Foreign funds have also been misused to help only the Hindu victims of poverty and disasters such as the Gujarat earthquake. Literacy and poverty alleviation are laudable objectives, but the problem with the anti-poverty programmes of the *sangh parivar* is that these activities have been conducted as part of a campaign against Muslims and Christians. It does not serve India's interests to create literate people who reject the citizenship rights of India's religious minorities which number well over 150 million people, making India into the world's largest Muslim country after Indonesia.

This overview of India's experience with globalization leads to the conclusion that India's economic integration is low but its political integration is high. The following sections of this chapter examine why this may be so. Before doing so, however, some general observations need to be made about how India's experience of globalization compares with international trends. Table 1 reveals some dramatic patterns. First, India shares with other large continental countries like China, Russia and the US a low level of economic integration. It is equally noticeable that the highest rankings for global economic integration go to relatively small nations. The case of the USA, however, is distinctively different from the other continental powers because America is highly integrated into global affairs according to technological parameters. India, China, Russia and the USA all receive high scores in terms of political integration. This derives from their claims to superpower status; but unlike the USA, the former planned socialist economies of Russia, China and India perform poorly on technology indicators. In other words, India's low economic integration is not unusual by world standards because it shares this characteristic with the USA. It is the combination of low economic with low technology integration that explains why India is relatively disadvantaged in the world economy and the USA, with its high technology rankings, is not.

THE REASONS FOR INDIA'S LOW ECONOMIC INTEGRATION INTO THE WORLD ECONOMY

India's low level of economic and technological integration into the world economy is caused by internal and external forces. Internally, India is still struggling to understand what it takes to establish an economic regime based on efficiency and competition. Whilst the underpinnings of the 'licence permit Raj' have been dismantled, India has not yet emerged from the fog of confusion about what is needed to build a new economic regime based on market principles. The developed countries of Europe and America, by contrast, are thoroughly familiar with the laws of market economics but staunchly refuse to observe these when it comes to giving foreign producers access to their domestic markets. These two sides of the problem will be discussed in turn.

Table 1. India's globalization relative to other selected countries

	Economic Integra-tion	Personal Integra-tion	Political Integra-tion	Technolo-gical Integration	Total Integra-tion
India	61	49	14	54	56
China	45	62	11	45	51
Australia	33	38	39	3	21
Britain	10	10	4	11	9
Ireland	1	1	22	17	1
France	12	17	1	21	12
Malaysia	8	24	32	23	18
Russia	51	54	3	43	45
Singapore	4	3	53	6	4
USA	50	33	2	1	11

Note: Ranking in 2003 of 62 countries from the least to the most globalized.
Source: A.T. Kearney/*Foreign PolicyMagazine*, January-February 2003 issue at:
    <http://www.foreignpolicy.com> accessed December 2002.

DOMESTIC BOTTLENECKS ON EFFICIENCY AND COMPETITION

The first sign that the Indian economy was in serious trouble emerged with the textile crisis that began in Mumbai in the 1970s and then manifested itself throughout the country's textile sector. Mill after mill began to close down, with the result that by the early 1990s Mumbai and other textile cities had 'de-industrialized'. The process by which this happened was very complex and cannot be described here, so readers are encouraged to consult the considerable literature that has emerged about this process (such as D'Monte 2002). The fundamental problem was that Indian textile production was too inefficient and too costly relative to the costs of labour and technology in China, Bangladesh, Pakistan and many other countries. To protect jobs in the textile sector, the Indian government intervened with the result that textiles became the core component of India's 'sick industries', surviving only because of government protection. Moreover, this protection was given not because the government had any plans for significant managerial or technological changes, but only because the textile workers constituted an important bloc of voters who had the sympathies of other public sector employees in equally moribund industries such as coal mining. Thus they constituted a significant vote bank. In more recent years, Indian manufacturing has found itself facing competition in many other products, in particular from Chinese substitutes. Whilst world manufacturing has increasingly shifted from the north to the south (Desai 2002), within the south itself considerable differences have emerged between the capacities of developing nations to meet the needs of global markets at prices which appear to be on a never-ending downward spiral as new and cheaper sources of labour emerge. During the last two years alone, India has lost its export markets for rubber gloves in Latin America and granite in Japan to Chinese competition, while the textile crisis also continues unabated.

One major reason for India's continued inefficiency in manufacturing is the slow speed of economic reform and technological change. During the period of socialist planning before 1991, the real costs of production in India were thoroughly distorted as a combined result of subsidies for industrial inputs, high tariffs that prevented the import of more competitive goods, and the policy of 'indigenous availability' that placed a premium on buying Indian components and raw materials (Mathur 1993, pp. 91-106). In particular, the mixed economy that emerged during the time of Indira Gandhi gave a privileged position to public sector enterprises and bureaucratic control of the private sector in a manner totally unrelated to market objectives. Government officials found themselves in the position of rentiers dispensing industrial licences to whomever they pleased whilst government appointees of public sector enterprises found themselves at the helm of vastly overstaffed production units which spent more time squabbling about wages and conditions than worrying about technological change or export-oriented growth. The Indian economy today has to live with the legacy of this because the slow speed of economic reform has been unable to reverse the fortunes of Indian industry fast enough. Slow reform, in turn, has seen the emergence of a major fiscal crisis that has pushed domestic debt to 60 per cent of GDP (*The Economic Times* 2003). According to some observers, India today is in the same precarious financial position that confronted the country in 1991 when it decided to deregulate the international sector of the economy.

The desperate fiscal state has compelled the government of India to engage upon an accelerated path of selling off profitable public sector units after a stop-go disinvestment policy during the last decade. A Disinvestment Ministry was set up in 2001 and the current Minister at the time of writing was determined to push through a wide range of strategic sales to rescue a cash-starved government. Funds from these sales were to go straight into Consolidated Revenue in an attempt to prevent the public debt from blowing out even further. However, the disinvestment policy was too narrowly conceived as a 'fire sale'. Disinvestment should provide India with an opportunity to boost its stock exchanges and promote private investment and confidence. The option of floating the profitable public sector units on the stock markets, however, was rejected in favour of strategic sales to a small number of large bidders. Only 16 per cent of the new capital was raised by public issue and only a third of this has been allocated to small investors ('Small investors left out from PSU selloffs', 2003). As a result, the process of disinvestment opened the Indian government to accusations of unfair bidding processes by coalition partners such as the Shiv Sena (Vicziany 2002). Political opposition and opportunism continue to slow down the reform process. But the overall problem is that the disinvestment process has missed an opportunity to throw decisions about ownership of former public assets back onto the marketplace. As a result, the Indian market is the weaker for this.

The sale of public sector enterprises is a good thing in its own right because it sends out strong signals to Indian and foreign entrepreneurs that the Indian state is now withdrawing from its role as the country's chief entrepreneur. This role has since the 1960s been one major reason for the relatively slow growth of the Indian economy because the PSUs had no agenda to act as a catalyst for technological change. Another reason why disinvestment is a positive move is that it coincides with emerging evidence about the degree to which Indian politics has become criminalized. The faster Indian production is removed from the influence of criminal politicians, the better for economic growth. In the old public sector system, for example, appointments to high managerial positions were overwhelmingly political decisions. And if a political decision could not be reached because of too much infighting, the PSUs went 'topless' for a time. Some PSUs were topless or without CEOs for months, even years.

The growing criminality of Indian politics is a major concern. One report estimates that 37 per cent of Indian politicians have criminal records. That figure does not include eminent Indian citizens like the Deputy Prime Minister himself, Mr L.K. Advani, who is about to stand trial for his role in inciting the destruction of the Babri Masjid in December 1992. This event gave birth to a violent communal movement that led to the anti-Muslim killings in Gujarat in 2002. In the Cabinet reshuffle that occurred on 29 January 2003, the Department of Personnel and Training (DoPT) was shifted to the portfolio of the Deputy Prime Minister. That department normally runs the Central Bureau of Investigation (CBI) which is prosecuting the Deputy PM. To avoid the obvious conflict of interest in the case of the Babri Masjid, the CBI was separated from the DoPT, and now reports directly to the Prime Minister, Mr Vajpayee ('CBI will remain under Vajpayee, not Advani' 2003, p. 1). It is not clear how long this arrangement will remain in place, but for the CBI to report to Vajpayee is no solution to the conflict of interest. Rather this example provides a dramatic illustration of the problem of governance in modern India: the organs of the state trusted with maintaining law and order are now run by a coalition government headed up by the BJP which, as an integral part of the *sangh parivar*, is itself the origin of communal hatred, violence and civil disorder.

Resistance to disinvestment is also a highly politicized matter not unrelated to *hindutva*. The most vocal resistance is coming from trade unions controlled by right-wing Hindu parties such as the Shiv Sena in Mumbai that has spearheaded the protest against the privatization of the Centaur Hotels (Vicziany 2002, pp. 47-48). Economic reform, in other words, is moving slowly because it is caught up with poor governance and the communal agenda of the BJP's coalition partners, such as the Shiv Sena. There is also the long-standing tension within the BJP's agenda between policies supporting more market liberalization and the older adherence to *swadeshi* or nationalist economics. This tension was first identified by Desai in the early 1990s (Desai 1994; 1996), but the continued oscillation between more disinvestment and then less disinvestment, for example, suggests that the tension has not been resolved.

Another reason for India's low level of economic and technological integration with the global economy is that a large part of India's energies is taken up with running the illegal black economy. One estimate has suggested that the black economy when measured as a percentage of India's GDP is about 44 per cent as big. This makes the black economy as large as the legal production generated by agriculture and industry together. Compared with Europe's worst-case scenarios, Italy and Spain, the size of the black economy in India is double their size: 44 per cent compared with 19 and 22 per cent respectively (Kumar 2002, pp. 303-304).

The size of the black economy in India is alarming because it is another index of why the official economy does not work properly. Almost every economic activity in the legal sector has its counterpart in the black economy, with the result that the official economy is drained of the capital, time and labour resources it so desperately needs. At the same time, the tax base of the Indian state continues to shrink, thereby worsening the fiscal crisis. In a number of revealing appendices to his book, Kumar documents how the illegal economy has enmeshed ordinary Indians – shopkeepers, school or university teachers, all kinds of professionals, police, army personnel and so on. Kumar has merely documented what is common experience in India. Prostitution, arms trading and drug smuggling – the core of the black economy in many other countries – are the least of India's problems. In Delhi, for example, street vendors who sell a wide variety of perishable and consumer goods are forced to pay between Rs.500 and Rs.10,000 a month to the police so that they can continue to run their stalls (Kishwar 2001, p. 6). The overplayed 'freedom of the press' in India has not generated any capacity to fight for changes that might result in financial transparency:

> It [the media] is supposed to act 'responsibly' and not rock the system. The

rewards for good behaviour have taken the shape of facilities like travel, housing, import of computers, jaunts and guest-house facilities (Kumar 2002, p. 149).

The few journalists who have been willing to pursue difficult issues have all too frequently been subjected to intimidation and coercion, especially in Mumbai and Maharashtra where the ultra-right wing Shiv Sena has resorted to violence to keep the press subdued (Sainath 1998b).

A final factor to consider as a reason for the slow pace of economic reform is the ideological resistance to globalization. The most potent example of such an ideology is contained within the *swadeshi* campaigns that began in the 1920s as part of the independence movement. *Swadeshi* stands for 'buy Indian products and boycott foreign goods'. Elements of *swadeshi* periodically re-emerge in India, primarily as political campaigns designed to mobilize votes amongst the poor, unemployed and disgruntled labouring classes who are more than willing to blame foreigners for their troubles. Although the BJP was the first party to systematically attack the economic controls that characterized four decades of Congress Party rule after independence (1947), it has also retained elements of *swadeshi* in its slogans 'computer chips not potato chips' and 'laptops not lipsticks'. However, as noted earlier, the BJP has not yet resolved the tension between its old ideological attachment to *swadeshi* and the pragmatic compulsions behind the need for serious economic reform and market liberalization.

What we can say, however, is that *swadeshi* has been an unreliable ally in the attacks on globalization because of the subtle ways in which foreign ideas in India have a habit of comfortably merging with local traditions. The values of the Indian elite in particular incorporate elements of US culture in matters of material consumption and education. At the same time, core values and cultural preferences have not been threatened nor have the popular items of Indian consumption been set aside – the *sari* remains perhaps the most enduring and elegant symbol of Indian confidence. The following discussion of *swadeshi* focuses on the Malegaon riots of October 2001 and shows that *swadeshi* is not the primary consideration within the Indian polity. The anatomy of that riot provides a bizarre example of how the gross negligence of the Indian state in the matter of the country's textile industry has now reaped harsh realities which, when matched with communal hatred, gave birth to civil violence and disorder.

After Friday midday prayers on 26 October 2001, an anonymous leaflet printed in Urdu was distributed by one Muslim youth outside the largest mosque in the rural town of Malegaon, Nasik district, in western India. The leaflet carried a heading in English: 'BOYCOTT: Drive Out the Foreign; Save the Country' (Nadeem 2001). A police constable standing nearby grabbed some of the leaflets and a scuffle broke out between police and worshippers that within a few hours grew into a full-scale riot – first between police and Muslims, and then between Muslims and Hindus when a Hindu structure was accidentally damaged in the scuffle.

The leaflet encouraged *all* Indians, not only Muslims, to boycott foreign goods and buy local manufactures. It had the hallmarks of a classic *swadeshi* document. The call for a boycott would have brought short-term benefits to both Muslim and Hindu residents in Malegaon, which emerged as a major textile centre in rural western India with the de-industrialization of Mumbai. None of this, however, is relevant to understanding what happened in Malegaon. The police intervened without bothering to find out what the leaflets were about. The circumstances were sufficient to arouse their suspicion; it has even been suggested that the police believed the leaflets had something to do with Osama bin Laden. In the ensuing violence, 12 Muslims were killed and one Hindu, most of the deaths being the result of police shootings. The total damage to the town was estimated at Rs.3 *crore* whilst insurance claims amounted to Rs.25 *lakh* ('CM Maharashtra visited Malegaon', 2001). How could a *swadeshi* campaign end up as one of the worst communal riots in western India?

The Malegaon riots are significant because they were, with hindsight, a precursor of the much greater Hindu-Muslim violence that erupted in the Gujarat in 2002. The one big difference is that whilst most of the victims in the Malegaon riots were Muslims, the town itself has a Muslim majority population representing 75 per cent of the local people (Concerned Citizens' Report on the Malegaon Riots, 2001). The riot was set off by the intervention of the police, who remain a largely Hindu force throughout most of India. Moreover, the police did not intervene to keep the escalating violence under control. Even in a Muslim majority town, the Muslims appear to have been defenceless and undefended. When the riot spread to the surrounding villages, the local Hindu population gave the violence more momentum – a reflection of their numerical dominance in the countryside.

As in the Gujarat in 2002 (see below), the police played a critical role in the outbreak of the violence and its sustainability. The general community of Malegaon was also divided along economic lines, with the minority Hindu population being engaged in cotton spinning and the sale of finished cloth whilst the Muslim majority were the cotton weavers who purchased yarn from the Hindus spinners and sold finished cloth to the Hindu middlemen. The financial basis of the textile industry resembled a 'putting out system' whereby the weavers felt increasingly squeezed between the spinners and cloth sellers. However, the call for a boycott of foreign goods by the Muslim weavers went beyond these divisions and appealed to the general population of Malegaon along a familiar *swadeshi* model first made popular by Mahatma Gandhi in the 1920s. Despite this, Malegaon is now best known as a centre of communal strife rather than a centre for the resurgence of *swadeshi.* This is only one example of how *swadeshi* has become a small and ineffectual voice within India, even if it is not totally irrelevant. The most powerful voice is preoccupied with religious and cultural divisions; in particular, it is anti Muslim and pro Hindu.

INTERNATIONAL CONSTRAINTS ON INDIA'S ECONOMIC INTEGRATION WITH THE GLOBAL ECONOMY

The previous section argued that the Indian economy is faced with many serious domestic problems that prevent it from establishing an economic regime that can turn things around fast enough at a time when China is emerging as a major global competitor. But the weak links between India and a globalized world economy also exist because powerful external forces prevent access to overseas commodity markets in which India could compete effectively. A stark example of this can be seen in the world rice trade, which has doubled in volume during the last decade (Gulati and Narayanan 2003, p. 45). Rice is a good example of how developed countries are distorting the potential benefits of globalization for developing nations. Rice is the world's largest cereal crop but the growth in rice trading has been driven largely by the artificial competitive advantages created by the EU and US governments through a combination of subsidies, export credit guarantees and food 'aid' programs to their own domestic producers. Gulati and Narayanan estimate that during the late 1990s about 65 and 22 per cent of rice exports from the EU and the USA respectively benefited from some form of domestic price support (Gulati and Narayanan 2003, p. 46). Developing countries, by contrast, tend to tax rice producers as part of their drive to generate capital accumulation for urban and industrial growth. To capture the extent to which rice from developed and developing countries is protected, Gulati and Narayanan calculated nominal protection coefficients (NPCs) to separate the competitive from the non-competitive producers:

> . . . Japan is at the high end of the spectrum with an NPC of 6.5 . . . Korea is also becoming uncompetitive, as are the United States and the European Union. On the other hand, countries such as China, India, Vietnam and Pakistan, with NPCs less than one, are competitive (Gulati and Narayanan 2003, p. 47).

Gulati and Narayanan argue, and their logic is sound, that if all trade barriers and price distortions were removed, the world rice trade would involve large quantities of rice being exported from the cheaper, competitive developing countries to the richer, high-cost developed countries. Such exports would generate jobs, income and development in rural Asia where about 70 per cent of the world's poor live. Freed from unfair restrictions, the world's trade in rice would be a powerful tool against mass poverty – more effective than aid or government attempts to generate public works (Gulati 2003, pp. 48-49). The growth of slums like Dharavi in Mumbai, Asia's largest, would be contained because the rural jobs created by cereal exports would keep people on farms rather than compelling them to search for jobs in the burgeoning cities of Asia (Vicziany and Vichare 2003).

There are plenty of other examples showing how the agricultural policies of developed countries are preventing the benefits of globalization from accruing to developing countries. According to Meghnad Desai:

> Each cow in Europe gets a subsidy of US2.25 cents a day. This is above the poverty line that the US applies to the poor in developing countries, i.e. the poor are defined as those that live below US$2 per day per capita (Desai 2002).

Cotton provides another example of unfair advantages accruing to developed countries. About 60 million people in India depend on the production and exchange of raw cotton. Its importance also derives from the fact that cotton can be grown in dry areas where other irrigated crops are not possible. During the last five years, however, Indian cotton production has declined, exports have virtually ceased and imports have been rising. Some of these shifts reflect the urgent need for technological change in raw cotton production, but much is also due to imported raw cotton being highly subsidized and sold to Indian mills on cheap credit terms that Indian producers cannot compete with (Mayee et al. 2002, p. 131). Unfair competition has also been blamed for the 25 per cent decline in Indian oilseed production in the four years 1996-97 to 2000-01 and the massive increase in imports (Singh 2002, p. 39).

In India between 30 and 45 per cent of the population live below the poverty line. The lack of employment opportunities in rural India is driving people into cities and those who can afford it seek to escape from India altogether to lands of opportunity in Europe, America and Australia. In these developed countries, the negative impact of anti-globalization agricultural protectionism is coming back to haunt policy makers in the waves of economic refugees who arrive to compete for jobs and welfare benefits. In the words of Stiglitz, the problem with globalization for countries like India is not the globalization of production and distribution but rather the way in which globalization has been managed by the developed countries and the global institutions that they dominate (Stiglitz 2002, p. 10). The unyielding market-conforming standards insisted on by the IMF and the World Bank have created much hardship. Sainath's case studies of the poor in rural India have thrown up multiple examples of how such mismanagement by international organizations has exacerbated poverty by introducing inappropriate technology (Sainath 1998a), creating new local 'community' structures that have dispossessed the poor (Sainath 2002a and 2002b) and insisting on tough 'user pays' principles which poor and marginal farmers cannot meet (Sainath 2001a). In drought-prone areas that are the most affected by these new 'development initiatives', suicide has become a way out for some farmers who have nothing left to sell to survive or cover their debts (Sainath 2001b; Sainath 2001c).

Critics of Indian agriculture argue that the rural sector is in trouble because of the lack of technological change and modernization. They point to examples such as the Indian tea industry that is having trouble facing competition from China, Kenya, Sri Lanka and Vietnam owing to low productivity driven partly by the fact that almost 40 per cent of India's tea plants are over 50 years old (Boriah 2002, p. 127). India is still the world's largest producer of tea, and the industry employs some 3 million people in production, processing and marketing. The failure to modernize an industry that is still a major earner of foreign exchange is a serious problem. At the same time, the woes of the Indian tea industry are small compared to the even greater difficulties faced by cereal and cotton producers where the unfair competition of developed countries is so overwhelming that the process of agricultural modernization within India itself is in jeopardy. How can India invest in agricultural modernization when at today's prices its principal commodities cannot compete with highly subsidized produce from the rich nations?

WHY INDIA'S POLITICAL INTEGRATION INTO GLOBAL AFFAIRS IS SO HIGH, AND ITS CONSEQUENCES

We saw in Table 1 that India punches above its economic and technological weight in matters of global politics. There are three reasons for this. First is the legacy of the first Indian Prime Minister, Nehru, who led the South's non-aligned movement in the 1950s. Vestiges of that early leadership survive today in India's involvement in a large number of UN peacekeeping missions. Second, although India no longer leads the South it is determined to be taken seriously as a power in its own right. As a demonstration of this, India formally entered the world's nuclear club in May 1998 when it conducted nuclear tests in the Rajasthan desert.

Third, India has for many centuries exported both cheap labour and talented entrepreneurs and scientists to many parts of the world. Today the Indian diaspora has come into its own. Some 30 million Indians live abroad as residents and citizens of other countries. Whilst this is a small number compared to the Chinese diaspora (which is probably three times as large), the overseas Indians command important positions in the affairs of the US,

Canada, Southeast Asia and Africa. The Sindhi community alone is known for its acumen and forms a business elite in London, Jakarta and Hong Kong. In America's Silicon Valley, about 40 per cent of IT companies have been established or are run by non-resident Indians. For decades, Indian economists have staffed key global organizations such as the UN, ILO and World Bank. American organizations such as NASA have depended on the brain drain of Indian mathematicians and scientists. In Africa, the Gujarati business community has been an influential elite for centuries, whilst in Britain many Indian-born citizens have risen to public prominence. Beneath this elite group lies a vast number of ordinary Indians who during the last 150 years have escaped from lives of poverty on the Indian subcontinent to become successful working and middle-class residents abroad. They contribute four times the remittances and investment in India that the elite overseas business groups do (Bidwai 2003).

What we have only come to appreciate during the last few years is how Indian migration across the globe has provided right-wing Hindu fundamentalist parties in India with opportunities for recruiting sympathy, supporters and funds from this diaspora. This is arguably the most powerful impact that globalization has had on contemporary India – and it is regrettably a very destructive one. The money flowing back to India has been used to fund programmes calculated to destroy the fabric of Indian secularism in order to promote the interests of *Hindu Rashtra* or the Hindu Nation (narrowly defined as a nation that privileges Hindu religious beliefs, values and customs to the exclusion of the rights of religious minorities such as Muslims and Christians). The softer version of *Hindu Rashtra* is *Hindutva*, which holds that Muslims and Christians are welcome to remain in India provided they demonstrate their loyalty to the Hindu Nation and concede the dominant rights of the Hindu majority. Unfortunately *Hindutva* establishes a paradigm that promotes and condones the harshest discrimination against non-Hindus. For many years, the Indian Prime Minister Mr Atal Behari Vajpayee, a long time devotee of the Rashtriya Swayamsevak Sangh (hereafter RSS), was regarded as the symbol of this softer *Hindutva*. However, the mass killings that occurred in Gujarat in 2002 convinced many loyal Indians that Mr Vajpayee himself was the most dangerous element of the *Hindutva* campaign, precisely because his stance provided a deceptive foil of respectability to a movement that on the ground turned out to be nothing less than an anti-Muslim campaign condoned by the ruling party in New Delhi.

The communal violence unleashed during the last two decades against India's Christian and Muslim communities has now been identified as the work of the *sangh parivar*, the name given to a corpus of organizations which all derive their legitimacy, guidance and instructions from the RSS, whose literal meaning in English is 'National Volunteer Corps'. Moreover, the *sangh parivar* has developed parallel organizations in America and Europe charged with the role of recruiting international support and money for the building of the *Hindu Rahstra* back home in India. The Indian diaspora remains closely linked to India through arranged marriages (which are still preferred to love marriages), remittances and employment networks. These same links have provided the *sangh parivar* with opportunities to promote its ideology of hatred and exclusion. Figure 2, reproduced from a report by Sabrang Communications (Mumbai) and the South Asia Citizens Web (France) in 2002, shows the relationship between the various Indian and US/UK components of the *sangh parivar*. Added to this diagram is information about the work of the *sangh parivar* in the UK. As the contours of these international connections have become known, there has been mounting criticism of the overseas activities of the RSS by many overseas Indians including Lord Desai, Lord Patel, Professor A.K. Sen, Kanwal Rekhi and hundreds of other European and US citizens of Indian origin. In the USA 250 eminent experts on South Asia signed a petition in December 2002 asking US corporations to oppose sectarianism in India by refusing to give donations to the NGO called 'India Development and Relief Fund' (IDRF) ('Academics against IDRF', 2002). This action was backed by the US State and Justice Departments, which added the IDRF to the list of organizations they are investigating for illicit donations and money laundering in the wake of 9/11 (Sevastopulo 2003). IDRF's responses to these criticisms have been unconvincing and unrepentant.

Figure 2 helps to explain why it has taken so long for the contours of the *sangh parivar* and its devastating activities to become understood, despite early warnings from journalists such as Praful Bidwai (cited in Prashad 2002). The institutions making up the *sangh parivar* are divided into branches that are not formally related. One needs to understand how the movement works in order to understand how the parts are interconnected. Moreover, despite its communal agenda of promoting *hindutva,* many of the public projections by the *sangh parivar* deny the communal character of the movement. Doublespeak insists that *Hindu Rahstra* is even more tolerant of minority communities than the fake secularism that defines the social agenda of non-*Hindutva* groups. The general image of the *sangh parivar* is of a shadowy and ill-defined group, partly because so much of the organization works as a brotherhood rather than through committees, elections and modern reporting structures. Despite this lack of transparency, the non-formal character of the *sangh parivar* has not prevented the movement from being a highly organized entity when it comes to collecting funds, fighting elections, recruiting supporters, victimizing opponents and minorities and arming Hindu militants and paramilitary. During the Gujarat carnage of

February-May 2002 there is evidence to suggest that the *sangh parivar*'s paramilitary, the youth-based *Bajrang Dal*, had computer-generated lists of the names of Muslim families and houses which it selectively targeted. Such lists could not have been created by a movement that was chaotic.

The core of the *sangh parivar* is the RSS which, since its foundation in 1925 in Nagpur, has over time increasingly come to resemble European fascism. In the words of Graham the RSS became:

> . . . the most successful of a class of associations which specialised in recruiting young men and adolescents into informal militia bands (known as *shakhas*) within a centralised framework presided over by full-time workers and teachers . . . a brotherhood dedicated to the improvement of Hindu society and to the eventual creation of a Hindu *rashtra*, or Hindu nation (Graham 1990, p. 7).

Figure 2. The Sangh Parivar in India and the USA and UK

RSS [HSS in USA and UK]
Generates the overall *Hindutva* ideology

BJP [OFBJP]	VHP [VHP-US]	SEVA VIBHAG [IDRF, USA & Sewa International, UK]
Political wing	Religious wing Bajrang Dal (Hindu Unity)	Social service wing Hundreds of individual 'social work' organizations throughout India, e.g.:
	Paramilitary youth wing	Sewa International Sewa Bharati Vidya Bharati Vanvasi Kalyan Ashram Ekal Vidyalay Foundation Vikas Bharati Sanskrit Bharati Janaseva Vidya Kendra

Note: The American and British parallel organizations are named in square brackets.
Source: Reproduced from Part 3, 'The structure of the Sangh Parivar', *The Foreign Exchange of Hate: IDRF and the American Funding of Hindutva*, Sabrang Communications Pty Ltd., 2002 at <http://www.mnet.fr/aiindex/2002/FEH/part3.html>, accessed December 2002. Sewa International, the peak *Hindutva* body in the UK, has been added to this diagram from Jonathan Miller (2002), 'Funding Gujarat Extremists', Channel 4 Transcript of TV documentary, December 12, <http://www.channel4.com/news/home/z/stories/20021212/guj.html>, accessed January 2003.

The RSS was not the only Hindu nationalist organization that evolved in response to British imperialism in the 1920s. The Hindu Mahasabha, a milder organization, found itself drifting by the 1940s into an increasingly fundamentalist position with Vinayak Damodar Savarkar, its chief ideologue and architect of the word 'Hindutva', warning India's Muslim League political party 'if we Hindus in India grow stronger in time these Moslem friends of the league will have to play the part of German-Jews' (Savarkar 1922, quoted in McKean 1996, p. 87; Chandra 2003).

During the late 1940s the leaders of the RSS and Hindu Mahasabha were arrested and the parties declared to be a 'threat to law and order' (Graham 1990, p. 11). The RSS was banned. These decisions by the new post-independence Congress Government were a reaction to the assassination of Gandhi by Nathuram Vinayak Godse, who was a member of both the RSS and the Hindu Mahasabha. Gandhi had been identified as the 'enemy' for his attempts to reconcile the Hindu majority and the remaining Muslims within India, after the partition of 1947 saw the creation of two states, India and Pakistan, the latter being a Muslim-dominant nation. Gandhi recognized that the partition immediately created a problem for the Muslim minority that continued to live within India and who today number some 150 million people. When the murder of Gandhi was confirmed to be a conspiracy by the 1970 *Report of Commission of Inquiry into Conspiracy to Murder Mahatma Gandhi*, the RSS was cleared of any involvement (Graham 1990, p. 11). This does not, however, absolve the RSS of responsibility for articulating a worldview that victimizes Muslims and rejects their basic citizenship rights.

Graham's book on the origins of the Bharatiya Jana Sangh party in October 1951 provides detailed documentation of why and how the socio-cultural agenda of the RSS took the form of this new political party. The Bharatiya Jana Sangh was the political ancestor of today's BJP. Both parties took issue with India's secularist traditions and both made the question of Pakistan (and by implication Kashmir and the Muslim minority within India) the centrepiece of their agenda. The work of the RSS today is carried out at three levels by organizations undertaking the political, religious and social work of the RSS. The BJP heads up the coalition government that rules India today and it also heads up state governments in Gujarat and Goa. In the USA and UK the parallel organization is called the Overseas Friends of the BJP (OFBJP). From time to time the leadership of the BJP falls out with the RSS, usually on tactical questions about how best to advance the *hindutva* agenda (Oberoi 2003). This creates the appearance that the BJP is separate from the RSS, but such a conclusion is dangerously wrong. The religious activities of the RSS are carried out by the Vishwa Hindu Parishad in India. Its counterpart in America and Europe is the Vishwa Hindu Parishad-US and UK. Fundamental to the mass appeal of both the political and religious wings of the RSS is the Seva Vibhag. This wing is engaged in a wide variety of social work, for which purposes hundreds of sub-organizations have been established with special agendas. It is the community work of the Seva Vibhag that has acted as the main conduit for channelling foreign funds into the *hindutva* program of the RSS within India. In America, funds are collected by the Seva Vibha's counterpart organization, the IDRF or India Development and Relief Fund.

For years, the IDRF described itself as an ordinary, non-profit NGO involved in community and relief projects in India. With the mounting communal violence in India, people who worried about the collapse of secular democracy began to ask questions about how it was possible for the BJP and its sister organizations to gain such widespread support from not only the Hindu community but also communities of tribal people who have traditionally stood apart from the Hindu mainstream. It was the search for an answer to these questions that unearthed compelling evidence about who has been funding the anti-Muslim and anti-Christian campaigns in India. Far from being an innocuous NGO, the IDRF has now been identified as a critical component of the overseas structure of the *sangh parivar*. The volume of money that the IDRF and parallel organizations in Britain, Europe, the Caribbean and Africa have sent to India is impressive. In 2000 alone, over US$3.8 million was collected by the IDRF in America ('The funding of Hindutva', 2002). In Britain, Sewa International raised £4 million in 2001 for the relief of the victims of the Gujarat earthquake, mainly for Hindu but not Christian or Muslim families (Miller 2002).

Other sectarian programmes funded by this international money include projects that will expand the size of the Hindu community through purification, reconversion[2] or education campaigns designed to create an aggressive Hindu consciousness amongst 'untouchables' and tribal peoples. Most worrying of all, much of the funding has been used to create inter-communal violence by intimidation, forcible reconversion, harassment and victimization of minorities and the training and arming of right-wing Hindu activists and paramilitary.

It is too early to say whether the bulk of international funding to the *sangh parivar* has come from people who have been tricked into giving support or whether there is a groundswell of sympathy for the RSS's communal agenda in Europe and America. In both the USA and UK public inquiries into the activities of the RSS have started. Prominent citizens such as Lord Patel in London have resigned as office-bearers of Sewa, claiming that they had been duped into joining an NGO presented to them as non-sectarian (Miller 2002). In the USA, leading software companies like Sun Microsoft, Oracle, Microsystems, Hewlett Packard, AOL Time Warner and Cisco have withdrawn their funding from IDRF. These large companies funded RSS organizations more generously than more deserving non-Indian associations, mainly because of the large numbers of employees of Indian origin. When these employees contribute to NGOs it is the policy of the US corporations to provide matching funds. The results are that in 1999, for example, Cisco gave 'Doctors Without Borders' less than 4 per cent of what they donated to IDRF (Ghosh 2002).

Rank-and-file membership of Sewa and IDRF might also, however, have its origins in Indian responses to European racial discrimination. Asserting one's Indian identity is the other side of being rejected by the host society. In the words of one teenage Indian recruited by the HSS and sent to India for further 'training':

> As most ethnic minority youngsters will tell you, it's important to know who you are and where you come from in order to face the rest of society; that's the way it is and that's how HSS has helped me coming to Shakha to develop a sense of identity (Miller 2002).

The terrible truth behind this statement is that for many overseas Hindu youth, *hindutva* hits back at European and American rejection and discrimination. Much of the racial conflict between Europeans and Indians in Britain also plays itself out in heightened inter-community animosity between migrants of Indian and Pakistani backgrounds; the animosity in turn feeds religious and cultural fundamentalism. This polarization within Europe and the US is quite extreme in some cities and suburbs because the majority of Indian migrants are Hindu and the majority of Pakistani migrants are Muslim. The fact that India has a huge Muslim minority is not something that Hindu fundamentalists claiming the supremacy of the Hindu nation wish to be reminded about. The emergence of a virulent *hindutva* in India, therefore, does have immediate consequences for civic harmony in Europe and the USA. Thus it does matter when Ashok Singhal, one of India's most prominent *hindutva* activists, convenes meetings in New Jersey to stir up local feelings by telling American Hindus that 'Hinduism' is facing a 'cultural onslaught' in India (Bahadur 2003). Another *hindutva* activist who has toured the US for fund raising is Sadhvi Rithambara (Ravishankar 2002). It also matters when the founder of IDRF repeats the hackneyed claim that India is suffering from a growing population imbalance caused by a shrinking proportion of Hindus. When this kind of demographic fear-mongering is wedded to the argument that 'US-Indian friendship is based on Hindu values not Islamic values' (Shane 2003) we know that we are dealing with the problem of Hindu fundamentalism within the US itself. As Rai Ravishankar argues, given the Indian government's support to the *sangh parivar*, the globalization of Hindu fundamentalism possibly poses a greater threat than Islamic fundamentalism within the US because there is no state actor prepared to contain its growth (Ravishankar 2002).

The Muslim killings that occurred in the Gujarat in 2002 were not, however, a spontaneous outbreak of Hindu frustration in either India or abroad. Rather they were part of a planned, anti-Muslim campaign carried out with a gusto only made possible because the *sangh parivar* had been fanning the 'politics of hate' since the BJP came to power in Gujarat in 1998 (Setalvad 2002, pp. 177-178). Muslim homes and families throughout urban and rural Gujarat were targeted before the violence broke out on 28 February 2002. Hindu houses were spared because they had been decorated with the symbols of *hindutva*, such as saffron flags (Concerned Citizens' Tribunal 2002b, p. 24). If Muslim houses were attached to Hindu homes, they were hacked apart before being torched. In all about 100,000 Muslim houses were destroyed, 1,100 Muslim hotels, 15,000 businesses, 3,000 handcarts and 5,000 vehicles (Concerned Citizens' Tribunal, 2002b, p. 27).

No one knows exactly how many Muslims died in February-May 2002, but the figure of 2,000 is widely accepted. The brutality of the slaughter was unprecedented in post-partition India. Women and children were gang-raped, mutilated, had objects inserted into their bodies, were quartered, burnt alive and subjected to extensive terror, beating, stripping, humiliation and molestation (Concerned Citizens' Tribunal 2002b, pp. 42-43; Dutta et al. 2002, pp. 214-246). When they did intervene, the police typically fired on the Muslims, even when they were being attacked by Hindu mobs (Setalvad 2002, pp. 181-183). At least 20,000 Muslims sought refuge in temporary camps set up by various NGOs. The brutish violence of Indian partition in 1947 replayed itself in countless incidents throughout rural and urban Gujarat in February-May 2002.

Beyond the events, the politics behind the communal slaughter are the most disturbing aspect of what happened in Gujarat in 2002 because there is a risk of its being replicated in the forthcoming state elections in 2003 and the national elections in 2004. The mass killing campaign against the Muslims in Gujarat was led by prominent citizens, members of parliament and heads of the organizations that constitute the *sangh parivar*. All the organs of civil society and government were suspended and ordered to allow the *sangh parivar* to act without restraint. What sparked off the violence? The ostensible catalyst was the burning to death of 59 passengers, mainly Hindus, on the Sabarmarti Express train as it pulled out of Godhra station on 27 February 2002. How the fire started in carriage S-6 and who lit it is still undetermined, but the BJP, the Chief Minister of Gujarat and the Home Minister of India all suggested that it was a deliberate act of terrorism planned either by Pakistan or other 'Jihadis'. These claims do not match the evidence, which overwhelmingly supports the view that the destruction of the carriage followed on from a series of unplanned, violent incidents that took place at the Godhra train station on that day. As Varadarajan has argued, the official response to Godhra shows how the *sangh parivar*'s propaganda campaign to stereotype Indian Muslims as disloyal citizens has since 9/11 been able to exploit the 'Global War Against Terror' by allowing Indian politicians, police and other office-bearers to justify anti-Muslim retribution as a response to Muslim terrorism.

> In the coded language that the *Sangh Parivar* has perfected, words like 'terrorist', 'fanatic' and 'fundamentalist' are subliminal signifiers for Muslim (Varadarajan 2002, p. 7).

According to many Indian observers, the events in Gujarat in 2002 were genocidal (Concerned Citizens' Tribunal 2002a, pp. 292-293; Concerned Citizens' Tribunal, 2002b, pp. 152-154). This is not an issue I wish to engage with in this chapter. Suffice it to say that despite the thousands of Muslims who were killed, the perpetrators of the violence have gone about their lives undisturbed, unfettered and unpunished for what happened. In fact, they have been rewarded by attaining high office. The BJP led by Chief Minister Narendra Modi won a sweeping electoral victory in the Gujarat state elections of December 2002. During the election campaign, the opposition Congress Party itself adopted a milder version of *hindutva* as part of its platform. It is now feared that the Gujarat election will provide a model for electoral successes in other parts of the subcontinent. A poll by India Today-ORG-Marg in January 2003 showed that throughout northern and western India there has been a wave of political support for the BJP and its *hindutva* platform (Dasgupta 2002, p. 26). For the first time since independence, the basic rights of all Indian citizens as expressed in the Indian constitution stand threatened by the country's office-holders and a public majority goaded into enthusiastically backing *hindutva.* International funding to the *sangh parivar* has had devastating consequences – financial donations by the Indian diaspora helped to build an infrastructure of violence whilst international support, whether willing or unwilling, gave *hindutva* confidence and respectability.

CONCLUSION

Reviewing India's experience with globalization until now leads to pessimistic conclusions. The evidence for India's integration into the global economic and technological world is weak. The domestic constraints on Indian efficiency and competitiveness are numerous, and act as serious barriers to India benefiting from the emergence of global markets. But far more damaging is the external straitjacket placed on Indian agriculture to prevent it from competing in areas of production where even without technological change India today could outperform the subsidized producers of America and Europe. It is the developed world that refuses to create the level playing field demanded by globalization. Where there is evidence for India's link to a global world in cultural and political terms, the conclusions are even more pessimistic. Hindu fundamentalism has re-emerged in India with a new virulence, partly funded by the overseas Indian diaspora. Until now India has been a poor, developing country evolving in the context of a secular democratic political system. Persistent poverty has always been made more palatable by the fact of free elections, a free press and a free judiciary. Now India faces the risk of persistent poverty within the political framework of *hindutva*, the successes of which in 2002 were based on murder, pillage, rape, a new politics of anti-Muslim hatred and a political and media system that connived with violence. The Indian Prime Minister's speech in Goa on 12 April 2002, soon after the worst carnage occurred, provides little hope for the resurrection of the institutions of civil governance and justice. In that speech the Muslim killings were justified as retribution for the burning of 58 Hindus in the Sabarmarti Express train, Hindus were portrayed as tolerant and secular and Muslims were described as intolerant and violent:

> Wherever Muslims live, they don't like to live in co-existence with others, they don't like to mingle with others; and instead of propagating their ideas in a peaceful manner, they want to spread their faith by resorting to terror and threats. The world has become alert to this danger. As far as we are concerned, we have been fighting against terrorism for the past 20 years . . . Now other nations in the world have started to realise what a great mistake they made in neglecting terrorism (Vajpayee 2002, p. 450).

As Vajpayee's speech makes clear, the rhetoric of *hindutva* today derives strength from the 'Global War on Terror' and the demonization of Muslims and Muslim culture in the aftermath of 9/11. Globalization, as it is currently structured and construed, seems only to deliver negative returns for India. Yet this is not the end of the story. In a fairer world, closer ties to the world economy would benefit India enormously. The natural economic growth that could flow from this would create jobs that would undermine the work of Hindu fundamentalist NGOs that appear to have captured control of a significant volume of international aid to India.

REFERENCES

'Academics against IDRF US Professor's Petition' (2002), *Siliconeer*, December, <http://stopfundinghate.org/resources/news/1202SiliconeerFP.htm>, accessed

January 2003.

A.T. Kearney/*Foreign Policy Magazine*, January-February 2003 issue at <http://www.foreignpolicy.com>, accessed December 2002.

Bahadur, Gaiutra (2003), 'Hindu Nationalists Tap Immigrant Guilt in US', *Philadelphia Inquirer*, 17 January, on <http://stopfundinghate.org/resources/news/011703Philly Inquirer.htm>.

Bidwai, Praful (2003), 'Flawed Bid to Woo Overseas Indians', *Asia Times,* 21 January, cited in <http://stopfundinghate.org/resources/new/012103AsiaTimes. htm>, accessed January 2003.

Boriah, G. (2002), 'India, World's Largest Consumer', *Survey of Indian Agriculture 2002,* Chennai: The Hindu.

'CBI will Remain under Vajpayee, not Advani' (2003), *Times of India*, 31 January.

'CM Maharashtra Visited Malegaon to Give Compensation' (2001), article from *The Tribune*, cited in Foundation for Civil Liberties, <www.ffcl.org/compensation/pages/p.80.html>.

'The Campaign to Stop Funding Hate', <http://stopfindinghate.org/resources>.

Chandra, Bipan (2003), 'Savarkar Cannot be a Role Model', The Rediff Interview, 3 March, <*rediff.com* www.rediff.com/news/2003/mar/03inter.htm>, accessed April 2003.

Concerned Citizens' Report on the Malegaon Riots (2001), <http://www.pucl.org/Maharasthra/2001/malegaon_concerned.htm>.

Concerned Citizens' Tribunal (2002a), *Crime Against Humanity: An Inquiry into the Carnage in Gujarat, vol I: List of Incidents and Evidence,* Mumbai: Citizens for Justice and Peace.

Concerned Citizens' Tribunal (2002b), *Crime Against Humanity: An Inquiry into the Carnage in Gujarat, vol II: Findings and Recommendations,* Mumbai: Citizens for Justice and Peace.

D'Monte, Darryl (2002), *Ripping the Fabric: The Decline of Mumbai and its Mills*, New Delhi: Oxford University Press.

Dasgupta, Swapan (2002), 'BJP's Finest Hour', *India Today,* 10 February, pp. 26-34.

Desai, Meghnad (2002), 'Globalisation and Mass Poverty', Public Lecture in Melbourne, 11 December, hosted by the Monash Asia Institute, Monash Institute for the Study of Global Movements and the Productivity Commission.

Desai, Meghnad (1994), 'The Economic Policy of the BJP', National Centre for South Asian Discussion Paper no. 1, Melbourne, January.

Desai, Meghnad (1996), 'India's Triple By-Pass: Economic Liberalisation, the BJP and the 1996 Elections', National Centre for South Asian Studies Discussion Paper no. 2, Melbourne, March.

Dutta, Bharka et al. (2002), 'Nothing New? Women as Victims', in Siddarth Varadarajan (ed.), *Gujarat: The Making of a Tragedy,* Delhi: Penguin, pp. 214-246.

The Economic Times, (2003), 'Moody about Ratings' (editorial), 5 February.

Foreign Policy/A.T. Kearney, January-February 2003, <http://www.foreignpolicy.com>, accessed December 2002.

'The Funding of Hindutva', *The Foreign Exchange of Hate: IDRF and the American Funding of Hindutva*, Part 4, Sabran Communications, 2002, <http://www.mnet.fr/aiindex/2002/FEH/part4.html>.

Ghosh, Deepshikha (2002), 'Stop Charities to U.S. Groups Funding Hindu Right in India', Indo-Asian News Service, 20 November 2002, <http://in.news.yahoo.

com/021120/43/1xzm9.html accessed in January 2003>.

Graham, Bruce (1990), *Hindu Nationalism and Indian Politics: The Origins and Development of the Bharatiya Jana Sangh,* Cambridge: Cambridge University Press.

Gulati, Ashok and Sudha Narayanan (2003), 'Rice Trade Liberalisation and Poverty', *Economic and Political Weekly,* 4 January, pp. 45-51.

International Telecommunications Union, 'Free Statistics', <http://www.itu.org/>.

Jalan, Bimal (2002), 'India and Globalisation', Speech by Dr Bimal Jalan, Governor of the Reserve Bank of India at the 36th Convocation Address of the Indian Statistical Institute, Kolkata, 15 January, <http://www.bis.org/review/020115 c.pdf>, accessed in January 2002.

Kishwar, Madhu (2001), 'Blackmail, Bribes and Beatings: Lok Sunwayi of Delhi's Street Vendors', *Manushi,* 124, May-June.

Kumar, Arun (2002), *The Black Economy of India,* New Delhi: Penguin Books.

Mathur, Shalini (1993), in Marika Vicziany (ed.), *Australia-India: Economic Links Past, Present and Future,* Perth: Indian Ocean Centre for Peace Studies and South Asian Research Unit, South Asian Issues Monograph, pp. 84-110.

Mayee, C.D., T.P. Rajendra, and M.V. Nad Venugopalan (2002), 'Surviving under Pressurised Trade', *Survey of Indian Agriculture 2002,* Chennai: The Hindu.

McKean, Lise (1996), *Divine Enterprise: Gurus and the Hindu Nationalist Movement,* Chicago: University of Chicago Press.

Miller, Jonathan (2002), 'Funding Gujarat Extremists', Channel 4 Transcript of TV documentary, December 12, <http://www.channel4.com/news/home/z/stories/20021212/guj.html>, accessed January 2003.

Nadeem, Naresh (2001), 'An Innocuous Leaflet that was Blamed for the Riots', *People's Democracy,* **25** (46), November 18, <http://pd.cpim.org/2001/non 18/2001_nov18_malegaon.htm.>.

Oberoi, Vitusha (2003), 'Togadia's Talk of Desertion Frightens BJP', *Midday,* 5 February.

Prashad, Vijay (2002), 'On the Tenth Anniversay of Ayodhya: At Least One Small Victory', *ZNET Daily Commentaries,* 6 December, <http://www.zmag.org/sustainers/content/2002-12/06prashad.cfm>, accessed January 2003.

Ravishankar, Rai (2002), 'Project Saffron Dollar', *Indymedia.org,* 3 December, on <http://www.stopfundinghate.org/resources/news/120302Indymedia.htm>.

Sainath, P. (1998a), *Everybody Loves a Good Drought – Stories from India's Poorest Districts,* Delhi: South Asia Books.

Sainath, P. (1998b), 'In Lawless Maharashtra', *Frontliine,* 4-17 July, <http://www.flonnet.com/fl1514/15141240.htm>, accessed January 2003.

Sainath, P. (2001a), 'Of Reptiles and Reforms', *The Hindu,* 11 November, http://www.hinuonnet.com/mag/2001/11/11/stories/20011111100010100.htm, accessed January 2003.

Sainath, P. (2001b), 'Where Stomachs are Terminal', *The Hindu,* 29 April, <http://www.hindunet.com//2001/04/29/stories/13290611.htm>, accessed January 2003.

Sainath, P. (2001c), 'Rajasthan's Drought', *The Hindu,* 18 March, <http://www.hinduonnet.com//2001/03/18/stories/13180611.htm>, accessed January 2003.

Sainath, P. (2002a), 'Little Pani, Less Panchayat', *The Hindu,* 15 September, <http://www.thehindu.com/mag/2002/09/15/stories/20091500080100.htm>, accessed January 2003.

Sainath, P. (2002b), 'Little Pani, Less Panchayat', Part 2, *The Hindu,* 22 September

<http://www.thehindu.com/mag/2002/09/22/stories/2002092200250100.htm>, accessed January 2003.

Savarkar, Veer V.D. (1964), 'Hindutva' (1922), in *Writings of Swatantrya Veer V.D. Savakar,* vol. 6, Poona: Maharashtra Prantik Hindusabha, pp. 1-91.

Setalvad, Teesta (2002), 'When Guardians Betray: The Role of the Police in Gujarat', Siddarth Varadarajan (ed.), *Gujarat: The Making of a Tragedy,* Delhi: Penguin, pp. 177-213.

Sevastopulo, Demetri (2003), 'US Widens Probe of Charities Tied to Militants', *Financial Times,* 14 February, <http://stopfundinghate.org/resources/news/021403FinancialTimes.htm>.

Shane, Scott (2003), 'India-relief Charity Criticised on Fund Use', *Baltimore Sun,* 4 December, <http://stopfundinghate.org/resources/news/120402Baltimore.htm>, accessed January 2003.

Singh, B.P. (2002), 'Can We Compete in International Markets?' *Survey of Indian Agriculture 2002,* Chennai: The Hindu.

'Small Investors Left Out from PSU Selloffs' (2003), *Times of India,* 3 February.

Stiglitz, Joseph E. (2002), *Globalisation and its Discontents,* New York/London: W.W. Norton.

'The Structure of the Sangh Parivar', *The Foreign Exchange of Hate: IDRF and the American funding of Hindutva,* Part 3, Sabran Communications, 2002, <http://www.mnet.fr/aiindex/2002/FEH/part3.html>.

Vajpayee, Atal Behari (2002), Reprint in English of the Hindi text of the Indian Prime Minister's speech in Goa on 12 April 2002 in Siddarth Varadarajan (ed.), *Gujarat: The Making of a Tragedy,* Delhi: Penguin, pp. 450-452.

Varadarajan, Siddarth (2002), 'Chronicle of a Tragedy Foretold', in Siddarth Varadarajan (ed.), *Gujarat: The Making of a Tragedy,* Delhi: Penguin, pp. 3-41.

Vicziany, Marika (2001), 'Opportunities in Information Technology: The Emergence and Growth of the Indian IT Sector', Research Consultancy for the East Asia Analytical Unit, Department of Foreign Affairs and Trade, Canberra, http://www.arts.monash.edu.au/mai/mas/index.html>.

Vicziany, Marika (2002), 'The BJP and the Shiv Sena: A Rocky Marriage?', in *Special Issue: The BJP and Governance in India,* **25** (3), pp. 41-60.

Vicziany, I. and S. Vichare (2003), 'India's Dharavi: Options for Asia's Largest Slum', 7th Baltic Region Seminar on Engineering Education, St Petersburg State Electrotechnical University, St Petersburg, Russia, 4-6 September 2003.

NOTES

1   I am enormously grateful to a large number of Indian colleagues, journalists, academics, activists and politicians from all religious and political persuasions for agreeing to meet me in December 2002/January 2003 to discuss the difficult times that India is currently experiencing. Given the sensitivity of the issues covered in this paper, I have not cited those interviews and discussions in this chapter.

2   Given that tribal people are not born as Hindus, they are regarded as being ritually impure. To bring them into the Hindu community they are required to undergo purification ceremonies conducted by Brahmin priests. In the case of Christians or Muslims whom the RSS wishes to bring back into the fold of Hinduism, the purification ceremony is known as *shuddhi. Shuddhi* alone makes reconversion possible.

7. Australian Roadmaps to Globalism: Explaining the Shift from Multilateralism to Imperial Preference[1]

Chris Nyland and Russell Smyth

In 1983 the Australian Labor Party (ALP) formed a national government committed to the globalization of the Australian economy and community. While there was wide support for this goal across the political spectrum, there was significant divergence regarding the pathway the nation should take in its effort to globalize. In short, there existed what Gill (2001) has referred to as a 'clash of globalizations'. This clash saw divergent schools of thought contend with each seeking to win support and to embed its preferred form of globalism within the culture and institutional structures of the nation. On the left, a grouping that initially appeared to have some influence advocated the pathway blazed by Swedish social democracy through the post-war years. This route involved a high level of engagement with the global economy, a sophisticated compensatory social protection regime and a participatory and activist state committed to developing an industrial structure that was highly competitive. In retrospect, it is clear that any commitment the ALP may have had to this approach was soon dissipated. With increasing enthusiasm, the leaders of the ALP chose instead to promote a route to globalism that emphasized the neo-liberal agenda associated with the Washington Consensus and the form of global governance advocated by the GATT. This agenda placed emphasis on extending and deepening market relations, limiting democratic control over key elements of economic policy and regulation, and locking in future governments to neo-liberal values and frameworks of wealth accumulation.

For almost two decades, a central tenet of those who embraced the neo-liberal vision of globalism was that multilateralism was a key element of this vision. It was deemed critical because it supposedly maximized the likelihood that resources would be allocated with greatest efficiency. This perspective enjoyed the support of all the major parliamentary parties and as a consequence all remained enthusiasts for such agencies as the WTO and

APEC. However, in the mid 1990s the conservative parties that make up the Coalition began to deviate from this position. While they remained committed to a neo-liberal vision of globalism, they began to insist that the best way to reach this goal was to place much greater emphasis on constructing a bilateral relationship with the United States. In this chapter we explore why the Coalition elected to take the latter path to globalism and hence why in 2003 it began the arduous process of negotiating an Australia and US free trade agreement (AUS-FTA). The chapter has two parts. First, we consider the economics of an AUS-FTA in the context of historical experience. We take this initial step in order to determine if the economic benefits likely to be achieved by this agreement justify the Coalition's claim that an AUS-FTA will significantly boost Australia's economic welfare and that it is this collective gain that explains its decision to turn from multilateralism. Having concluded that this claim cannot be supported we propose an alternative explanation which suggests that domestic and global political influences better explain the Coalition's policy choice. We argue that the Coalition's new approach to trade is in fact part of a 'wedge'-based political strategy that aims to: (a) ensure that Australians continue the march toward the neo-liberal vision of globalism the Coalition shares with the ALP; (b) distinguish the conservative parties from Labor and preserve the Coalition in government, and (c) capture some of the benefits that can accrue to those willing to play a subaltern (deputy) role in the United States' current reconfiguration of the notion of globalism that will return Australia to a position similar to that which prevailed under the interwar Imperial Preference system.

A GLOBALIZED AUSTRALIA AND THE US-AUSTRALIA FREE TRADE AGREEMENT

From the late 1980s, the concept of globalization came to dominate debate surrounding Australia's place within the global economy and community. For many observers, the key element in this debate was the assertion that the competitiveness of Australian industry had declined because of the nation's long history of industrial protectionism and consequent lack of market discipline. From 1983 this was a message promoted with great enthusiasm by neo-liberal activists within both the ALP and the Coalition parties. As Conley (2001, p. 223) has observed, the mantra constantly repeated was that:

> Australia had to economically discipline itself or suffer the consequences of global punishment. Alternative policy responses were simply not viable given the 'reality' of a global economy: Australia had to shift from a protectionist past to an

economic liberal, globalised future.

Informed by this perspective, in 1983 the ALP floated the Australian dollar and launched the nation along the path of deregulation, privatization, streamlined and targeted social protection, and an embrace of globalism that placed emphasis on multilateral governance. By the time the ALP was voted from office in 1996 this sustained effort had arguably rendered Australia the most open economy in the OECD but had also induced a suspicion of, and in many cases an abiding aversion to, globalization within a large part of the population.

Given Australia's geographic location and the fact that much of Asia boomed from the early 1980s, the multilateral approach to globalism reshaped the character of Australia's trade pattern. Most importantly, it caused Asia to become of greater significance in terms of both imports and exports (Bell 1997; Lambert 2000). The United States, nevertheless, remained a major trading partner. In 2001, Australia's merchandise exports to the US were valued at $A11.9 billion, making it the second largest destination for Australian exports after Japan. Australian merchandise imports from the States, by contrast, were worth $A21.4 billion, easily making that nation the largest source of Australian imports (see Table 1). Relatively, the bilateral relationship is more important to Australia than to the US. The latter is the destination of 11 per cent of Australia's exports and the source of 20 per cent of its imports. In contrast, US exports to Australia account for just 1.6 per cent of total exports, while Australia is the source of only 0.7 per cent of imports to the USA (Centre for International Economics 2001). The US is also important to Australia as a destination of outward foreign direct investment (FDI) and a source of inward FDI. Table 2 shows inward and outward FDI in Australia in 2000. The US was the biggest source of inward FDI (30 per cent of the total) and the major destination of Australia's outward FDI (41.7 per cent of the total).

The biggest benefit to Australia of an FTA with the United States would lie in opening up agricultural markets. In a clean FTA all sectors including politically sensitive areas such as grain, meat and sugar would be included. However, in a dirty FTA, key agricultural products would be excluded. Many observers have argued that the prospects for a clean FTA between Australia and the US are virtually non-existent because of political opposition from the farm lobby in the United States. This lobby wants Congress to defer negotiations with Australia over an FTA until the WTO multilateral negotiations on agriculture are completed, which is expected to be in 2005. The reason for this is that the farm lobby fears an FTA with Australia will force farmers in the US to compete with more efficient Australian farm products without opening up new markets to US primary producers (Brennan

2002; Schuff 2002). The political influence of the farm lobby is reflected in the fact that in 2000 US farmers received subsidies worth $US28 billion (AFR 2001b). In addition to the ongoing political opposition from US farm groups, the reality is that extant agricultural subsidies under the Farm Bill are inconsistent with entertaining the prospect of free trade in agriculture with Australia. As Garnaut (2002, p. 133) notes:

> Congressional deal-makers have not thought much about the content (of an FTA). When asked they say that trade in meat, sugar, dairy products and some other agricultural goods would be excluded. There is no mechanism for maintaining free trade in grain with Australia alongside United States subsidies, so there is a presumption that free trade in grain would not even be discussed.

Table 1. Australia's major trading partners in 2001

Market	Exports	
	$A million	Growth % (from 2000)
Japan	23,703	8.7
United States	11,904	8.4
South Korea	9,538	5.4
China	7,587	26.3
New Zealand	7,152	8.9
Taiwan	5,356	-3.6
Singapore	5,354	-8.6
United Kingdom	5,192	38.4
Hong Kong	4,184	17.0
Indonesia	3,215	11.1

	Imports	
	$A million	Growth % (from 2000)
United States	21,413	-7.4
Japan	15,260	-0.4
China	10,314	13.7
Germany	6,666	13.3
United Kingdom	6,279	-9.8
New Zealand	4,741	5.7
South Korea	4,635	-3.5
Singapore	3,968	6.9
Indonesia	3,905	44.7
Malaysia	3,899	-8.6

Source: Davis (2002a).

Table 2. Australia's inward and outward foreign direct investment in 2000

Inward Investment as at 30 June 2000 (% of total)	
United States	30
United Kingdom	24.8
Japan	6.9
Hong Kong	3.4
Singapore	2.8
Netherlands	2.8
Others	29.3
Outward Investment as at 30 June 2000 (% of total)	
United States	41.7
United Kingdom	17.3
Japan	6.1
New Zealand	5.3
Singapore	2.6
Hong Kong	2.2
Others	24.8

Source: Davis (2002a).

HOW BIG ARE THE ECONOMIC BENEFITS?

Initially the supporters of an AUS-FTA on the Australian side argued that there are dynamic benefits from linking up with the world's 'new economy', though their enthusiasm for this perspective became more muted following the collapse of the IT bubble (Oxley 2001). In a report commissioned by the Department of Foreign Affairs and Trade (DFAT), the Centre for International Economics (2001) evaluated the economic impact of an AUS-FTA using McKibbin's APG-Cubed model and the Global Trade Analysis Project (GTAP) model. The report estimates that the gains to the United States will be 0.02 per cent of GDP or $US2.1 billion per annum by 2006, while the benefits to Australia will be 0.4 per cent of GDP or $US2 billion per annum by 2010. The Centre for International Economics further estimates that over the next 20 years, in net present value terms, an AUS-FTA would add $US15.5 billion to the GDP of Australia and $US16.9 billion to the GDP of the United States.

These results, however, make a number of heroic assumptions, which were imposed by DFAT. In particular, the modelling exercise by the Centre of International Economics assumes that all tariffs are reduced to zero without exception. and that quota restrictions on imports are 'in the main' converted to tariffs and reduced to zero. Most of the benefits to Australia would flow from Australia abolishing its own tariffs on imports from the United States (McKibbin 1998). The remaining benefits would largely accrue from the US dropping its trade barriers against a small number of Australian agricultural exports, such as dairy products and sugar, which if post-war history is taken as a guide will not happen.

Another problem with the modelling is that several of the main targets for US negotiators in discussions over an FTA are assumed unchanged. For example, Democrat Senator Max Baucus, Chairman of the US Senate's Finance Committee, has stated that Australia would need to make significant reforms to its quarantine regulations before the United States would sign an FTA (Davis 2002c). However, the claimed benefits are predicated on the assumption that the quarantine regulations remain unchanged. Similarly, the modelling exercise assumes that the Australian Wheat Board monopoly over wheat exports would be retained, while its removal is likely to be a precondition for Congressional support for a bilateral FTA with Australia (Garnaut 2002, p. 131).

With an FTA there will be both trade creation and trade diversion. Trade creation would occur when high cost domestic production in Australia (or the US) is replaced with imports from the United States (or Australia). Trade diversion occurs when higher cost imports from Australia (or the US) replace cheaper imports from third parties. Whether the benefits of trade creation outweigh the costs of trade diversion is an empirical issue. Using the APG-Cubed model, the Centre for International Economics purports to show that an AUS-FTA would lead to net trade creation. However, as Garnaut (2002, p. 132) notes, the APG-Cubed model is not suitable for assessing the importance of trade diversion because it is too aggregated. In contrast, the GTAP model, which is better suited to assessing the effects of trade diversion because it has more commodity detail, suggests that Australia may experience significant trade diversion from East Asia. First, a high proportion of Australian imports of motor vehicles and components that Australia currently sources from Japan and South Korea would be diverted to the United States. Second, a sizeable amount of Australian imports of textile, clothing and footwear products from China would be diverted toward much higher cost producers in the USA (Centre for International Economics 2001, pp. 39-44). Thus the level of trade creation generated by the type of dirty FTA that post-war history suggests is likely to be achieved will be less than the modelling by the Centre for International Economics suggests, while there is likely to be the same trade diversion.

Overall, the usefulness of the estimates compiled by the Centre of International Economics regarding the benefits that could accrue in an ideal world for Australia is limited. Past experience suggests that the economic benefits to Australia of an AUS-FTA are likely to be negligible. Garnaut (2002, p. 139) sums up the situation well. After stressing that 'All that is politically feasible is a heavily compromised bilateral free trade agreement', he points out that 'such compromise would remove the main sources of potential gains to Australia, other than those that derive from Australia removing its own barriers to imports'.

EFFECT ON INVESTMENT

Given the paucity of the trade argument, advocates of an AUS-FTA have come to place increasing emphasis on investment inflow. From the perspective of the US, Australia is more important in terms of investment than trade. Australia ranks fifteenth among the United States export markets and is only twenty-ninth as a source of imports. However, in terms of investment, there has been significant growth in US interests in Australia since the mid 1990s. Between 1995 and 2000 US FDI in Australia grew at an average annual rate of 25 per cent, such that in 2000 the total value of US investment in Australia was $A215 billion (Davis 2002b). As a result, Australia now ranks eleventh among destinations for US direct investment abroad (Australian APEC Study Centre 2001, p. xii). Therefore it is likely that the United States would want strong investor rights provisions included in the FTA. In this respect it is expected that the North-American Free Trade Agreement (NAFTA) Chapter 11 investment provisions would serve as a blueprint for the investment component of an FTA agreement between Australia and the US (Edwards 2001; International Trade Strategies (ITS) 2002).

Prominent amongst the supporters of an AUS-FTA who insist that an agreement will boost United States investment in Australia is the Australian APEC Study Centre (2001, p. xiii). The Centre argues that an

FTA could improve conditions for investors from both countries through putting in place legal guarantees and implementing other measures aimed at providing a further sense of certainty for investors. Such measures would not only encourage US investors to invest in Australia, but may also further encourage them to use Australia as a base for operations in the Asia-Pacific region.

This is consistent with economic theory which suggests that codified regulatory frameworks which enshrine the sanctity of private property against unaccountable government action are important for attracting foreign investment (Caves 1960). Much of the business sector has endorsed an FTA on this basis. In July 2001 a coalition of 16 Australian industry associations and 10 major Australian corporations wrote to the Bush administration supporting an FTA, arguing that it would 'provide a further spur to investment, enterprise, employment and growth to the benefit of both nations' (AFR 2001d).

However, the empirical evidence on the effects of the NAFTA investment provisions on foreign investment flows between Canada, Mexico and the United States is inconclusive. While it is clear that FDI in the three countries has increased (Gestrin and Rugman 1994; Nossal 2001; ITS 2002), it is uncertain whether this is due to the investor rights enshrined in the Chapter 11 provisions or the liberalization process in a more general sense. The more common view is that increases in investment flows among NAFTA countries were due to the latter. This is reflected in an ITS (2002) report on the effect of the Chapter 11 provisions on FDI in Canada, Mexico and the United States. It argues (at p. 11):

> Foreign Direct Investment increased in all three countries, but the relationship with the investment provisions is likely to be correlative rather than causal, reflecting the effects of general liberalization of trade and investment policies before, during and after the agreement.

From Australia's standpoint, the inclusion of Chapter 11 provisions would be contentious. Chapter 11 is a controversial component of NAFTA because it undermines national sovereignty through removing governmental discretion to deal with foreign investors (Mann and von Moltke 2002). Davidson (2002) puts forward this view in the Australian debate, arguing against an FTA on the basis that Chapter 11-type provisions would be a direct assault on Australian sovereignty. He suggests that the FTA would be another route through which the United States could achieve the purpose behind the failed Multilateral Agreement on Investment (MAI), which was based on the Chapter 11 provisions. The anti neo-liberal globalization movement in Australia was at the forefront of public opposition to the MAI, suggesting that there would be strong opposition to including such provisions in an FTA (Capling and Nossal 2001). The problem is that, under Chapter 11-type provisions, US investors would get rights that could be exercised against the Australian government which go much further than those found in WTO agreements. Under NAFTA these rights can be exercised through tribunals set up under NAFTA for which, unlike the WTO dispute settlement mechanism, there is no appeal process. This represents a significant departure from accepted WTO practice where only states are capable of bringing international legal proceedings (Capling 2001a, pp. 23-24).

At the core of an FTA, the United States will want a major overhaul of Australia's foreign investment laws. At the least, the current situation where the Treasurer can reject foreign investment proposals on undefined 'national interest' grounds would have to be modified (Edwards 2001, p. 32). It is likely that Australia would have to offer removal of foreign investment restrictions, which has the potential to produce a kind of 'big bang' ownership deregulation in several industries including aviation, banking, media and telecommunications (Kohler 2002). The Chapter 11 provisions of NAFTA allow for 'national interest' reservations, which include restrictions on foreign investment.

Edwards (2001, p. 33) suggests that Australia might be able to make exceptions for aviation and the media on these grounds. However, NAFTA's experience with the national interest clause shows that whenever one party invokes a national interest reservation, at the least the other side removes any guarantees not to impose a similar restriction. This would have implications for Australian investments in the United States, which would need to be considered. For example, if Australia retained its media restrictions as a reservation to an AUS-FTA it might make it very difficult for a company such as News Corporation to get approval for a takeover in the United States (Kohler 2002). This is an important consideration given that there is an imbalance in direct investment, defined as a holding of more than 10 per cent, between Australian companies investing in the United States and US companies investing in Australia. Australian direct investment in the United States (such as News Corporation's film and television businesses, Lend Lease and Westfield's property investments and James Hardie's fibre board factories) totals $A95 billion. Meanwhile US direct investment in Australia (including companies such as GMH, Ford, the tobacco industry and much of the food industry) is worth $A62.8 billion, which is about two-thirds of Australian direct investment in the US (Kohler 2002).

BILATERALISM VERSUS MULTILATERALISM

Another argument advanced by supporters of an AUS-FTA is that it will provide Australia with more room to manoeuvre in representing its trade interests in Washington. Pearson (2002) makes this point, arguing that while Australian lamb, wheat and steel exports have incurred US protectionism, '[i]t has not gone unnoticed [in Canberra] that the partners to NAFTA, Mexico and Canada, have been spared the wrath of the US steel [and agricultural] lobbies. In short, a free trade deal with the US will give Australia some protection from the caprice of American trade politics'. Peter

Watson, a US trade lobbyist who represented Australia in appealing the US decision to penalize Australian lamb in the WTO, makes a similar point about Australian lamb exports to the United States. He suggests, 'while an FTA would not rule out the possibility of another lamb-type problem in the future, it would make it much less likely' (AFR 2001a).

It is also argued that bilateral FTAs give countries such as Australia more negotiating power in multilateral forums. Kunkel (2002, p. 240) suggests that

> Australia's trading interests are . . . broadly-based and geographically diverse. But without a natural home in a trading bloc, its room to manoeuvre may not always be what it is today.

This reflects the growing importance of regional trade agreements (RTAs) in world trade. According to the WTO (2001) there are 170 RTAs in place, and this number is expected to increase to 250 by 2005. More than half of world trade occurs within RTAs or prospective RTAs. While Australia has missed out on ASEAN plus three, if Australia cements its economic relationship with the United States through an FTA, this would shore up US support for reducing agricultural tariffs in multilateral forums such as Doha.

In this vein, the Australian APEC Study Centre Report (2001, p. xvii) for DFAT argues that a bilateral agreement between Australia and the United States would promote 'economic integration that can then be used as benchmarks in the global negotiations'. The Australian government has continually argued that Australia's best hope of achieving reform in world agricultural trade is to persuade the US to take a leadership role in the WTO on agriculture (Davis 2002d, 2002e). The Bush administration appears committed to multilateral trade liberalization as evidenced in both Doha and the APEC leaders' meeting in Shanghai; however, Bush argued that what he could achieve in multilateral forums was limited given the fractured Congress. This has changed following the Congressional elections in November 2002, for the Republicans now have control of the House of Representatives and the Senate.

Historically, the problem with Australia pinning its hopes on the commitment of the US to freer trade is that the United States has shown that it is more than willing to thumb its nose at free trade when doing so is in its best interests. While the Bush administration has been at pains to emphasize its commitment to free trade as 'an important engine of economic growth and a cornerstone of its economic agenda', its free trade rhetoric has always played second fiddle to domestic political considerations (Hewson 2002). There are several recent instances where Australian exports to the US have suffered because of domestic political considerations in the United States.

These include steel tariffs (Hewson 2002), lamb quotas (AFR 1999), sugar quotas (Pearson 1999a) and excise tax exemptions for US wine producers (Pearson 1999b).

On top of this, the opportunity cost to Australia of negotiating an FTA is potentially high. Australia, at least prior to the 2003 Iraq war, has had limited diplomatic access to the United States at the highest levels and it is arguable that Australia would be better served using this time to argue its interests on a case-by-case basis (Garnaut 2002, p. 134). Indeed it is likely that far from furthering Australia's interests by getting the US to take a leadership role on agriculture in the WTO, an AUS-FTA by its very nature would hinder Australia's credibility to argue for multilateral reductions on agriculture in the WTO. This stems from the fact that an AUS-FTA would be compromised on agricultural trade. As Garnaut (2002, p. 139) emphasizes, 'a [compromised] bilateral FTA would break the formal rules of the WTO, encourage Japanese and European supporters of agricultural protection, and weaken the prospects of securing Australian and US interests in a new round of multilateral trade negotiations'.

In ending this part of the chapter it is noted that our observations are in accord with two reports regarding the impact of an AUS-FTA released in the first half of 2003. The first report by ACIL Consulting determined that a free trade deal would cost the Australian economy more than it can deliver. Indeed, ACIL has concluded that the economy would be worse off, estimating that the deal would reduce GDP by 0.02 per cent. In reaching this conclusion ACIL observed: 'The US would have most of the bargaining power, as it needs the [agreement] less than Australia . . . Worse still, the strains and disappointments of a negotiation with the US, in which it gradually became clear that much agriculture would be excluded, could harm overall Australia-US relations rather than improve them.' The report was commissioned by the Rural Industries Research and Development Corporation (RIRDC) and guided by a steering committee with representatives from the Department of Foreign Affairs and Trade, the Department of Agriculture and the National Farmers Federation. Garnaut (2003) argues that the study was commissioned because there existed a 'strong view in DFAT' that a free trade deal could be shown to be worth more than $4 billion. However, when the results fell short of expectations the report was 'nobbled' by DFAT officials. He adds that the primary reason its conclusions were less favourable than previous DFAT modelling is that it is not assumed that total trade liberalization is achievable. The study also rejects the

assumption that services sector productivity would improve by 0.3 per cent due to the elimination of foreign ownership restrictions in telecommunications, banking and other areas. This assumption had accounted for the largest component of the department's claimed $4 billion in gains (Garnaut 2003).

ACIL's negative assessment was echoed in May 2003 in a working paper produced by four Productivity Commission researchers (Adams et al. 2003). The central finding of this study was that most preferential trade deals negotiated over the previous forty years had depressed rather than expanded trade. It was found that a number of agreements with innovative investment provisions, by contrast, have had a positive impact on investment flows; but how the trade-investment balance nets out remains unclear. In concluding this section of the chapter we suggest that in the light of the post-war history of US-Australia trade relations the economic case for an AUS-FTA is weak. If the observer is informed by the trade norms established through that period one is led to conclude that Australia would be better served by concentrating on forging a common front with the US to further the liberalization of agriculture in the current WTO round of negotiations.

A GLOBAL DEPUTY

Similar conclusions to those reached in the foregoing section have been advanced by a great many observers. In short, the views of economists who have considered the AUS-FTA proposal from the conventional perspective have been overwhelmingly negative. But the arguments of these analysts have tended to fall on deaf ears. We suggest that this is because the economics of the recent past is not what the trade deal is about. Rather, the government's decision to embrace a bilateral pathway to globalism is based primarily on the electoral security an AUS-FTA can provide to the Coalition parties and on the government's decision to have Australia play the part of deputy in the current US effort to refocus the globalization project.

From his analysis of international negotiations Putnam (1988) concluded that such negotiations are best understood as a two-level game – one level involving domestic interest-group politics and the other international deal-making to avert threats to national interests. He also observed that the interaction that occurs between the two levels can create important opportunities in both.

Each national political leader appears at both game boards. Across the international table sit his foreign counterparts, and at his elbows sit diplomats and other international advisers. Around the domestic table behind him sit party and parliamentary figures, spokespersons for domestic agencies, representatives of key interest groups, and the leader's own political advisers. The unusual complexity of this two-level game is that moves that are rational for a player at one board . . .

may be impolitic for that same player at the other board. . . . On occasion, however, clever players will spot a move on one board that will trigger realignments on other boards, enabling them to achieve otherwise unattainable objectives. This 'two-table' metaphor captures the dynamics of . . . negotiations better than any model based on unitary national actors (Putnam 1988, p. 434).

We accept the applicability of this metaphor to the AUS-FTA and suggest that the Coalition's decision to embrace the bilateral path to globalism is best explained by the fact that the leaders of the government are aware that they need to distinguish themselves from their domestic opponents. And they are also aware that moves on the global stage have created a rare opportunity to achieve this goal in a manner that can both advantage the Coalition and make the attainment of a profitable AUS-FTA at least possible. To explain this turn of events we begin by discussing Australia's 'domestic politics of globalization'. Conley coined this phrase to make the point that while many developments in the world of political economy occur outside the control of nations 'it is in the domestic arena that interpretations are constructed and policy choices made, explained and justified' (Conley 2001, p. 223). Given that this is the case, liberal democratic governments committed to a particular path to globalism must strive to 'educate' the domestic community as to the benefits and if possible the inevitably of the chosen route. This need is heightened when the goal and the path taken are prone to induce anxiety in a significant section of the electorate. Such a situation can assist the government to traverse the way forward but can also induce a backlash against those deemed responsible for protecting the population from the source of this anxiety.

Through the 1980s, both the ALP and Coalition parties took up the task of convincing Australians that the neo-liberal path was the best route to a desirable form of globalism. The fact that both parliamentary groupings promoted a similar vision and agenda facilitated the change process required to globalize Australia. However, this consensus was Janus-faced as far as the major political parties were concerned. While facilitating acceptance of change, it concomitantly made it difficult for many within the electorate to distinguish what it was that the respective parties had to offer and, as a consequence, over time party allegiance was weakened. This was a development furthered by the fact that the two parliamentary groupings utilized a similar strategy to encourage acceptance of their common vision. In short, both sought to overcome resistance by manipulating the anxiety invariably generated within any population compelled to embrace the many changes associated with a shift from domestic protectionism to globalism. This was done in many ways but most importantly by constantly reiterating the mantra that if Australians did not embrace the neo-liberal global vision then social decay and 'Banana Republicanism' were bound to be their lot.

Australia's party leaders chose to manipulate – if not encourage – anxiety regarding the nation's place in the global economy because such an approach can be a very effective change management strategy. However, this strategy generally requires that those who put themselves forward as leaders offer a means to enable the population to break free from the identified sources of anxiety. If leaders fail to offer this escape, they risk the danger that those they seek to manage may turn to others. Accordingly, Australians were told repeatedly that while the changes associated with globalization might be discomforting, the competitive outcomes produced by these very changes would ensure that the good times would roll once again. Indeed, once the needed changes were in place, Australians would find themselves on the upswing of a 'J-curve' that would carry the nation to unprecedented levels of security and prosperity.

Constant reiteration of this message proved a highly effective electoral strategy for the ALP from 1983. Or rather, it remained effective for as long as their parliamentary opponents remained an easy target by constantly depicting themselves as the more extreme enthusiasts for the global neo-liberal agenda. However, the Coalition eventually ceased to be so obliging. From the mid 1990s, while the conservative parties continued to adhere to the vision they shared with the ALP, their leaders finessed their means of promoting their message. Under John Howard's leadership the Coalition continued promoting the idea that if the population did not embrace neo-liberal globalism their well-being would be undermined, but in so doing it sought to manipulate popular anxiety by pointing to new threats that it suggested only the Coalition had the capacity to keep at bay.

Central to Howard's strategy was a recognition that the common vision and strategy of the major political parties had weakened the party allegiance of a great many Australians (Bell 1997). The electoral opportunity thus generated was made apparent to Howard by the outcome of the 1993 federal election. In that contest the Coalition had been led by John Hewson, an economist who had called for an acceleration of the global neo-liberal project, with the result that his message and his party were unexpectedly defeated at the polls. Howard subsequently seized the leadership and, having done so, ensured that the Coalition did not make the same mistake in the 1996 election. In the midst of the latter campaign he outflanked the ALP by putting himself forward as a 'compassionate conservative' who promoted policies that would make Australians 'relaxed and comfortable'. In so doing he drew on US Republican Party experience with 'wedge politics'. This strategy has been explored by Wilson and Turnbull (2001, p. 384), who define it as '*a calculated political tactic* aimed at using divisive social issues to gain political support, weaken opponents and strengthen control over the political agenda'. Embraced by the Republicans from the time of the Reagan presidency, the tactic is sharpened by drawing attention to issues and groups likely to attract resentment or antipathy in the population. The tactical effect is two-fold: the opponent is compelled to retreat from supporting those targeted and, if it fails to take this step, is made to appear weak and incapable of strong leadership.

In his use of this tactic Howard singled out for vilification both domestic and global targets. Domestically, he marked both welfare recipients, who he claimed were bleeding the 'Aussie battler', and the 'elites' who stressed the value of multiculturalism (Wilson and Turnbull 2001). Globally, he situated two primary groups in his sights. The first was made up of those who wished to build 'special relationships' with Asian nations rather than with Australia's more traditional friends in Europe and North America. His second target was those individuals who gave encouragement to global institutions, which Howard claimed were 'meddling' in Australia's internal affairs (Lambert 2000). In promoting the global part of this strategy, Howard played on a long-held ambivalence in the Australian communities' view of Asia and the fact that it has always been easier to sell insecurity rather than a positive vision of what benefits might accrue from closer economic, social and defence ties with the region.

While playing on these xenophobic tendencies the Howard leadership also sought to win over the electorate in 1996 by offering to slow the rate at which Australia was being opened to the global economy. By contrast, the ALP continued trumpeting its commitment to multilateralism, Asian engagement and the whole global neo-liberal agenda. By so doing, Labor managed to paint itself as the more extreme enthusiast for globalization and continued to expound this message throughout the election campaign. As a consequence, the ALP was decimated at the polls, with the largest swing from Labor occurring in the party's working-class heartland.

Following the 1996 election the Coalition sought to consolidate its victory by advancing the global neo-liberal agenda with more caution than had been the norm within Australia since 1983. This step was heightened by a challenge that emerged from within its own electoral base. The clearest expression of this resistance was the rapid rise of One Nation, a right-wing party that was grounded in rural areas that traditionally gave unswerving support to the Coalition and that was xenophobic, populist and overtly opposed to the global neo-liberal project. The enthusiasm with which One Nation's message was taken up by large sectors of society normally supportive of the Coalition rattled the government. Howard responded by expressing his sympathy for those attracted to One Nation's policies. But in so doing he had to confront the problem that he remained deeply committed to the economic policies that were a key reason the Coalition's traditional supporters had turned to right-wing populism (Conley 2001). In short, Howard's problem was that repeatedly declaiming that the Coalition sympathized with the fears felt by many in their heartland, as a consequence of their leaders' embrace of neo-liberal globalism, was simply not an effective response to One Nation. Consequently, if the government was to remain in office it needed to show these individuals that it could contain the dangers posed by the outsiders who it claimed were threatening Australians' way of life.

Given its continued commitment to the global neo-liberal project, the outsiders that the Coalition could target for vilification could not be the global investors and traders pointed to by One Nation. Instead, the spotlight was focused on those international human rights agencies that, it was claimed, 'pandered' to such groups as the Australian Aborigines and in so doing challenged Australian sovereignty (Leaver 2001b, p. 20). In undertaking this effort at political camouflage the UN was selected for particular vilification:

> The deep distrust of economic globalisation felt in many parts of rural and suburban Australia had made it attractive for the government to adopt an anti-international stance. Unwilling, however, to shake loose from the extensive web of international economic treaties to which it is a party, and having only a limited capacity to influence the global economic forces that press in at every point, the Government has chosen skilfully to displace domestic concern about the loss of economic sovereignty on to international agencies promoting a global social democratic agenda of which the UN human rights system is one. Economic globalisation remains unchecked while, popularly, no interference from international political and social organisations will be tolerated (Zifcak 2003, p. v).

In promoting this strategy the Coalition drew from a period in its own history that Howard much admires. Through the 1950s and 1960s an important factor enabling the Coalition to remain in office had been the ability of Liberal leader Robert Menzies to drive a wedge into the working-class electoral base of the ALP. Menzies had been able to achieve this goal by targeting those individuals sympathetic to any form of collectivism whom he depicted as communists or 'fellow travellers'. Given that a great many members of the ALP were sympathetic to a mild form of collectivism, even while despising the Soviet option, this proved a very effective electoral strategy. Labor found it could not emulate the Coalition's attack on all forms of collectivism; and when it attempted to restrain this assault, the ALP members who were willing to engage in the attack split from the Party. Those who remained were charged with being 'soft' in their response to dangerous forces supposedly poised to strike at Australia from the immediate North. In most cases these Northerners were nationalists seeking to free their countries from colonialism. But in Australia throughout the two decades after 1950 all the resistance forces of Asia tended to be depicted as communists – or at the very least as communist sympathizers – and as such a threat whose advance could only be halted if the Australian people continued to return Coalition governments.

In pointing constantly to the 'threat from the North' through the 1950s and 1960s, the Coalition had needed to calm the anxieties thus generated by showing it could meet this challenge. Its primary means of so doing was to highlight its commitment to Australia's alliance with the United States. Ensuring the protection the latter could offer, Australians were informed, was a task impossible for the ALP because it was soft on collectivism and indeed wished to introduce into Australia 'socialism by stealth'. This was a fiction that the US allowed the Coalition to sustain, but in return a heavy price was demanded. The cost was that Australia had to adopt a 'forward defence' policy which in practice meant that Australian troops would support the US in any military engagements it undertook with Australia's immediate and near neighbours. This eventually meant that Australians were amongst the very small group of nations that actively participated in the US attack on the Vietnamese war of independence.

In the second half of the 1990s Howard's capacity to appeal to xenophobia, denigrate global human rights agencies and rerun the 'threat from the North' message was heightened by the arrival of an increasing number of individuals seeking refugee status under UN treaties. This time the outsiders were not communists. However, it was noted, even if *sotto voce,* that being Muslims or from Islamic countries, they differed from both 'old Australia' and recently settled immigrants from East Asia and as such constituted a new and unknown threat. The extent to which the Coalition was able to exploit the anxiety around this issue was at first muted. However, once the strategy was confirmed as a winner at the ballot box and the Coalition realized that the ALP had great difficulty emulating the tactic, it was promoted with a vengeance. This was the more so once the Howard government came to appreciate that it was a strategy capable of redirecting many of the fears associated with globalization away from the Coalition's neo-liberal agenda.

But in reactivating the 'threat from the North' story the government needed to offer some way of showing that it alone could contain the new dangers it had identified. The 'fortress Australia' notion promoted by One Nation had shown that inducing anxiety in the population was insufficient. The Coalition needed not only to engender anxiety but also to show that it could overcome the source of these fears. Howard's means of resolving this dilemma was once again to draw on the Menzies experience he so much admired. From the time he became Prime Minister he had constantly reiterated the need for Australia to strengthen its bilateral economic and military ties with those nations in North America and Europe with which Australia had traditionally sustained 'special relationships'. As part of this process, Australians were told, they should reconsider the notion that emphasis should be placed on multilateral trading arrangements and the building of many new special relationships across Asia. In a 1999 interview with *The Bulletin* magazine Howard made plain his enthusiasm for this notion and in the process raised what became known as the 'Howard Doctrine'. This amounted to nothing less than the notion that Australia should again take up a forward defence policy and act as a US 'deputy' in Asia. It was an offer that caused offence to governments across Asia, the more so when Australia sent troops to confront rampaging militia in Timor while an American fleet sat off the coast with the clear understanding that they would strike Indonesia if the latter resisted the Australians (Beeson 2000; McDougall 2002).

While Clinton may have been willing to make use of the Australians in Timor, he was less interested in the idea that Australia should be publicly anointed the US satrap for its region. The idea that Australia might play this role under a Republican Party administration, however, had been canvassed by Robert Zoellick (the next US Trade Representative) in 1999. In the same year, the idea was given greater substance by Dick Armitage who suggested that if the ANZUS alliance was to survive it would need an enhanced Australian military commitment and Australians would have to accept that there would need to be a closer link between trade and strategic policy (Leaver 2002, pp. 2, 5). But in 1999 trying to sell this message within Australia remained difficult. This was the more so given that as late as 2000 an official Green Paper concluded that Australia was one of the most secure places on the planet and observed that it was difficult to identify the context in which an attack might occur or from where it might originate. In such circumstances it was hard for the Coalition to sustain the message that it alone could protect the Australian people from obscure external forces. But then a series of fortuitous developments unfolded that were useful for the government's strategy. First, the Bush administration, with its commitment to a level of global unilateralism without post-war precedent, captured the White House. Second, several boatloads of refugees managed to reach Australian waters immediately prior to the 2001 federal election. Third, the Twin Towers came down and Bush declared his 'war on terrorism'.

The Coalition exploited the subsequent fears unleashed within Australia with a level of vigour and ruthlessness not seen since the 1950s. Actively replicating the campaign that has been undertaken by the Bush administration, the Coalition initiated an unrelenting effort to create a political environment in which Australians perceive themselves to be endangered and are convinced that the Coalition is the only parliamentary grouping able to protect them from the looming forces to the North. In so doing it has shown a willingness to support and indeed assist the unilateralism and adventurism that has become part of the US global agenda. Moreover, while continuing to insist that Australia remains committed to its involvement with Asia, the government has made the region patently aware of its willingness to play the part of deputy sheriff in a manner similar to that which a great many Europeans believe is being undertaken by Tony Blair in Europe.

Unwilling or unable to convince its supporters to follow suit, Labor has been compelled to limit its response to complaining that the Coalition is not doing enough to protect Australia from external dangers. In the 1950s, when confronted by a similar criticism, the Coalition reacted by muddying the waters by legislating to ban the Communist Party. This step was illegal under the Australian Constitution, a reading that was subsequently supported by the High Court. Nevertheless, the attempt to ban the party proved a major victory for the Coalition because the ALP felt compelled to resist the government's assault on the basic political rights of Australian citizens. By so doing Labor was placed in a situation where it was able to be depicted as 'soft on communism'. Similarly, in mid 2003 the government announced that it intended to pass wide-sweeping legislation that would allow it to proscribe political organizations and in so doing pointed specifically to the resistance body Hezbollah. Again it appears that the intention is to drive a wedge into the Labor Party and into its electoral base, this time by depicting the party as 'soft on terrorism'. When the ALP sought to elude this feint by proposing a bill that would target only the external militant wing of Hezbollah, the Attorney-General replied that Labor was weak and unwilling to protect the people of Australia. Indeed he accused the ALP of actively working to create an environment in which Australians were put at risk by the terrorists from the North that he claimed were a threat to Australia (Lewis 2003, p. 4).

CONCLUSION

In bringing our discussion to a close, we note that earlier we observed that conventional economic analysis does not justify an AUS-FTA and that Australia would be better served by continuing with the multilateral path to globalism. However, this conclusion was premised on an orthodox understanding of the post-war pattern of US-Australia trade relations. In the light of the foregoing discussion of the Coalition's use of wedge politics, we suggest that this conclusion needs to be modified or at least advanced with caution. Putman's observation that on 'occasion ... clever players will spot a move on one board that will trigger realignments on other boards, enabling them to achieve otherwise unattainable objectives' seems to have marked relevance in relation to the US-Australia relationship. We suggest that when George Bush seized the US presidency and made clear his intention to reconfigure the US approach to the trade-strategic relationship, the Coalition saw a great opportunity at the global level. In short, they recognized that if they showed a clear willingness to support the Bush global adventure they could achieve what had previously been unattainable objectives in both the domestic and global arenas. At home they could utilize anxiety management and wedge politics with a degree of abandon and success that had hitherto been impossible. And at the global level, they could with some justification entertain the hope that they could win a trade deal with the US that could actually be of economic benefit to Australia. Seizing this opportunity, immediately following the US election that returned Bush, Howard's cabinet authorized the pursuit of an AUS-FTA and made clear Australia's intention to fully integrate its defence strategy in Asia with that of the US (Leaver 2002).

What now remains in question is whether the US will adequately reward Australia for abandoning any attempt to develop a defence and trade strategy that has elements of independence and self-reliance. Leaver (2002) has suggested that the US could achieve this goal by manipulating its use of trade quotas and suggests that if the US takes this path Australia will in effect be returned to the Imperial Preference system which Menzies reluctantly abandoned when the UK joined the European Union. Under that regime, member states of the British Empire were offered tariff concessions by the UK that were not available to non-Empire states and in return were expected to favour Britain's exports and give unquestioning support to Britain's strategic designs globally. If the US is to replicate this strategy it will need to find a way to reward those willing to play the part of subaltern. In the case of Australia, the most effective rewards are agricultural trade concessions; but under the circumstances that were previously the norm, ceding the required indulgences would have generated an unmanageable level of resistance from within the US. However, with the war on terror in full swing, the circumstances are not 'normal' and what were previously 'unattainable objectives' have in many cases been rendered attainable. In short, given the Bush government's exploitation of the Twin Towers outrage, an environment has been created which just might make it possible for the US to overcome domestic resistance and make the required concessions.

That the foregoing just might occur is suggested by the fact that since the invasion of Iraq the Bush administration has striven to show that it rewards those willing to embrace its global efforts without question. Immediately following the fall of Baghdad, Bush invited Howard to stay at his private ranch and it was made very clear to the world that this was a sign that the 'US appreciates allies that stand by it' and that he wanted this appreciation to be reflected in the forthcoming trade negotiations. As Hartcher (2003, p. 23) has noted, besides the personal hospitality Bush offered Howard, there are a number of indications Australia may have increased its capacity to benefit from an AUS-FTA because of its willingness to actively support the war on Iraq. These include the fact that the US has given the highest possible priority to the AUS-FTA negotiations and set a timetable that, if met, will be the quickest free trade agreement the US has ever negotiated.

That there is a direct connection between Australia's willingness to serve in America's wars and trade has been denied by the Coalition. However, it is an understanding that has been highlighted in the US by Richard Fisher, Deputy US Trade Representative under Clinton, who declared: 'There's no question – Australia is a beneficiary of the administration's trade priorities for having stood shoulder-to-shoulder with us in Iraq' (cited in Hartcher 2003, p. 25). Bisley (2003, p. 32), by contrast, has argued that 'the one constant in American post-Cold War trade policy is the fact that the US draws a firm distinction between its security and trading interests. There is no reason to believe that the US, or Japan for that matter, is likely to behave any differently in the current environment.' The reality, however, is that there is reason to so believe. Indeed in May 2003 Zoellick took pains to make it explicit to the world that the US now perceives a direct relationship between trade and strategic policy, and in so doing he also made clear what the US believes is the nature of FTA relationships. Having observed that henceforth the US will demand that countries seeking free trade status agree to cooperate with it on its foreign policy and national security goals, he added that America's partners must understand that negotiating an FTA with the US 'is not something one has a right to. It's a privilege' (Krebs 2003).

Further indications that Australia may benefit from its proven willingness to embrace US foreign policy include the fact that the US has allowed Australia a share of the booty won by the occupation of Iraq. Thus Bush made it clear that Australian wheat sales to Iraq would be allowed to continue and granted this boon in the face of explicit resistance from the US wheat industry. Similarly the Bush administration has persisted with its intention to negotiate an AUS-FTA despite the fact that the US National Cattlemen's Association, a staunch. supporter of the Republican Party, has expressed strong opposition to any agreement and is bound to intensify its resistance to Australia's demand for greater access to the US market (Krebs 2003). All this bodes well for the Coalition's dream that it will be able to repeat Menzies's success in consolidating the Coalition as the 'natural party of government' in Australia. If Howard's dream is realized and if the US is successful in its determination to impose a new unilateral stamp on the globalization process, Australia will be returned to its earlier position as a satrapy that sits anxiously at the edge of Asia, plays the role of local military base, and is rewarded by being allowed special trade privileges. In short, Australia will complete the turn away from a multilateral world of alliances and open markets to a version of the subject relationship it formerly sustained with Britain when it was both empire and hegemon.

REFERENCES

Adams, Richard, Philippa Dee, Jyothi Gali and Greg McGuire (2003), 'The Trade and Investment Effects of Preferential Trading Arrangements – Old and New Evidence', Productivity Commission Staff Working Paper, May.

Alcorn, Gay (2001), 'Us and Them – for Now', *The Age* (Melbourne), 11 September, p. 11.

Australian APEC Study Centre (2001), 'An Australia-USA Free Trade Agreement: Issues and Implications', Australian APEC Study Centre, Monash University, Report for the Department of Foreign Affairs and Trade.

Australian Financial Review (AFR) (1999), 'US Flirts with Protectionism', *Australian Financial Review*, 30 March, p. 16.

Australian Financial Review (AFR) (2001a), 'Countdown to a Free Trade Agreement with Uncle Sam', *Australian Financial Review*, 9 March, p. 12.

Australian Financial Review (AFR) (2001b), 'Farmyard Diplomacy', *Australian Financial Review*, 12 March, p. 12.

Australian Financial Review (AFR) (2001c), 'In Hot Pursuit of US Trade', *Australian Financial Review*, 12 April, p. 21.

Australian Financial Review (AFR) (2001d), 'Business Backs Free-trade Pact', *Australian Financial Review*, 31 July, p. 4.

Beeson, Mark (2000), 'Debating Defence: Time for a Paradigm Shift?', *Australian Journal of International Affairs,* **54** (3), 255-259.

Bell, Stephan (1997), 'Globalisation, Neoliberalism and the Transformation of the Australian State', *Australian Journal of Political Science* **32** (3), 345-367.

Bisley, Nick (2003), 'The Return of Bilateralism', *The Diplomat,* **2** (1), 30-33.

Brennan, Geoffrey (2002), 'US Deal may be Strategically Smart or a Dangerous Liaison', *Australian Financial Review*, 21 September, p. 50.

Capling, Ann (2001a), 'An Australia-United States Trade Agreement?' *Policy, Organisation and Society,* **20** (1), 11-27.

Capling, Ann (2001b), 'Clutching for Apron Strings? Assessing the Prospects for an Australia-United States Trade Deal', Speech to the Sydney Institute, 30 April.

Capling, Ann and Kim Nossal (2001), 'Death of Distance or Tyranny of Distance? The Internet, Deterritorialisation and the Anti-globalisation Movement in Australia', *Pacific Review* **14** (3), 443-446.

Caves, Richard (1960), *Multinational Enterprise and Economic Analysis*, Cambridge: Cambridge University Press.

Centre for International Economics (2001), *Economic Impacts of an Australia-United*

States Free Trade Area, Sydney: Centre for International Economics.

Conley, Tom (2001), 'The Domestic Politics of Globalisation', *Australian Journal of Political Science*, **36** (2), 223-236.

Davidson, Kenneth (2002), 'Free Trade with America? Read the Blueprint and Weep', *The Age*, 1 August.

Davis, Mark (2002a), 'Push to swell ranks of exports', *Australian Financial Review*, 11 April, p. 8.

Davis, Mark (2002b), 'Exports to US Grow Rapidly while Imports Head Down', *Australian Financial Review*, 26 July, p. 9.

Davis, Mark (2002c), 'Quarantine Hurdle to Trade Deal', *Australian Financial Review*, 9 September, p. 6.

Davis, Mark (2002d), 'Howard Embraces American Values', *Australian Financial Review*, 13 June, p. 1.

Davis, Mark (2002e), 'Howard Talks up Closer US-Australia Trade Ties', *Australian Financial Review*, 12 June, p. 3.

Davis, Mark (2002f), 'US Selects Nations for Trade Deals', *Australian Financial Review*, 3 October, p. 5.

Davis, Mark (2002g), 'Trade-security Link "Not in our Interest"', *Australian Financial Review*, 11 September, p. 11.

Edwards, John (2001), 'An American-Australian Free Trade Agreement?' *Policy, Organisation and Society*, **20** (1), 29-37.

Garnaut, John (2003), 'Free Trade Comes at a Painful Price', *Sydney Morning Herald*, 26 February, p.1.

Garnaut, Ross (2002), 'An Australia-United States Free Trade Agreement', *Australian Journal of International Affairs*, **56** (1), 123-141.

Gestrin, Michael and Alan Rugman (1994), 'The North American Free Trade Agreement and Foreign Direct Investment', *Transnational Corporations*, **3** (1), 77-95.

Gill, Stephan (2001), 'Constitutionalizing Inequality and the Clash of Globalizations', Paper presented at the International Studies Association, 42nd Annual Convention, Chicago, 21-24 February.

Hamilton, Clive (2001), 'The Case for Fair Trade', *Journal of Australian Political Economy*, **48**, 60-72.

Hartcher, Peter (2003), 'What Australia Won from the War', *Australian Financial Review*, 10 May, p. 25.

Hewson, John (2002), 'Bush's Blatant Self-interest', *Australian Financial Review*, 8 March, p. 74.

International Trade Strategies (ITS) (2002), *NAFTA Chapter 11 – Issues and Opportunities: Research Paper on NAFTA Chapter 11 and its Use for Illuminating Debate on Investment Provisions in an Australia-US FTA*, Melbourne: International Trade Strategies.

Jackson, Allison (2002), 'Singapore Pact Frees Trade Route', *The Age* (Melbourne), 4 November, Business Section, p. 1.

James, Craig (2002), 'Afghan Venture to Aid Free Trade Accord', *Australian Financial Review*, 5 April, p. 16.

Kelly, Paul (2001), 'What Price Free Trade?' *Weekend Australian*, 24-25 March.

Kelton, Maryanne and Richard Leaver (1999), 'Issues in Australian Foreign Policy: January to June 1999', *Australian Journal of Politics and History*, **45** (4), 526-543.

Kevin, Tony (2002), 'Australian Foreign Policy at Crossroads', *Australian Journal of International Affairs*, **56** (1), 31-37.

Kohler, Alan (2002), 'Foreign Investment the Flip Side of Trade', *Australian Financial Review*, 5 September, p. 63.

Krebs, A.V. (2003), 'U.S. will Demand Countries Seeking "Free Trade" Status must "Cooperate" with U.S. on its Foreign Policy and "National Security" Goals', *The Agribusiness Examiner*, **20** (May), No. 250.

Kunkel, John (2002), 'Australian Trade Policy in an Age of Globalisation', *Australian Journal of International Affairs*, **56** (2), 237-251.

Lambert, Rob (2000), 'Globalization and the Erosion of Class Compromise in Contemporary Australia', *Politics and Society*, **28** (1), 93-118.

Leaver, Richard (2001a), 'Is Australia Being Economically Excluded from Asia?', *Policy, Organisation and Society*, **20** (1), 141-156.

Leaver, Richard (2001b), 'The Meanings, Origins and Implications of "the Howard Doctrine"', *The Pacific Review*, **14** (1), 15-34.

Leaver, Richard (2002), 'Australian Trade Policy: the Return of Imperial Preference', working paper, Department of Political and International Studies, Flinders University.

Lewis, Steve (2003), 'Dockyard brawl over outlawing Hezbollah', *The Australian,* 28 May, p. 4.

Lloyd, Christopher (2002), 'From Labourist-Protectionism to Globalisation in Australia: A Case of Necessary Regime Adaptation?' Paper presented at the 13th World Congress of Economic History, Buenos Aires.

Lyon, Rod (2001), 'Issues in Australian Foreign Policy, January to June 2001', *Australian Journal of Politics and History*, **47** (4), 516-530.

Mann, Howard and Konrad von Moltke (2002), 'Protecting Investor Rights and the Public Good: Assessing NAFTA's Chapter 11', Background Paper to the International Institute for Sustainable Development Tri-National Policy Workshop, March-April, Mexico, Ottawa, Washington.

McDonald, Hamish (2000), 'Trading Places: Asia or America?' *Sydney Morning Herald*, 23 December.

McDougall, Derek (2002), 'Australia's peacekeeping role in the post-Cold War era', *Contemporary South East Asia*, **24** (3), 590-608.

McKenna, Bernard (2000), 'Labour Responses to Globalization: the Australian Experience', *Asia Pacific Business Review*, **7** (1), 71-104.

McKibbin, Warwick (1998), 'Regional and Multilateral Trade Liberalisation', in Peter Drysdale and David Vines (eds), *Europe, East Asia and APEC: A Shared Global Agenda*, Cambridge: Cambridge University Press.

Nossal, Kim (2001), 'Bilateral Free Trade with the United States: Lessons from Canada', *Policy, Organisation and Society* **20** (1), 47-62.

Oxley, Alan (2001), *New Directions in Australia's Trade: Trends and Strategies to 2010,* accessible at <www.tradestrategies.com.au>.

Pearson, Brendan (1999a), 'US Sugar Policy Sours Trade', *Australian Financial Review,* 5 November, p. 13.

Pearson, Brendan (1999b), 'Australian Wine Exporters to the US Disadvantaged by Excise', *Australian Financial Review,* 16 June, p. 11.

Pearson, Brendan (2002), 'Diplomacy is Learning to Work with a Scoundrel', *Australian Financial Review*, 7 March, p. 8.

Putnam, Robert D. (1988), 'Diplomacy and Domestic Politics: The Logic of Two-level Games', *International Organization,* **42** (Summer), 427-460.

Rasmussen, Mikkel Vedby (2002), 'A Parallel Globalization of Terror: 9-11, Security and Globalization', *Cooperation and Conflict,* **37** (3), 323-349.

Schuff, Sally (2002), 'Farm Froups Urge Bush to Reject Australian FTA', *Feedstuffs,* 30 September, p. 6.

Simpson, Kate, James Ensor and Sarah Lowe (2001), *The Globalisation Challenge: Australia's Role in a Rapidly Changing World,* Fitzroy, Melbourne: Oxfam Community Aid Abroad.

Solomon, Russell (2000), 'Trading Places: Steering Globalisation and National Interest', *Australian Quarterly,* **72** (4), 36-39.

Tang, William (2001), *Multilateral Regime in Crisis and the Strategic Trade Agreements in Asia-Pacific,* accessible at <http://home.kimo.com.tw/liutaho/MultilateralRegime.htm>.

Thawley, Michael (2002), Speech to the Los Angeles World Affairs Council, 2 April, accessible at <http://www.lawac.org>.

Trebilcock, Michael and Robert Howse (2001), *The Regulation of International Trade* (2nd edn), New York: Routledge.

Vaile, Mark, (2002), 'Vaile Hails Breakthrough for Australia-US Trade Relations', Media Release MT147/2002, 14 November 2002, accessible at <http://www.trademinister.gov.au/releases/2002/mvt147_02.html>.

Wesley, Michael (2002a), 'Australia's Department of Foreign Affairs and Trade and the Challenges of Globalisation', *Australian Journal of International Affairs,* **56** (2), 207-222.

Wesley, Michael (2002b), 'Perspectives on Australian Foreign Policy, 2001', *Australian Journal of International Affairs,* **56** (1), 47-63.

Wilson, Shaun and Nick Turnbull (2001), 'Wedge Politics and Welfare Reform in Australia', *Australian Journal of Politics and History,* **47** (3), 384-402.

WTO (2001), *Overview of Developments in the International Trading Agreement,* WT/MIN(01)/2.

Zifcak, Spencer (2003), 'The New Anti-Internationalism: Australia and the United Nations Human Rights Treaty System', Discussion Paper Number 54, Canberra: The Australia Institute.

NOTE

1   We thank Ed Morrison for research assistance with this project.

8. Globalization: A New Zealand Perspective

John Ballingall, Phil Briggs and Joanna Smith[1]

WHAT IS GLOBALIZATION?

According to an International Monetary Fund (IMF) definition, globalization refers to the growing economic interdependence of countries worldwide through the increasing volume and variety of cross-border transactions in goods and services, capital, technology, information, and people (Prasad and Gable 1997, p. 5).

Two factors in particular have played an important role in the growing integration of the world economy. One is technological innovation, particularly in transportation and communications. The advancement of technology has greatly reduced natural barriers in space and time. This allows firms to co-ordinate production activities in different locations easily, and makes possible the rapid and expansive flow of trade, investment, and people. Policies have also played a part in the international integration process. Countries have lowered barriers restricting the movements of trade, investment, and people. International organizations such as the World Trade Organisation (WTO) and its predecessor, the General Agreement of Tariffs and Trade (GATT), have also facilitated a more open international economic system.

The past two decades have witnessed increased economic integration between countries. But global economic integration is not a new phenomenon. It began to intensify from the mid 1800s until it was interrupted by the first and second world wars. The process of economic integration has resumed in recent decades, in part spurred by the experience of the wars. While there are fundamental economic reasons underlying the increased integration, one important political reason is the belief that increased exchange between nations will reduce the possibility of destructive wars. As the saying goes: if goods don't cross borders, soldiers will.

The salient features of recent economic integration are its intensity and comprehensiveness. There has been an unprecedented flow of goods, services, capital, information, and tourists and migrants. Integration is not limited to industrialized countries. Many developing countries and formerly centrally planned economies, the so-called transitional economies, are now active participants. This chapter looks at how globalization is affecting New Zealand in terms of movements of people, trade, global trends and the international flow of ideas.

PEOPLE

On arriving in New Zealand, visitors are asked whether they intend to stay for less than 12 months. These people are short-term visitors (tourists) while those staying for 12 months or more are regarded as permanent and long-term (PLT) migrants.

SHORT-TERM MOVEMENTS

With New Zealand being located far from major visitor markets, air travel has been a critical factor in the development of its tourism industry. In 1950, two-thirds of all passengers travelled to or from New Zealand by sea. By 2000 air travel accounted for over 99 per cent of arrivals (Statistics New Zealand 2000).

Tourism plays a key role in the growth of the New Zealand economy through employment, foreign exchange earnings, investment and regional development. Tourism's direct contribution to the New Zealand economy in the year to March 2000 totalled $4.8 billion, or 4.9 per cent of GDP.

Tourist arrivals to New Zealand have grown strongly over the last 20 years, with growth averaging 7.3 per cent per annum. Total arrivals reached 1.96 million in the year to June 2002; New Zealand's total population at this time was 3.94 million.

New Zealand's source countries (or markets, in this case) have been expanding and diversifying. Over the last 20 years, the significance of Australia has waned. Although it remains New Zealand's single most important tourist market, its share of visitor arrivals has been declining. Europe is still a significant market, as is the USA. But Asia's share of visitors has climbed from 7 per cent in 1981 to 24 per cent in 2002. Although a large proportion of these people are from Japan (indeed Japan's share of the market has doubled over the last two decades), it is countries such as Korea and China that are exhibiting the most spectacular growth. Growth in visitor arrivals from these, and other non-traditional source countries, is likely to continue.

Figure 1. Visitor arrivals

Annual

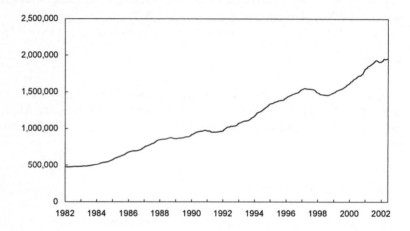

Source: Statistics New Zealand.

Clearly New Zealanders have seen a dramatic increase in the number of tourists visiting their country, with a growing proportion of these tourists coming from Asia.

The number of short-term trips by New Zealanders overseas has also increased considerably over the last 20 years. Growth has averaged 5.8 per cent per annum since 1982. In comparison New Zealand's population growth averaged 0.9 per cent per annum over the same period.

PERMANENT AND LONG-TERM MIGRATION

Refugees

New Zealand has long accepted refugees and displaced persons. German Jews entered New Zealand from Nazi Europe during the 1930s; other refugees from Europe arrived between 1949 and 1958. A 1950 agreement with the Netherlands government enabled the assisted passage of thousands of Dutch migrants. Chinese refugees from Hong Kong and Indonesia, as well as Czechoslovakian refugees, arrived during the 1960s. The 1970s saw an influx of refugees from Uganda and Chile and the first Indo-Chinese refugees, from Cambodia, Laos and Vietnam. Assyrian Christian refugees from Iraq came into the country between 1985 and 1994, and refugees from Somalia and Bosnia in the 1990s.

But it was not until the late 1980s that the number of *individual* claims for refugee status in New Zealand began to surge. Prior to 1987, an average of ten individual claims had been made each year; in 1991, 1,124 people claimed refugee status (New Zealand Immigration Service 2002).

Other migrants

The level of inward migration has not altered markedly over the last 20 years; government has kept tight control on the number of entry permits issued. But what has altered significantly is the origin of migrants. The UK and Australia have traditionally been the major source countries of migrants. This is partly a reflection of migration policy (see discussion below). But arrivals data for recent years show a significant increase in the number of immigrants from non-traditional source countries (the 'other' series in Figure 3). Immigrants in this category now comprise over half of all arrivals. There has been particularly strong growth in arrivals from Asian countries, most notably India, Pakistan and China.

Figure 2. Market shares of visitor arrivals

Per cent of total annual visitor arrivals, as at June

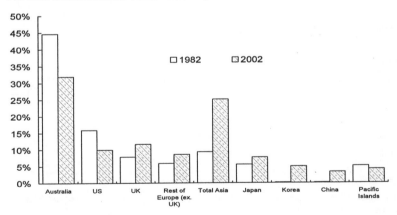

Source: Statistics New Zealand.

Figure 3. Permanent and long-term arrivals by country of last permanent residence

Annual, per cent of total PLT arrivals

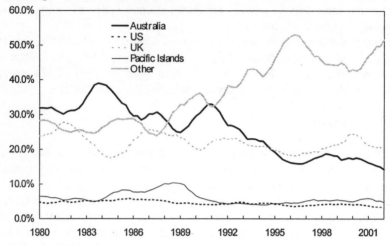

Source: Statistics New Zealand.

The unprecedented growth in arrivals from non-traditional countries has resulted in marked changes in the ethnic composition of New Zealand society. Between the 1991 and 2001 censuses, the proportion of the population identifying as European declined, whilst other categories, particularly Asian, increased (Table 1).

Table 1. NZ resident population by ethnicity

Per cent of population

Ethnic category	1991	2001
European	83.2	80.0
Māori	13.0	14.7
Pacific peoples	5.0	6.5
Asian	3.0	6.6
Other	0.2	0.7

Note: Figures sum to more than 100%. This is because respondents may select more than one ethnicity.
Source: Statistics New Zealand.

THE ROLE OF IMMIGRATION POLICIES

The prime focus of immigration policies from the 1940s to the early 1990s was combating immediate shortages of skilled labour. Through the 1970s and 1980s, entry on this basis was controlled via the 'occupational priority list', which designated those occupations for which employers could recruit overseas. Workers from 'traditional source countries' were given priority; these were countries from which New Zealand had traditionally taken substantial numbers of immigrants, or which had similar vocational training schemes.[2]

A policy review in 1991 acknowledged the inefficiencies in reactive policies that focused on specific skills. A 'points' system was brought in which scored potential migrants on the basis of human and investment capital, and was intended to attract skilled migrants from a more diverse range of countries. The new system resulted in a dramatic increase in the number of immigrants from Asian countries. The policy was fine-tuned in 1995, introducing an English language standard.

Clearly the changes in policy in 1991 had a marked impact on the composition of New Zealand's inward migration. There were political pressures for this change: the priority given to migrants from 'traditional source countries' appeared unfair, particularly to applicants from non-traditional source countries.

It seems that another factor was reinforcing the changed migration pattern over the 1990s, and this was tourism. Some tourists, on returning home after seeing New Zealand, probably started the process of applying for permanent entry. For example tourist arrivals from South Korea, which were negligible in the early 1990s, climbed very rapidly in the mid 1990s. Then when the results of New Zealand's 2001 population census were released, they revealed that of all the ethnic groups, the Korean group showed the fastest growth over the 1996-2001 period.

Another factor that is probably affecting immigration from Asia is the number of students coming to New Zealand to study. The number of such students has climbed markedly over recent years. Like tourists, these people come in on short-term visas. However, it is likely that a proportion of these people are also returning later as permanent migrants.

NEW ZEALANDERS GOING OVERSEAS

The number of permanent and long-term departures has fluctuated over the last few decades, but the level for the year to March 2002 is not vastly different from that of 0 years earlier (Figure 4). This is a little surprising.

Perhaps it partly reflects tight migration policies in prospective destination countries, especially the USA.

Figure 4. Permanent and long-term departures

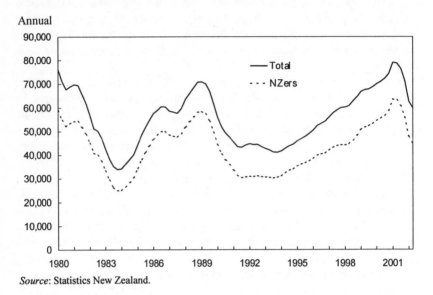

Source: Statistics New Zealand.

Age profile

As shown in Figure 5, young adults accounted for the bulk of departures in 1982. 'Overseas experience' has long been a part of New Zealand culture – a rite of passage – with young New Zealanders undertaking overseas travel (including working abroad) after finishing school or university, and before settling into permanent work.

The age profile of departing people has flattened out over the last few decades, however, with older working-age people comprising a larger proportion of departures. This may reflect dissatisfaction with the scale and nature of employment opportunities within New Zealand. Factors commonly regarded as contributing to this include: little room for advancement in a chosen career, the limited range of industries and occupations, and restrictive salaries. These are partly a feature of the small size of the economy and the focus on primary-based industries.

Figure 5. Permanent and long-term departures by age

Per cent of total PLT departures

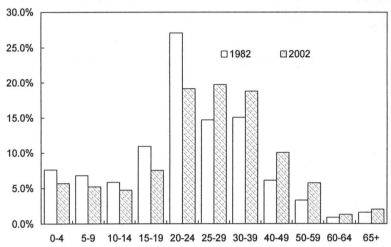

Source: Statistics New Zealand.

Destination countries

The destination of PLT departures from New Zealand has changed over the last 20 years. In 1982, 62 per cent of all departures were headed for Australia. By 2002 this was down to 46 per cent. While there has been some diversification with respect to destination countries, Australia and the UK still account for the bulk of departures. As the composition of New Zealand's resident population continues to diversify, expansion in the popularity of 'other' destination countries is likely.

POLICY INFLUENCES

Dual citizenship with the UK, or patriality due to British parents or grandparents, entitles many of New Zealand's young people to live and work in the UK without a work permit. And since the 1920s, all New Zealanders have been entitled to live and work in Australia without visas or permits.

In 2001 Australia made policy changes making it more difficult for New Zealanders to claim social welfare benefits. Whilst New Zealanders continue to be able to live and work in Australia indefinitely, social security payments are restricted to New Zealanders who become permanent Australian residents. The impact of this policy change is visible in Figure 4; departures leapt in late 2000-early 2001 as people moved in advance of the policy taking effect in February 2001, then fell back sharply.

Figure 6. Permanent and long-term departures by country of next permanent residence

Annual, per cent of total PLT departures

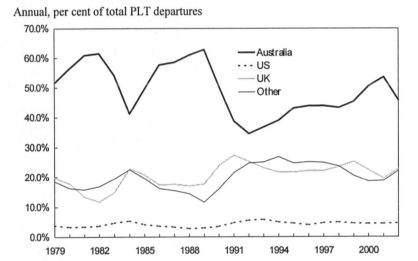

Source: Statistics New Zealand.

The New Zealand government, while retaining strict control of the level of permanent migrants, has taken steps to increase the numbers of short-term working visits. In 2000, the government announced a doubling of the number of 'working holiday visas', to 20,000. This has also allowed the government to negotiate new reciprocal schemes with other countries, allowing more New Zealanders to go overseas on working holidays. Agreements were already in place with the UK, Ireland, Canada, Japan, South Korea, Malaysia, Singapore, France and the Netherlands, and new agreements have been negotiated with Germany, Hong Kong, Italy, Chile and Sweden (Statistics New Zealand 2000).

TRADE

The New Zealand economy is heavily dependent on external trade. This has been true for all of New Zealand's short economic history, and will remain so in the future. There are a number of reasons for New Zealand's reliance on the rest of the world. First, and most obviously, New Zealand is economically small. Its population of less than four million cannot provide large domestic markets for New Zealand producers. In order to continue expanding, New Zealand firms have to begin looking overseas to larger markets. Second, New Zealand's endowments of the key factors of production – its fertile soil and a favourable climate – have led to a comparative advantage in primary products such as dairy, meat, forestry, and horticulture (Ballingall and Briggs, 2002a). New Zealand's domestic market takes only a fraction of the output from these sectors. The rest is sold overseas. Third, New Zealand's manufacturing sector is relatively limited, and is largely made up of food processing, light manufacturing, and some aluminium smelting. Most other manufactures are imported. In addition, New Zealand is heavily reliant on imported capital machinery, and the technology embodied in that capital.

However, a particular problem that New Zealand faces, as an exporter of primary products, is agricultural protectionism. For various reasons, most of New Zealand's major trading partners continue to protect their own agricultural sectors, inhibiting trade in this area.

The success or otherwise of the export sector has huge flow-on effects for the rest of the New Zealand economy. When export returns are high, exporters – and in particular farmers – increase their expenditure in the domestic economy. The 'multiplier' effect of this additional spending leads to strong household consumption expenditure and business investment. As shown in Figure 7, export revenue takes around 18 months to filter through the rest of the economy. It remains to be seen how well the high export earnings of the early years of the millennium will act as a buffer against the recent global slowdown.

NEW ZEALAND AND TRADE LIBERALIZATION: A BRIEF HISTORY[3]

New Zealand's staple export in the country's early colonial days was wool, with the UK being the major destination. Gold exports boomed for a time following the successive gold discoveries of the 1860s. But with the introduction of refrigerated shipping in 1882, meat and dairy products also became major export commodities. Again, the UK was the major destination. The historian James Belich refers to this time as the period of recolonization.[4]

New Zealand introduced relatively high tariffs on manufactured goods as early as 1888. In the period prior to the Second World War it went even further, introducing a system of import licensing for manufactures. The objective of these protective policies was to diversify the economy, which had become narrowly focused on the lucrative market for primary products in the UK. New Zealand's standard of living was one of the highest in the world in this period.

Figure 7. Export revenue and domestic spending

Annual average per cent change

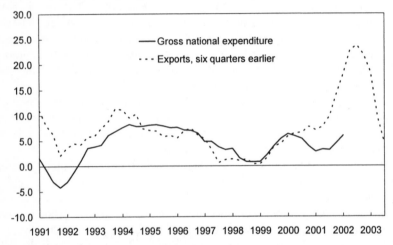

Sources: Statistics New Zealand, NZIER forecasts.

In the post-war period, New Zealand entered a new phase of economic development. These developments coincided with a new period of globalization. The UK withdrew its guaranteed export prices in 1955 and Western Europe began to draw together under the Common Market (now the EU) from 1958. When the UK joined the EEC in 1973, New Zealand had to focus on world market opportunities outside the UK, which it did with mixed success (Brownie and Dalziel 1993, p. 235).

New Zealand's relative living standards had begun to slip in the 1960s. The country suffered a sharp recession in the late 1960s as a result of falling prices for coarse wool. These price falls were largely due to increased competition from synthetic fibres. The World Bank advised the New Zealand government to revise its entire trade policy stance and to reduce import protection measures. But import policy changes came slowly and sporadically over the next 20 years. This is perhaps not surprising given the conjunction of other external shocks that accompanied the UK's entry to the EEC – two major oil shocks (1974 and 1979) and slow world growth.

Figure 8. Goods exports by type of commodity

Per cent of total

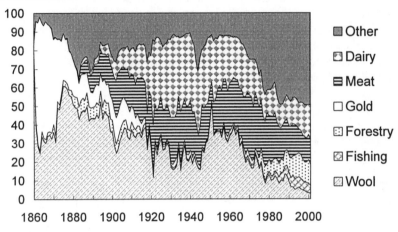

Source: Briggs (2003)

Trade policy reform quickened in the early 1980s. The Closer Economic Relations (CER) free trade agreement was signed with Australia in 1983 and a process of removing import licensing quotas for Australia was introduced. The fourth Labour government accelerated the removal of import quotas and reductions in tariffs after 1984. Currently the remaining tariffs protecting New Zealand firms are mainly on textiles and related sectors.

On the export side, New Zealand has become an active promoter of bilateral, regional and multilateral trade liberalization. On the bilateral front, New Zealand has the CER and a closer economic partnership (CEP) with Singapore, and is considering or pursuing further CEPs with Hong Kong, South Korea, Chile and (optimistically) the USA. New Zealand has also been a committed participant in regional trade discussions, such as APEC, and in GATT/WTO rounds. These multilateral negotiations have much to offer New Zealand, as one of the key aims of the WTO has been to reduce barriers to trade for agricultural products. According to the Ministry of Agriculture and Forestry (2002, p. 9), 'it would be reasonable to estimate that total gains to New Zealand agriculture since the conclusion of the [Uruguay] Round have already exceeded $1.5 billion'.

These historical events have led to a diversification of export commodities (Figure 8) and also in export destinations (Figure 9). The effects of the UK's entry into the EEC are clear to see; the share of New Zealand's merchandise exports into the UK fell from nearly 50 per cent in 1970 to just 27 per cent in 1980.[5] The other obvious trend is the emergence of the Asia Pacific area as the major destination for New Zealand's exports – APEC's share of New Zealand's merchandise exports rose from 41 per cent in 1970 to 72 per cent in 2002.

Within these regional groupings, on a country by country basis, New Zealand's export destinations have also changed significantly. Figure 11 shows the shares of New Zealand's merchandise exports going to its then top 18 trading partners in 1970.[6]

Figure 9. Goods exports by region of destination

Per cent of annual merchandise exports (June)

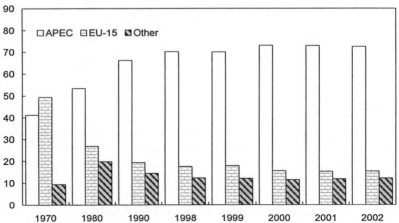

Sources: Ministry of Foreign Affairs and Trade (MFAT), New Zealand Institute of Economic Research (NZIER).

If we now look at the export shares of the same 18 countries in 2002, the change is dramatic. The importance of Asian nations has increased, and Australia's share has trebled, which would be largely due to the CER agreement.

So, overall, it can be said that New Zealand has become more globalized in its trade patterns. However, as the next section shows, it appears that New Zealand has not fully latched on to the globalization process.

Figure 10. Goods exports by country of destination, 1970

Per cent of annual merchandise exports (June)

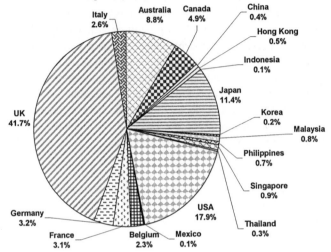

Sources: MFAT, NZIER.

THE RELATIONSHIP BETWEEN TRADE AND GROWTH

One way of measuring the extent of a nation's openness to trade is the ratio of its trade (exports plus imports) to its gross domestic product (GDP). This is denoted in this chapter as the 'trade ratio'. Larger countries tend to have lower trade ratios than smaller countries since they are less reliant on trade. For example, the sheer size of the US economy allows a wider range of industries to produce at efficient scale and to buy and sell within its borders. However, we would expect globalization – part of which entails an increase in international trade – to increase the trade ratios of most countries.

To get some impression of the way that globalization has affected New Zealand and 26 of its top trading partners and suitable comparators, we plotted nominal GDP against trade ratios for each country.[7] We did this for 1989, for every second year through to 1999, and for 2000, taking logarithms of both variables to reduce their variability.

The economies covered range from the US (far right scatter point), which has a low trade ratio, to Singapore (top left point), whose exports and imports total more than twice its GDP. The regression line represents an 'average' level of globalization for a given economic size. New Zealand is below the trend line, indicating that for an economy of its size its trade ratio is relatively low. The dot adjacent to (or virtually on top of) New Zealand is the Philippines.

Figure 13 shows the same figure for the year 2000. While the majority of New Zealand's trading partners have moved upward and rightward, including the Philippines, New Zealand's position has barely shifted. This would suggest that New Zealand has not kept pace with the globalization trends exhibited by its main trading partners and comparator countries.

Table 2 shows the coefficients and goodness-of-fit statistics of the regression lines produced for each year. The slope of the line has remained fairly constant over the years. Given this, the increasing intercept over time indicates that for any given level of GDP, the average level of globalization (as measured by trade ratios) has increased.

Figure 11. Goods exports by country of destination, 2002

Per cent of annual merchandise exports (June)

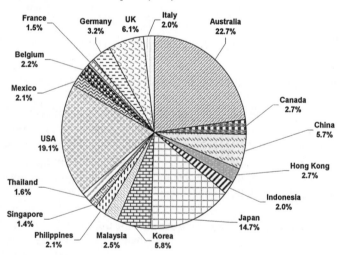

Sources: MFAT, NZIER.

Figure 12. Trade ratios and GDP, 1989

Both axes are in logs

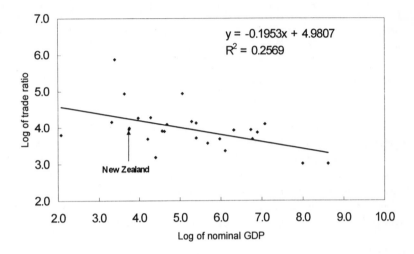

Sources: IMF (1996, 2001b), NZIER.

Figure 13. Trade ratios and GDP, 2000

Both axes are in logs

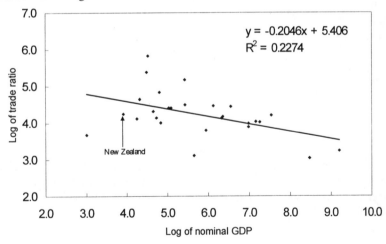

Sources: MF (2001a, 2001b), NZIER.

Table 2. Regression line coefficients

	1989	1991	1993	1995	1997	1999	2000
Intercept	4.981	5.073	5.124	5.231	5.250	5.316	5.406
Slope	-0.195	-0.206	-0.213	-0.207	-0.199	-0.207	-0.205
R^2	0.257	0.238	0.246	0.216	0.207	0.227	0.227

Sources: IMF (1996, 2001a, 2001b), NZIER.

We can obtain some indication of how far off the globalization trend New Zealand is by using the regression equations in Table 2. These equations show the expected level of globalization (trade ratio) for a given level of GDP. By plugging New Zealand's actual GDP into the equations, and looking at the difference between its expected and actual trade ratios, we can see how much New Zealand needs to lift its trading performance to be in line with global averages. These results are shown in Table 3.

Table 3. New Zealand's expected and actual trade ratios

	1989	1991	1993	1995	1997	1999	2000
Actual trade ratio, %	52.2	54.7	59.1	58.1	55.7	62.1	69.9
Estimated trade ratio, %	70.1	73.9	75.4	80.1	82.8	88.9	100.0
Difference, % of GDP	-17.9	-19.2	-16.3	-22.0	-27.1	-26.8	-30.1
Difference, $US billions	-7.6	-8.1	-7.0	-13.2	-17.8	-14.8	-15.1

Sources: IMF (1996, 2001a, 2001b), NZIER.

Table 3 suggests that for a country of its economic size, New Zealand needs to be exporting and importing around $US15 billion more each year in order to keep up with current trends in globalization and economic growth around the world.

WHY IS NEW ZEALAND OFF THE PACE?

The simple analysis presented above poses the question: why has New Zealand not kept up with the globalization trend? Previous work completed at NZIER provides some insights (Briggs et al. 2001; Ballingall and Briggs 2001). This analysis suggests that New Zealand's relatively low long-run economic growth is mainly due to low export growth. This poor export growth can, to a large extent, be attributed to the fact that world growth in demand for primary-based products has been lower than demand for other products, especially manufactures. Much of this low growth is due to agricultural protectionism, which was mentioned earlier. Nearly half of New Zealand's total exports in 1999 were in sectors that, at the world level, were growing more slowly than average.

New Zealand faces restrictive trade barriers in many of its export markets, particularly for dairy products and meat in the USA, Europe and Southeast Asia. Tariffs, quotas, tariff-rate quotas and non-tariff barriers such as phyto-sanitary standards all prevent New Zealand exporters from fully exploiting their comparative advantage in primary goods. These trade restrictions act as a brake on New Zealand's potential regarding globalization.

There has been a policy focus in recent years of trying to move the New Zealand economy towards exporting goods and services with a higher 'knowledge' content. Policy makers want to encourage sectors which demonstrate high levels of innovation and 'Kiwi ingenuity', and which result in higher value-added production processes. This shift has become known as economic transformation.[8] However, recent work by Ballingall and Briggs (2002b) suggests that there are few signs of economic transformation at the industry level.[9] Their analysis of revealed comparative advantage for 706 export sectors indicates that New Zealand's comparative advantage remains firmly in the production of resource-based commodities. However, there are some indications that the manufacturing and processing industries associated with these commodities are growing in importance.

IDEAS

A key facet of globalization is the international exchange of ideas. In the early days of its history, New Zealand tended to share many economic and political ideas with Britain. For example, the Liberal party, which came to power in 1891, had much in common with Gladstone's party and its policies. Labour's arrival in government in the mid 1930s coincided with the emergence of Keynesianism as the dominant paradigm for managing the economy. By the time the fourth Labour government was elected, in 1984,

Labour was on a different course. It set about reforming the economy along market lines. The Keynesian approach of managing the economy via fiscal spending gave way to the monetarist approach of controlling the money supply. Markets were deregulated and government agencies were corporatized and in some cases privatized (Bollard 1988).

In the social area, three issues in particular have come to the fore in the last 30 years or so: the changing roles of women, the emergence of the indigenous Māori community as a social and economic force, and the increasing awareness of the importance of the environment. All of these have become major factors influencing the formation and implementation of New Zealand public policy.

Similarly in terms of business ideas, which can be taken to include organizational matters and also the development and implementation of technology, New Zealand has largely participated in broad international trends. One area where New Zealand is ahead of global trends is in 'farming without subsidies' (Sandrey and Reynolds 1990). Virtually all subsides to the primary sector were removed by Labour in 1984. The policy has been largely successful, with farmers adapting quickly to the new environment. A key accompanying policy has been the adoption of a floating exchange rate. When world prices for agricultural commodities fall, the New Zealand exchange rate also tends to fall. Hence, the negative effects of the world price movements on producers' incomes tend to be offset by the positive effects arising from the movements in the exchange rate.

THE PRESENT AND THE FUTURE

Ideas now flow across borders at near the speed of light, via telecommunications networks. The business sector has played the lead role in New Zealand in implementing this technology. Faxes, cell phones and internet websites have all been taken up quickly by businesses. However, the drive behind this may have been a defensive one; the focus may not have been so much on trying to get a competitive edge as on trying to keep up with competitors, especially those overseas. This situation is likely to continue, with businesses leading the way in the application of technology.

An irony regarding information technology for New Zealand is that the country still largely makes a living from moving people (tourists) and goods (primary exports) rather than information and ideas. Perhaps the most important ideas in the future will be those little ones – not large ideas like those in the social and political areas, but those little ideas that firms have which lift their productivity.

CONCLUSION

Regarding the movement of people, New Zealand shows similar patterns to other countries. Growth in the number of trips by short-term visitors – by both overseas visitors and New Zealanders travelling overseas – has been very high. And the range of countries from which significant numbers of visitors are arriving is expanding. Flows of permanent migrants continue to be heavily constrained by government policies – inward flows are constrained by New Zealand government policies, and outward flows by policies of other governments. However, as with tourism flows, the range of countries from which inward migrants are arriving is increasing.

On the trade front, it is worth noting that New Zealand has weathered some severe shocks over the last 40 years. The first was the collapse of prices in the mid 1960s for coarse wool – which had until then been a staple export commodity – as synthetic fibres replaced wool in the manufacturing of carpets. The second was the entry of Britain into the EU in 1973, which severely limited access to what had been New Zealand's major market. The third was the oil shocks of the 1970s, which hit hard given that New Zealand's own oil supplies are close to negligible. The fourth was various international slowdowns, including: the 1987 sharemarket collapse; the severe global recession of the early 1990s; the Asian crisis of the late 1990s; and the current global slowdown.

Good progress has been made in diversifying the markets to which New Zealand exports. Some progress has also been made in diversifying the products that the country exports, although this progress has been more limited (Ballingall and Briggs 2002b). Despite this, it is probably fair to say that the nation as a whole is not sufficiently outward-looking. Perhaps it has been mesmerized by local issues: implementing economic reforms, developing environmental protection procedures, settling longstanding grievances with Māori. Whatever the reason, New Zealand, which has for most of its history been an outward-looking county, is in danger of getting left behind in global trade. The size and location of the New Zealand economy are undoubtedly factors that are hindering performance. But location cannot be changed – although transport and communication costs can be – and size will change relatively slowly. There appears to be no option: this small, relatively unified country will have to sharpen its focus on exporting, utilizing all the resources and skill it can muster.

REFERENCES

Ballingall, J. and P. Briggs (2001), 'A Comparison of Australia's and New Zealand's

Export Performance Using Shift Share Analysis', New Zealand Institute of Economic Research (NZIER) working paper 01/05.

Ballingall, J. and P. Briggs (2002a), 'Economic Transformation and Agriculture: Has New Zealand's Comparative Advantage Shifted?' Paper presented at the 2002 annual conference of New Zealand Agricultural and Resource Economics Society, Blenheim, New Zealand, 5-6 July.

Ballingall, J, and P. Briggs (2002b), 'A Look at New Zealand's Comparative Advantage: Updating the Porter Study's Analysis of Axports', NZIER working paper 02/04.

Belich, J. (2001), *Paradise Reforged. A History of New Zealanders: From the 1880s to the Year 2000*, Auckland: Penguin.

Bollard, A. (ed.) (1988), *The Influence of United States Economics on New Zealand: The Fulbright Anniversary Seminars*, NZ-US Education Foundation and NZIER, Wellington.

Briggs, P. (2003), *New Zealand's History: Looking at the Data*, Wellington: NZIER.

Briggs, P., P. Bishop and E. Fan (2001), 'New Zealand's Economic Growth: Why Has it been Low?' NZIER Working Paper 2001/2.

Brownie, S. and P. Dalziel (1993), 'Shift-Share Analyses of New Zealand Exports, 1970-1984', New Zealand Economic Papers, **27** (2).

Easton, B. (1997), *In Stormy Seas: The Post-War New Zealand Economy*, Dunedin: University of Otago Press.

Fan, E., P. Briggs, J. Smith, and P. Gardiner (2001), 'New Zealand's Export Performance and Outlook: An aAalysis Based on Gravity Modelling', Report to Trade New Zealand, October 2001.

Hawke, G. (1985), *The Making of New Zealand: An Economic History*, Cambridge: Cambridge University Press.

International Monetary Fund (1996, 2001a), *Balance of Payments Statistics Yearbook: Part 2, World and Regional Tables*, Washington, D.C.: IMF.

International Monetary Fund (2001b), *The World Economic Outlook* (WEO) Database, online at <http://www.imf.org/external/pubs/ft/weo/2001/01/data/index.htm>.

Lattimore, R. and J. Ballingall (2001), 'Trade Liberalisation and New Zealand: A Resource Base', NZIER report to the New Zealand Trade Liberalisation Network, December 2001.

Ministry of Agriculture and Forestry (2002), 'Rewinding the Uruguay Round of Multilateral Trade Negotiations', online at <http://www.maf.govt.nz/mafnet/rural-nz/profitability-and-economics/trends/uruguay-trade-round-negotiations/uruguay-trade-round-results.pdf>.

Ministry of Research, Science and Technology (1998), 'Foresight needs Hindsight Too', online at <http://www.morst.govt.nz/foresight/info.folders/press/press4.html>.

New Zealand Immigration Service (2002), Refugee data from website: <www.immigration.govt.nz/workshop/hist.htm>.

Prasad, Eswar S. and Jeffery A. Gable (1997), 'International Evidence on the Determinants of Trade Dynamics', IMF Working Paper WP/97/172.

Sandrey, Ron and Russell Reynolds (1990), *Farming Without Subsidies: New Zealand's Recent Experience*, Wellington: MAF and GP Books.

Statistics New Zealand (2000), 'Reference Report: Tourism and Migration 2000', downloaded from <http://www.stats.govt.nz/domino/external/pasfull/pasfull.nsf/ eb/Reference+Reports+Tourism+and+Migration+2000?open>.

NOTES

1 The authors gratefully acknowledge the assistance of John Yeabsley. The report was prepared for the New Zealand Institute of Economic Research (NZIER). Based in Wellington, the NZIER was founded in 1958 as a non profit-making trust to provide economic research and consultancy services. Best known for its long-established *Quarterly Survey of Business Opinion* and *Quarterly Predictions*, the Institute also undertakes a wide range of consultancy activities for government and private organizations. It obtains most of its income from research contracts obtained in a competitive market and trades on its reputation for delivering quality analysis in the right form, and at the right time, for its clients. Quality assurance is provided on the Institute's work: by the interaction of team members on individual projects; by exposure of the team's work to the critical review of a broader range of Institute staff members at internal seminars; by providing for peer review at various stages through a project by a senior staff member otherwise disinterested in the project; and sometimes by external peer reviewers at the request of a client, although this usually entails additional cost. The Institute, its contributors, employees and Board shall not be liable for any loss or damage sustained by any person relying on this report, whatever the cause of such loss or damage.

2 'Traditional source countries' were: Austria, Belgium, Canada, Denmark, Finland, France, Germany, Iceland, Ireland, Italy, Luxembourg, the Netherlands, Norway, Sweden, Switzerland, the UK and the USA.

3 Much of this section is sourced from Lattimore and Ballingall (2001, pp. 7-9). For a more in-depth examination of New Zealand's economic history see Hawke (1985), Belich (2001), Easton (1997) and Briggs (2003).

4 Belich suggests that 'from the 1880s, came the era of re-colonisation. It developed fully between the 1900s and 1920s and began petering out in the 1960s. During this era, New Zealand's relations with Britain became closer and more junior. We relinquished expectations of the steady development of independent nationalism' (cited in Lattimore and Ballingall 2001, p. 7).

5 We focus here on New Zealand's exports of goods. Country-specific data on New Zealand's exports of services are patchy and only available for a very short time frame. However, we do know that tourism and education exports have become increasingly important to the New Zealand economy.

6 The source of the GDP data was the IMF's online database, and the data are in nominal US dollars. The trade ratio data were sourced from the IMF's *Balance of Payments Statistics Yearbook*. The countries in this analysis are Canada, the USA, Mexico, Chile, Argentina, Uruguay, Australia, Japan, France, Germany, the UK, Belgium, Italy, Portugal, Spain, Denmark, Sweden, Greece, China, Indonesia, Korea, Malaysia, Singapore, Thailand, the Philippines and South Africa.

7 The source of the GDP data was the IMF's online database, and the data are in nominal US dollars. The trade ratio data were sourced from the IMF's *Balance of Payments Statistics Yearbook*. The countries in this analysis are Canada, the USA, Mexico, Chile, Argentina, Uruguay, Australia, Japan, France, Germany, the UK, Belgium, Italy, Portugal, Spain, Denmark, Sweden, Greece, China, Indonesia, Korea, Malaysia, Singapore, Thailand, the Philippines and South Africa.

8 A number of background papers on the prospects for, aims of and possible impediments to economic transformation can be found on the New Zealand Treasury website at <www.treasury.govt.nz>.

9 A series of papers by Colin Campbell-Hunt suggest that there is evidence of economic transformation at the firm level (see the Competitive Advantage New Zealand website at <http://www.vuw.ac.nz/fca/research/canz/index.htm>).

9. Globalization and Japan after the Bubble

Ross Mouer

THE RISE AND FALL OF THE JAPANESE MODEL

As the first non-Western nation to develop, Japan has always been the case *par excellence* when it came to testing notions about the impact of outside ideas and technology on local norms, customs and practices. Its experience has featured in debates on convergence and divergence. One key to the debate is the distinction between form and function and the relative importance attached to either dimension. This delineation allows for cultural forms to be retained while functionally equivalent outcomes are achieved. Bendix (1967) and others have argued that:

> the functional requirements for operating a modern industrial system are such that they can be met by a wide variety of structural and cultural forms (as noted in Dore 1967, p. 22).

Convergence has also been a key concept in the debate. Few have maintained that the domain culturally peculiar to Japan has expanded (that is diverged). Many have argued that it has held its own in the face of a spreading 'Western industrialism' (that is parallel development). Recognizing the staying power of certain traditional cultural features in absolute terms, others have acknowledged that their importance has declined over time in relative terms. The Japanese experience has shown that the relationships between social and cultural change, technology, government policy and the processes of diffusion are complex.

Many of Japan's post-war institutional arrangements – especially with regard to the involvement of the state and the reliance on regimented corporatistic arrangements – were explained in terms of Japan's being a latecomer to development. However, the success of the Japanese economy in generating huge balance-of-payments surpluses resulted in many suggesting that its 'premodern-postmodern' institutions had allowed Japan to leap to the forefront in terms of its economic institutions and the cultural orientations that supported those institutions. Vogel's (1979) popular volume was one of many that drew attention to Japan's across-the-board success in creating a society of highly motivated citizens from which America and other developed nations could learn. Among Japan's achievements he counted: high levels of literacy and basic education; strong commitment and high levels of productivity at work; a high quality of governance through a meritocratic bureaucracy; the extensive provision of corporate welfare (without entitlement); an egalitarian distribution of societal rewards; low levels of alienation and crime; remarkable levels of social cohesion; and many cultural and artistic achievements.

These perspectives gave way to the idea of 'reverse convergence' – the possibility that, after a century of modernization premised on catching up with the West, convergence would occur as the Western world adopted Japanese-style management and its institutions came to look more like those found in Japan. The Japanese achievements that drew the most attention related to the organization of work. Many Japanese management practices came to be praised in the late 1970s and throughout the 1980s, the studies by the OECD (1972 and 1977), Ouchi (1981) and Athos and Pascale (1981) being the best known. Those practices were the core of what came to be known as the 'Japanese model'. A new literature on corporate culture and the merits of enterprise bargaining emerged and drew heavily on what was perceived to be the Japanese experience. However, when Japan's economic bubble suddenly burst in the early 1990s, pundits were returned to a simple truth highlighted a decade earlier by Kassalow (1983) in his survey of the rise and fall of various models of industrial relations. In terms of the diffusion of social practices, Kassalow suggested that any given society's ways of conducting life would become a standard for other societies only if

- that society's national economy generated surplus
- there was consensus among members of the society that their model was a good one, and
- there was enough confidence in the model for leaders in the society to want to export it.

Although Kassalow was sceptical as to whether the second two conditions had been met, the first was so well met with Japan's mammoth balance of payments surpluses that enthusiasts abroad tended to overlook the other two, or to assume that the second had been met, while encouraging Japanese to be more confident in transferring the model so that the third condition would inevitably be met.

However, the bursting of Japan's economic bubble economy undercut the interest in Japan as an economic model. This resulted in several outcomes.

One was a greater awareness of other Japanese exports (for example in the cultural domain). Another was a greater appreciation for the position of those who saw Japanese-style management as ultimately being ultra-Fordist, and not post-Fordist as those promoting the model had believed. Third was a shift in the focus from 'reverse convergence' back to earlier notions of Western-led convergence and the spread of liberal-democratic ideas through the flow of finance, goods, people, technologies and other ideas (that is globalization).

In considering the impact of globalization on contemporary Japan, it is not especially fruitful to debate the history of globalization. Japanese have been particularly aware of the nation's absorption of outside ideas and goods from ancient times, a process that accelerated following the Meiji Restoration. Most informed Japanese are aware of the huge changes wrought by Japan's new internationalization (*kokusaika*) or deregulation (*jiyuka*) of the economy in the 1960s. However, much of that globalization, as well as the notion of reverse convergence, was conceived largely in the context of international competitiveness and the popular belief that the economy could be internationalized while maintaining Japan's unique cultural integrity.

With the bursting of the bubble, however, there was a considerable change in how Japanese thought about this process and an openness to globalization occurring as a more comprehensive and inevitable process than internationalization. The data provided on the usage of terms for civil society by Mouer and Sugimoto (2003) suggest that there was first an introspective concern with Japan's adequacy as a civil society (a theme developed from concerns with Japan's democratization in terms of universal standards) and then a growing outward-looking appreciation that 'the game' was about a much more broadly conceived process of globalization.

Rather than delineating the forces associated with globalization and then following them through in Japan, the approach taken here is to discuss a few master trends already present in Japan over the past decade to highlight some of the forces shaping the way Japan is responding to globalization. In this way a more complex picture of Japan's globalization will emerge, one in which Japan is both an agent shaping globalization and a respondent to change. It is also a picture in which it is difficult to disentangle independent universal trends (for example the drive for a higher standard of living) from the impact of ideas, goods and people spontaneously flowing into Japan from outside (as they have done for centuries) and from the international politics involved in formulating and implementing newly conceived global standards. The reader is left to decide what is and what is not globalization in terms of their own definitions.

THE 'LOST DECADE' AND THE POST-BUBBLE CONUNDRUM

For the first 50 years after the war, economic growth was popularly seen in Japan as being the engine driving change in other areas. At the same time, much of Japanese life was subverted to support rapid growth. It is not surprising, then, that a decade without such growth would be seen by many as Japan's 'lost decade'. Unemployment doubled from 2.3 per cent in 1989 to 5.3 per cent by 2002. During the same period the growth rate fell from 5.2 per cent in 1989 to -0.7 per cent in 2002. While only one firm listed on the upper stock market became bankrupt in 1985 and none did so in 1989, 29 did so in 2002. The pension and health-care funding systems were in financial trouble, and the funding for higher education was also in for a serious rethink. By 2003 references to the Japanese model were hard to find in the Japanese media, whereas those to the 'Japanese disease' had come to the fore.

How could this change have occurred so rapidly and on such a scale? Observers have pointed to Japan's own financial crises and to bad debts that had accumulated behind a veil hiding the true situation from the public and even from employees in affected firms. A series of lead articles on the Japanese disease in Japan's leading economic newspaper, the *Nihon Keizai Shimbun* (morning edition, 1-2 January 2003), advanced four reasons for Japan's plight at the beginning of the twenty-first century. In each explanation globalization was a key factor.

One reason was the failure to implement structural reforms in terms of how corporate society is organized and run in Japan. Failures in structural reform were cast largely in terms of low standards in accounting and transparency both within firms and in the way the national economy had been run by the state. Other deficiencies were highlighted in the Structural Impediment Initiatives talks begun in the late 1980s by a United States bent on reducing its large trade deficit with Japan. The talks led to the dismantling of many protective practices. US-Japan trade aside, the greatest impact was that many domestically produced products were displaced by cheaper imports manufactured elsewhere in Asia. In both cases, domestic practices were seen as inferior to outside practices, with external pressures generating a concern with international competitiveness and the need for Japan to respond.

Second was the attachment of Japan's conservative leadership to the now outdated mercantilist strategies that had brought success in the past. Japan's economic performance in the 1980s fostered a renewed sense of national confidence and an ethnocentric assertion of Japan's cultural superiority. A fundamental assumption had been that the structural features of Japanese-style management would continue to give Japan an advantage because they could not be borrowed without also importing the cultural ethos of the Japanese. The speed with which companies abroad sifted through the model and picked out the structural features most relevant to competitive advantage startled many Japanese conservatives who had assumed that the social values underpinning Japanese-style social organization and human resource management were unique to Japan. Given their lower labour costs, the availability of foreign capital (including the shift of simple manufacturing processes out of Japan) and their already fragmented labour markets with a latent capacity for tiering production processes, many nearby countries in Asia were quite capable of introducing many features of the Japanese-style management model such as quality control mechanisms, internal labour market practices and other techniques used by Japanese management to co-opt labour into a strictly regimented framework for enhancing productivity. For Japan this was an example of globalization in reverse: rather than outside forces foisting a foreign process onto Japan, something allegedly unique to Japan had been sucked out of Japan and its ownership shifted abroad. Here was an external response to internally generated pressures arising from a concern with international competitiveness.

Third was an indifference or imperviousness to key changes in Japanese society. The changes included new levels of consumer sophistication, shifts in attitudes toward work (especially dangerous, dirty or demanding tasks), an increased interest among young working-age adults in 'actualizing' themselves through a range of experiences in differentiated settings, the ageing of the population, a growing interest among middle-aged and older Japanese in various forms of community service, immigration, and the return of some from the corporate sphere to family life. The population's ageing created a new awareness of the 'need' for new social welfare services well beyond what Japan's highly differentiated and non-portable corporate welfare schemes could supply. While much of this change was internally generated as a result of new levels of affluence (which had in turn resulted from the diffusion of manufacturing processes), rapid advances in information and communications technologies fed a rapacious appetite for travel abroad, overseas information and knowledge about standards in other societies.

The fourth reason for Japan's difficulties at the beginning of this century was an overwhelming loss of confidence as many Japanese came to fear risk-taking following a deflation of the collective ego after the collapse of the bubble economy in the early 1990s. Growing levels of alienation were accompanied by an increased awareness that Japan was not the mass middle-class society envisaged in the 1970s and 1980s, by further disclosures of political corruption and corporate mismanagement, and by the rapid turnover of political leadership at home. Behind this has been sensitivity to the feeling that Japanese must yet again 'pull up their socks' and measure up to externally generated global standards (seen largely as being American standards). The acclaim given the Japanese model in the 1980s allowed for a certain measure of cultural confidence from knowing that Japanese ways were contributing to the formation of international standards. 'McDonaldization' and 'Disney-fication' of consumer culture aside, proudly Japanese companies such as Nissan now employ foreign-born CEOs who have pushed for leaner approaches to human resource management, for new levels of transparency, and for bilingualism in the workplace.

To summarize, for most of the post-war period Japan's rapid economic growth had been couched in terms of the ability of Japanese to manage Western technology with the 'Japanese spirit' and the cultural nuances it embodies. The Japanese economy has now reached a stage where the import of soft technologies is more important than the acquisition of the hard technologies associated with manufacturing. The debate concerning the future of Japan is partly about the future of Japan's corporate culture and its social ethos – the need to be internationally transparent in ways that facilitate both a new level of integration into the global economy and the increased movement of people into and out of Japan. The sections below illustrate some of the ways in which Japan is responding to this challenge.

INEQUALITY IN JAPAN AT THE TURN OF THE CENTURY: A UNIVERSAL TREND

Japan is no longer the mass society that was seen by many as underpinning most of its post-war development. Japanese debate in the 1950s and early 1960s revolved around the extent to which Japan had democratized. By the early 1970s many had come to believe that Japan's rapid economic growth had produced the first truly mass society, in which nine out of ten Japanese believed they were middle class. It was commonly assumed that Japan's distribution of income was more egalitarian than that in other similarly developed economies and that serious pockets of poverty or wealth did not exist.

This perception was widely accepted into the 1990s despite a good deal of research documenting

- the segmentation of Japan's labour market
- similarities elsewhere in wage and income differentials,
- diversification in Japan's consumer markets
- stratification in the education system at all levels, and
- institutionalized unevenness in the distribution of social welfare.

During the 1990s several global developments contributed to a greater recognition of these facts. The end of the Cold War reduced the pressure on the conservative establishment to embrace the view that Japan was more egalitarian than other societies. Greater flows of information and people contributed to a growing awareness that most other advanced economies are similarly stratified. Japanese capital and a growing Japanese diaspora abroad found it beneficial to accept views facilitating the integration of their interests with those of persons abroad.

Within Japan a new generation of intellectuals began to re-articulate concerns about social justice, and studies began to challenge the perception that Japan was no longer a mass society. Sato (2000), for example, argued that Japan's elites had increasingly come to be rewarded for qualifications acquired through inherited access to higher education. His major concern was that lower mobility would undermine belief in the value of hard work, the ethic of many Japanese for much of the first half century after the war. A sense of national identity had been undermined by embourgeoisement, multiculturalization and globalization as employees came to have a broader interest in family life, community service (voluntary work), the enjoyment of material goods already acquired, and opportunities in the world beyond Japan.

These changes are not unique to Japan; similar tensions have come to the fore in Australia as its egalitarian ethos also gives way to greater inequality and the increased channelling of opportunity over the 1990s (see, for example, the editorial in *The Sunday Age* (Melbourne), 18 August 2002, p. 16). In both countries change has resulted from a universal drive to rationalize economic activity in the course of capitalist development. Globalization simply accelerated such change.

Although the collapse of organized labour and radical unionism contributed to a perception that disgruntled labour no longer has a coherent discourse, disenfranchised workers obviously exist in Japan in an objective sense. Sato's research is best understood in the context of a broader debate on increased inequality in contemporary Japan as brought together by the editors at Bungei Shunju (1999) and Chuo Koron (2001) as well as those of the *Nihon Rodo Kenkyu Zasshi* (480, July 2000). Tachibanaki (1998 and 2000), for example, has argued that Japan's income differentials have widened significantly since the early 1980s and that the amount of inequality in Japan is on a par with that found in most other advanced economies. Kariya (2001) has argued that educational outcomes for students from middle-class families have increasingly come to depend upon the educational background of their mothers. Hashimoto (2001) has also underlined the usefulness of class as a heuristic category for understanding Japanese society.

The effect of educational background on career paths and the age/wage-earning profile of white-collar and blue-collar employees has been known for some time, and it was obvious from the early 1970s (as discussed in Mouer 1975 and 1991) that Japan was re-stratifying and that social class distinctions were being reproduced. Although some such as Koike and Watanabe (1979) argued some time ago that the importance attached to one's place of education had diminished in Japan and that one's demonstrated ability at work had become the important consideration in determining career, others wrote that such change was occurring only at the lower levels of management. In the early 1980s it still made sense for Kitagawa and Kainuma (1985) to write about the continuing influence of Japan's pre-war elites as a force in post-war Japanese society. While regional differentials were marginal and gender-based differentials were perhaps narrowing, the pattern of occupational differentials remained fixed, an indication that there would be cumulative effects.

The debate on inequality in Japan has been driven internally. It represents a continuation of the debate on democracy in post-war Japan, and is concerned largely with the nature of Japanese capitalism and the dynamics of change within Japan. At the same time, Japanese capitalism can best be understood as a variant of capitalism, and the dynamics of inequality in Japan are fruitfully understood in terms of:

- the global flow of symbols and information shaping class consciousness and the sense of civil society on the subjective level: and
- the role of labour markets in distributing wealth on the objective side as they respond to the pressures to remain internally competitive.

GLOBAL COMPETITIVENESS AND LABOUR MARKET REFORM: DIFFERENT APPROACHES TO ACHIEVING FUNCTIONAL EQUIVALENCE

The decision of many Japanese to work is fundamentally shaped by their options in a highly segmented labour market where the threat of under-employment or redeployment looms large, with Japan's official rates of unemployment currently over 5 per cent. In the 1990s Japan's labour markets were fundamentally altered by changes in the industrial structure, a record number of bankruptcies and the introduction of government policies to deregulate the labour market. One outcome has been more unemployment. Another has been the willingness of more individuals (especially young persons) to assess critically their options in the labour force. A third has been the willingness of individual firms to adopt new strategies for dealing with these kinds of changes.

THE PUSH FOR MORE FLEXIBLE MARKETS

While internationalization in the 1960s had initially worked to open markets to Japanese goods in the advanced economies of North America and Europe, globalization is now working to reinforce moves to open Japanese markets to imports from Asia. In addition to trade liberalization at home, the rising costs of domestic production, the advantages of producing on the other side of non-tariff barriers elsewhere (in China, for example), rapidly accumulating reserves of foreign exchange and the appreciation of the yen led to an increasing number of Japan's manufacturers speeding up the transfer of production overseas, a process begun in the late 1970s. Kruger and Fuyuno (2002) describe the way cheap Chinese imports have undercut the centuries-old ceramic and textile industries in Gifu, arguing that products from China are produced with a labour cost one tenth to one 30th of that in Japan.

The revitalization of Japan's labour economy is one key to Japan's repositioning of itself in a more competitive world economy. Labour market deregulation had been conceived as a means to move labour from high-productivity industries that are losing their competitiveness to newly emerging industries with even higher levels of productivity. On the other hand, after a long period of believing that they were staffing the factory of the world, many Japanese now seem to have accepted the inevitability that China has taken over that mantle. As Japan loses its international competitive edge in manufacturing, employment is shifting to the tertiary sector and the IT industry.

In the internal labour markets of the past, tiered subcontracting and the use of multiple employment statuses to casualize the labour force enhanced the leverage of management in the allocation of Japan's human resources. However, the renewed pressure from global competition is now highlighting inefficiencies in those approaches. Globalization has come to require that firms have a more complex or sophisticated mix of employees who are more differentiated and specialized than in the past, and that they can make much quicker adjustments to their human resources portfolio. In this context, employers have pushed for further deregulation of the labour market. Their immediate goal has been to lower the ratio of:

- permanent (core) employees in supervisory positions and in more inflexible forms of employment to
- replaceable staff engaged in repetitive tasks; and to
- professional types with specialized skills critical to the achievement of important short-term goals.

ONGOING LABOUR MARKET SEGMENTATION

The need for labour market reform was recognized long before the 1990s. However, legislation was passed in the 1990s as a response to heightened pressures to remain competitive in the face of the raised levels of competition that have accompanied globalization and have been in line with universal capitalist processes already under way in Japan. Deregulation has had to be balanced against union concerns with the maintenance of employment security (*Shukan Rodo Nyuusu*, 1717, 1997, p. 3). Nevertheless, management's push to deregulate has made headway overall, and further changes are likely to follow. Deregulation has not yielded less segmentation and may indeed have strengthened it, even though some movement from the market for full-time regular employees to the other markets for non-regular employment may have resulted. A recent White Paper on smaller businesses (Chusho Kigyo Cho 2001, pp. 26-28) states that non-regular employees are increasingly being employed by enterprises of all sizes. At the turn of the century 71.8 per cent of Japan's labour force worked for firms with less than 100 employees, up from 69.72 per cent in 1986.

THE HOUSEHOLD AS A SUPPLIER OF LABOUR

Obi (1968) noted some time ago that decisions concerning the labour force participation of secondary earners in Japan depend not just on the wage/hour packages available but also on the opportunity cost of shifting labour from important unpaid activity in the home to the overall operation of the household. Other long-term factors include a decline of three-generational households from 19.7 per cent of all households in 1968 to 10.6 per cent in 1999. Over the same period the number of single-person households rose from 19.8 to 23.6 per cent, and the proportion of all families with children under the age of 15 fell from 41.2 to 34.4 per cent. The percentage of single-parent households has remained fairly constant at 5.3 per cent (Tominaga 2001, p. 246). These trends seem to be universal phenomena accompanying industrialization and not the result of globalization per se. However, a recent White Paper (Kosei Rodo Sho 2001, pp. 50-100) revealed that thinking about the division of labour within Japanese households is quickly changing. It indicated that the established male-female division of labour which assigned women to the home and part-time work was breaking down. Adding to the changes in household size mentioned above, sensitivity to international standards regarding gender roles in North America and Europe has contributed to the erosion of distinctly male and female labour markets in Japan.

THE IMPACT OF AFFLUENCE

New levels of affluence and appreciation of the yen present Japan's youth with options outside the labour market. *Furiitaa* and 'parasite singles' (see for example Yamada 1999 and 2000) form a new floating work force. The former stay in casual employment for extended periods. The latter, even when fully employed, stay at home and live off their parents. Japan's high standard of living allows parents to subsidize the freedom these youths enjoy on their relatively low wage income. Unlike the part-timer wife supporting the family system, the *furiitaa* and 'parasites' challenge what has always been seen as the stable pattern of employment for single males and females.

While the lifestyles of these new types may depend upon Japan's domestically produced affluence, their thinking is often shaped by global flows of information about other lifestyles. Numerous observers have commented on the increasing number of persons who have given up pressured employment in a profit-driven business for meaningful engagement with a non-profit organization (NPO). Hanami, Mitsuhashi and Tachigi (2000) note that firms too have quickly responded to this multiculturalization of lifestyle. They also point to two other new phenomena in the labour market. One is the use of traditional franchising arrangements to allow outstanding employees to establish their own place of work. The second is the expansion of telework. Changes of this kind put in place mechanisms that allow Japanese not only to be employed away from the place of business, but also to work across national boundaries.

FOREIGN FIRMS

Over the last decade, foreign firms in Japan have come to be seen as attractive employers. A survey by Recruit Research in 1997 and 1998 revealed that the popularity of such firms rose rapidly in the late 1990s (*Asahi Shimbun*, morning edition, 6 June 1998, p. 14). While restructuring brought on by the last decade's recession and increased international competition has undermined the confidence of graduates in the ability of Japanese firms to provide secure employment, a March 2002 survey by the Ministry of Welfare, Labour and Health revealed that foreign firms experienced a fairly high labour turnover but provided shorter working hours and better leave provisions, which are attractive to those seeking the 'new lifestyle' (*Shukan Rodo Nyusu*, 9 April 2001, p. 4). Through this experience, international norms regarding working conditions are diffused.

THE MARKET FOR FOREIGN WORKERS

The changing power relationship in the labour market between increasingly 'fussy' Japanese suppliers (that is workers who do not wish to do dirty, dangerous or demanding tasks) and cost-conscious buyers has seen an increase in the number of foreign workers in the Japanese labour market. It is estimated that some 700,000 legal and illegal migrants work in Japan. While the term 'foreign worker' has often been used to connote prostitutes, dancers and other female entertainers brought in from Southeast Asia, since the mid-1980s other foreign workers have been employed in ever-increasing numbers in manufacturing to offset labour shortages. While these workers tend to be underpaid and exploited, many socially concerned Japanese have worked quite independently from their government and foreign influences to improve the lot of Japan's newcomers. The critical mass necessary to impel the system to compromise has been reached, and the newcomers have been accommodated in a wide range of ways, some of which are mentioned below.

In this regard, the Japanese government has been caught between the anti-foreigner sentiment found in Europe and the reality that migrants were underpinning the Japanese economy with their cheap labour. During the bubble years the Japanese government allowed distinct labour markets for legal and illegal entrants to coexist. However, as the economy fell into recession in the early 1990s and the unemployment rate began to rise, the government became ever more sensitive to the backlash against foreign workers. As the recession lengthened, the government sought to tighten its control over the immigration of those who were most different visually and culturally (for example, those from Islamic nations such as Iran, Pakistan and Bangladesh). Between July 1989 and May 1993 the number of legal immigrants tripled over a four-year period from 106,000 to nearly 300,000 (Kuwahara 2001, p. 8). While the recession has since resulted in the door being closed to more foreign workers, it did not produce a large exodus. It is likely that an economic recovery in the future will be accompanied by more immigration, a prospect that points to Japan becoming even more multicultural.

DIFFUSION: MIGRATION, MULTICULTURALIZATION, ENGLISH AND THE NATURE OF JAPAN'S CIVIL SOCIETY

Globalization is fundamentally altering the *seikatsu kukan* (living space) within Japanese society and thereby the essence of civil society in Japan. The Japanese term *'kokusai shakai'* (international society) is used in a loose fashion to refer to the 'living space' which citizens of a state can comfortably access outside the confines of that state. The term *'kyosei'* has frequently been used over the past five years to refer to multicultural arrangements which allow people of different backgrounds to function peacefully together in the living space of countries which have been internationalized. Writers such as Ohmae (1999) (economically), Fukushima (1992) (politically) and Huntington (1992) (culturally) have all speculated about the nature of the borderlessness of states and about the possibility of other criteria resulting in cross-cultural identities and 'denizenship'. Four areas of change are considered below to illustrate how globalization is impinging upon Japan.

CIVIL SOCIETY

The Japanese experience with globalization cannot be understood apart from the emergence of its own civil society. After 1945 leftist intellectuals were outspoken in their wish for the state to provide for new civil minimums and human rights associated with civil society. Although the idea of 'civil society' existed in pre-Meiji Japan, conservatives dismissed such thinking as a foreign individualist ideology that had no place in a collectivistic Japan. In the early 1990s *'hibiru sosaitei'* came to be associated with an interest in the potential for voluntarism in societal affairs, an orientation acceptable to conservatives concerned about the costs of social welfare.

Over the past decade the term 'non-profit organization' (NPO) has become widely used in Japan to differentiate groups with an ongoing interest in 'serving society' from those with clear economic interests to serve long-term specialized political agendas (Keizai Kikaku Cho 2000, p. 8). Although Japanese have in the past joined service clubs such as Rotary or Lions, local management groups, labour unions and various movements to effect political change (for example, those spawned by consumer, environmental or student groups), Sugishita (2001, pp. 5-8) argues that the use of 'NPO' in contemporary Japan was stimulated by public discussion of the NPO bill which was passed in the Japanese Diet in March 1998 and provided tax relief to officially recognized NPOs. The Japanese move was stimulated by the enactment of similar legislation in the USA in the mid-1990s and is another example of Japan seeking to conform to international (that is American) standards.

A recent *White Paper on Information and Communication* (Somu Sho 2001) suggests that some 47.08 million Japanese (approximately 37 per cent of the adult population aged 15-79) are Internet users, and that the majority of these users log in every day. This enables many Japanese citizens to expand their 'living space' beyond the borders of the Japanese state. The enhanced ability of ordinary Japanese to enter and access space outside the confines of local and national communities has obviously had ramifications on how Japanese think about their life-cycle options within Japan. For example, the influence of civil society and local NPO activity can be seen in Japan's regional political dynamics. Yabuno (1995) describes the period after the oil shocks of the 1970s as a time during which peripheralized local communities experienced depopulation, rapid ageing, feminization, unemployment and various other changes. He argues that many local communities responded by establishing their own international relations, thereby circumventing the national government in activities traditionally seen to be within its exclusive domain. This grass-roots diplomacy has allowed many Japanese to expand the horizons of their world.

IMMIGRATION

Japan's 'foreign' population has always been small. Including naturalized Koreans and Chinese, it has traditionally been less than 1-2 per cent of Japan's total population. However, the number of foreigners living in Japan began to increase markedly from the late 1980s, owing in part to labour shortages. Based on his reading of many disparate studies on Japan's new migrant population, Komai (2001) hints that Japan's newcomers are now reaching a critical mass that can fundamentally change Japanese society.

Many barriers previously circumscribing the world of the foreigner in Japan are being lowered as contact with 'foreigners' has expanded in a wide range of areas. Until the 1990s the National Sports Competition had been closed to foreigners. In the 1990s the senior high, junior high and universities divisions were successively opened to non-Japanese students. In 1997 the 'open' division became truly open. The Sumo Association has also had to grapple with calls to limit foreign involvement, but the Association decided on selection according to ability from the Kyushu Tournament in January 1998. Foreign wrestlers won most of the top divisions in the January 2003 Grand Tournament. Baseball used to limit teams to three *gaijin senshu* (non-Japanese players), but that ban was lifted in 1996. Many of the restrictions governing the appointment of foreigners to senior academic positions at national universities have been relaxed over the last two decades. An oddity on Japanese television in the 1970s, foreigners now commonly appear. Increasingly a multi-ethnic composition has come to be accepted in most public arenas in Japan. The presidents of several large Japanese firms are foreign-born, the best known being Carlos Ghnos (President of Nissan). In 2002 a naturalized citizen from Finland was elected to the Diet, Japan's national parliament.

These changes are reflected in notions of Japanese identity. Both Mouer and Sugimoto (1995a and 1995b) and Fukuoka (2000) observed in the mid-1990s that citizenship, blood, language and ethnicity no longer went together in defining Japaneseness.   The country's new wealth attracted a growing number of non-Japanese to work in Japan.   At first they came mainly as singles and entered as temporary residents.   By the 1990s, however, familes started to arrive and longer-term settlement began.   While this influx was first felt in factories, several rural areas sought to overcome shortages of household labour by 'importing' brides from overseas.   Burgess (2003) reports that about one out of every 20 Japanese entering matrimony today marries a non-Japanese, up from one in every 200 only 30 years ago. He also notes that in about 80 per cent of those marriages the Japanese partner is male, a reversal of the situation in the early 1970s. Most significant, perhaps, are his findings that foreign-born wives in Japan are not simply assimilating into Japanese society in an official sense.   Rather, he found them to be actively participating in civil society and shaping the way officially recognized social institutions were evolving around them.

EMIGRATION

Until the 1970s Japan's foreign exchange restrictions meant that few Japanese could freely enter or access the domain beyond the Japanese state. Since then the number of Japanese travelling abroad has increased exponentially. In 1970 about 1.7 million Japanese exited Japan and about 270 thousand nationals lived overseas. Just four years later those figures had jumped to 3.1 million and 380 thousand. By 2000 they stood at about 18 million and 800 thousand.

A Japanese diaspora has been slow to form.   The growth of overseas Japanese communities has been linked to Japanese direct foreign investment. A survey of 4800 major Japanese companies in the early 1990s (Tokyo Keizai Shimposha 1995, pp. 7-13) revealed that many were adopting an integrated approach to production and attached value to localization, underlining the likelihood that Japanese would be communicating and interacting much more closely with their counterparts overseas. Tsuchiya (1995, p. vi) also pointed to the growing appreciation by Japanese that they must 'get their hands dirty' in the everyday affairs of people elsewhere. Although Sedgwick (2001) suggests that Japanese globalization is driven by its multinational corporations, it is important to remember that the movement of Japanese capital to Asia in the late 1960s and early 1970s was driven by small manufacturers of textiles and other light manufactured goods. Not until the 1980s did Japan's large firms seriously move offshore. Furthermore, cultural exchange has been an important element in the 'normalization' of

Japan's relations with the world elsewhere, and much of the contact Japanese have had overseas has been through tourism and other types of person-to-person contact not related directly to Japan's presence abroad. Finally, Sato (2001) indicates that a portion of the Japanese diaspora consists of 'spiritual migrants' wanting to get away from the social controls which characterized their life in Japan.

ENGLISH

Another change is the accelerated absorption of English. An easy measure of this would be the increased use of foreign words in the discourse used for many public debates in Japan. Japanese are actively adopting English words into Japanese, often with a uniquely Japanese nuance, and Japanese have been quite adept at creating their own English. Sometimes English words appear so quickly in Japan that it is difficult to trace their origins back to any major English-language centre. Although 'Japlish' has been a derogatory term used to refer to quaint renditions of English-like words or phrases that did not communicate to native speakers of English, some of the lexicon generated in Japan is now being accepted as local variants of English after the manner of 'Singlish' (Singaporean English) and other forms of English. A small number of Japanese firms have introduced English as a second language in running their business, and it seems to serve as an important adjunct for many educated Japanese. It is time to acknowledge the permanence of English in Japan and to accord to Japanese some of the rights of cultural ownership that go with its extensive usage in that society.

In recent years vigorous public debate was stirred when an advisory group of the Prime Minister in 2000 suggested the desirability of having English as Japan's second official national language (see for example Funabashi 2000). While not receiving wide support (given the climate at a time when English was being criticized for being the conveyor of cultural imperialism, as described in Oishi 1997), the debate underlined the importance of English for Japan's international interface and the extent to which English was impacting on the Japanese language. That importance was further underlined in July 2002 when the Japanese Government introduced to schools a new six-point strategy to raise the English skills of Japanese children.

Considering the extent to which other cultural forms are being infused to create a kind of 'McJapan culture', there is room to speculate about the extent to which bicultural literacy is now required to reap the full benefits of living in Japanese society and to shape the directions that society will take in the global era. Although English has been used to infuse the Japanese language with additional vocabulary (rather as Latin and Greek derivatives did for

English elites some centuries ago), the use of English nevertheless tends to set Japan's more privileged citizens apart from many of its ordinary citizens. Language lies at the core of cultural identity, and the impact of globalization will be most deeply felt at this level by those who are likely to be left behind in the monolingual segments of Japanese society. At the same time, while elitist biculturalism may in some ways undermine the emergence of civil society in Japan, the Internet and other aspects of globalization also have the potential to open up the outside world to Japanese at many more levels than would otherwise have been the case.

RETHINKING JAPANESE BEST PRACTICE WHILE LINKING INTO A GLOBALIZED WORLD: TOWARD A BICULTURAL SOCIETY?

While borderlessness may be accompanied by a relative decline in the role of the state in regulating the interface of its citizens with international society, the discourse and many of the symbols for nationalistic consolidation remain. The role of the Japanese government is by no means negligible, and its policies are shaping the way Japanese interact with the world. Democratically elected governments often choose to respond to populist demands in a democratic fashion by implementing policies that ultimately serve to retard globalization and the development of civil society. Nevertheless, although Japan's post-war conservative governments have structured Japan's foreign policy around a carefully considered line known as 'economic diplomacy', there is also pressure to involve Japan with the world across a broader range of areas.

The debates on 'convergence' and 'divergence' and on the role of 'Asian values' in shaping the course of development have focused attention on Japan as the most advanced economy in Asia. Many have speculated about the lessons to be gleaned from Japan's experience, especially as a model providing a route to development and to alternative forms of social organization and governance in advanced economies. However, as already noted, Japanese social structures and values are not now seen as necessarily unique, as was previously thought to be the case in the 1970s when *nihonjinron* was at its height as an ideology of cultural difference and national superiority.

Change in Japan over the past decade has been far-reaching and complex. Some change has clearly been shaped by inflows of people and ideas from abroad. At the same time the changes have not been inevitable, at least in the short term. While the government gropes for a way forward, individual Japanese have taken the initiative to make Japan more internationally competitive. This has resulted in Japan being attuned to, and adopting, global best practice. While many of those initiatives may be considered as a response to global forces, it is difficult to separate in a causative sense universal processes already occurring from those due mainly to globalization. It is likely that the functional imperatives universally associated with further capitalist development will result in changes which incorporate forms derived from Japan's cultural heritage. Globalization will no doubt heighten the need to respond to a growing set of universally recognized problems. The extent to which each successive search for functional equivalence further dilutes that which is culturally distinctive about Japan remains to be seen. As Japanese society becomes more multicultural and more multilingual, two-way flows of information and of ideas will facilitate Japan's interface with the increasingly globalized world. Japan's impact back on that world is likely to increase, but such things as *karaoke* and *anime* become less Japanese as they become part of other cultures. These processes are likely to result in Japan becoming less 'Japanese' as it borrows and lends in an increasingly globalized environment.

Growing inequality on a functional basis (in terms of occupational groupings delineated in the first instance by educational background) will continue to temper Japan's globalization. To negotiate that interface and maximize the benefits they receive from it, Japan's bilingual elite will become increasingly conversant in English, participating fully in the emerging global society being formed by an emerging international elite. If that is the scenario, it is likely that the ways in which people of the Japanese diaspora organize their affairs will come to reflect that mosaic of inequality. The major question concerning the integration of Japanese society into the global scene concerns the capacity of other Japanese to become bilingual and utilize that bilingualism to invigorate the NPOs and other grass-roots bodies which support their interests.

REFERENCES

Athos, Anthony G. and Richard Tanner Pascale (1981), *The Art of Japanese Management*, New York: Simon & Schuster.
Bendix, Reinhard (1967), 'Preconditions of Development: A Comparison of Japan and Germany', in Ronald P. Dore (ed.), *Aspects of Social Change in Modern Japan*, Princeton: Princeton University Press, pp. 27-68.
Bungei Shunju Henshushu Bu (The Editorial Department, Bungei Shunju Publishers) (1999), *'Shin Kaikyu Shakai Nippon'* (Japan: the New Class Society), *Bungei Shunju* (May), 94-107.
Burgess, Christopher (2003), 'The Challenge of Globalisation and International Migration for the New Japan', draft Chapter One of PhD thesis, tentatively titled '(Re)Constructing Identities: Permanent Migrants as Potential Agents of Social

Change in a Globalising Japan' for submission to Monash University (Melbourne).

Chuo Koron Henshu Bu (Editorial Board, Chuo Koron) (2001), *Ronso Churyu Hokai* (The Debate on the Collapse of the Middle Class in Japan), Tokyo: Chuo Koron Sha.

Chusho Kigyo Cho (The Agency for Small and Medium-Sized Enterprises) (2001), *Chusho Kigyo Hakusho 2001 Nenpan: Mesame Yo! Jiritsu shita Kigyo e* (The 2001 White Paper on Small and Medium-Sized Enterprises: Time to Wake Up and Build Strong Firms), Tokyo: Gyosei.

Dore, Ronald P. (1967), 'Introduction', in Ronald P. Dore (ed.), *Aspects of Social Change in Modern Japan*, Princeton: Princeton University Press, pp. 3-24.

Fukuoka, Yasunori (2000), *Lives of Young Koreans in Japan*, Melbourne: Trans Pacific Press.

Fukushima, Francis (1992), *The End of History and the Last Man*, New York: Free Press.

Funabashi, Yoichi (2000), *Aete Eigo Koyogo Ron* (A Humble Proposal to Have English as One of the Official Languages), Tokyo: Bungei Shunju.

Hanami, Hiroaki, Hideyuki Mitsuhashi and Nami Tachigi (2000), 'Hatarakikata-Mitsuketa Kojin to Shakai no Atarashii Kankei' (Work Ways: Toward a New Relationship Between the Individual and Society), *Nikkei Bijinesu*, **1139**, 29 April, 26-40.

Hashimoto, Kenji (2001), *Kaikyu Shakai Nihon* (Japan as a Class Society), Tokyo: Aoki Shobo.

Huntington, Samuel P. (1992), 'The Clash of Civilizations?' *Foreign Affairs*, **72** (3), Summer, 22-49.

Kariya, Takehiko (2001), *Kaisoka Nihon to Kyoiku Kiki – Fubyodo Saaiseisan kara Iyoku Kakusa Shakai e* (The Crisis in Education and the Stratification of Japan: From Inequality in Class Reproduction to a Difference in Incentives), Tokyo: Yushindo.

Kassalow, Everett M. (1983), 'Japan as an Industrial Relations Model', *Journal of Industrial Relations*, **25** (2), June, 201-219.

Keizai Kikaku Cho (The Economic Planning Agency) (2000), *Neisei Juni-nenpan Kokumin Seikatsu Hakusho* (The 2000 White Paper on the Lifestyles of the Populace), Tokyo: Okura Sho Insatsu Kyoku.

Kitagawa, Takayoshi and Jun Kainuma (1985), *Nihon no Eriito* (Japan's Elite), Tokyo: Otsuki Shoten.

Koike, Kazuo (1981), *Nihon no Jukuren* (Skill Formation in Japan), Tokyo: Yuhikaku.

Koike, Kazuo and Ikuro Watanabe (1979), *Gakureki Shakai no Kyozo* (The Myth of Education-Based Credentialism in Japan), Tokyo: Toyo Keizai Shimposha.

Komai, Hiroshi (2001), *Foreign Migrants in Contemporary Japan*, (trans. by Jens Wilkinson) Melbourne: Trans Pacific Press.

Kosei Rodo Sho (The Ministry of Welfare, Labour and Health) (2001), *Kosei Rodo Hakusho Heisei Jusan Nendo: Shogai ni Wataru Kojin no Jiritsu no Shien suru Kosei Rodo Gyosei* (The 2001 Welfare and Labour White Paper: Toward a Labour and Welfare Police Which Will Support the Development of Individuals Through Their Life Course), Tokyo: Gyosei.

Kruger, David and Ichiko Fuyuno (2002), 'Innovate or Die: Reinventing Japan', *Far Eastern Economic* Review, **165** (16), 25 April, 28-33.

Kuwahara, Yasuo (ed.) (2001), *Guroobaru Jidai no Gaikokujin Rodosha: Doko kara Kite Doko e* (Foreign Workers in the Globalized Era: Their Origins and Future), Tokyo: Toyo Keizai Shinposha.

Mouer, Ross (1975), 'Nihon ni Okeru Ka-I Taikei Betsu no Shotoku Bunpu no Jotai: Kakei Chosa Kenkyu o Tsujite' (A Subsystems Approach to Income Distribution in the Japanese sStting: A Study of the FIES Data, 1963-1972), *Kikan Riron Keizaigaku* (The Quarterly Journal of Theoretical Economics) **25** (1), April, 30-44.

Mouer, Ross (1991), 'Income Distribution in Japan: Change and Continuity, 1962-1990', paper presented to Sixth Biennial Conference of Japanese Studies Association, Canberra: The Australian National University, July.

Mouer, Ross and Hirosuke Kawanishi (2003), 'Change and Challenge Confronting Japan's Labor Market in the Globalized Era", *Waseda Studies in Human Sciences,* **16** (1), 59-108.

Mouer, Ross and Yoshio Sugimoto (1995a), '*Nihonjinron* at the End of the Twentieth Century: A Multicultural Perspective', Asian Studies Papers, Research Series, No. 4, Bundoora: School of Asian Studies, LaTrobe University.

Mouer, Ross and Yoshio Sugimoto (1995b), 'Japanese Studies – *Nihonjinron* at the End of the Twentieth Century: A Multicultural Perspective', in Johann Arnason and Yoshio Sugimoto (eds), *Japanese Encounters with Postmodernity*, London: Kegan Paul International, pp. 237-269.

Mouer, Ross and Yoshio Sugimoto (2003), 'Civil Society in Japan', in David Schak and Wayne Hudson (eds), *Civil Society in Asia*, London: Ashgate, pp. 209-224.

Nihon Rodo Kenkyu Zasshi (2000), **480**, July.

Obi, Keiichiro (1968), 'Rodo Kyokyu no Riron: Sono Kadai Oyobi Kiketsu no Gan-I' (The Theory of Labor Supply: Some New Perspectives and Some Implications), *Mita Gakkai Zasshi*, **61** (1), January, 1-25. (Translation available in Nishikawa Shunsaku (ed.), *The Labor Market in Japan: Selected Readings*, trans. Ross Mouer, Tokyo: University of Tokyo Press, pp. 41-66).

Ohmae, Ken-ichi (1999), *The Borderless World: Power and Strategy in the Interlinked World*, New York: Harper Collins.

Oishi, Toshikazu (1997), *Eigo Teikoku Shugi Ron – Eigo Shihai o do suru ka* (Arguments About English Language Imperialism: What Can be Done About the Way English Controls the World?), Tokyo: Kindai Bungei Sha.

Organisation for Economic Cooperation and Development (1972), *OECD Tainichi Rodo Hokokusha* (The OECD Report on Labor in Japan, trans. Rodosho, Ministry of Labor), Tokyo: Nihon Rodo Kyokai.

Organisation for Economic Cooperation and Development (1977), *Roshi Kankei Seido no Tenkai – Nihon no Keiken ga Imi Suru Mono* (The Development of Industrial Relations in Japan: Some Implications of the Japanese Experience), Tokyo: Nihon Rodo Kyokai.

Ouchi, William G. (1981), *Theory Z: How American Business can Meet the Japanese Challenge*, Reading: Addison-Wesley.

Sato, Machiko (2001), *Farewell to Nippon* (Melbourne: Trans Pacific Press), a translation of *Shin Kaigai Teiju Jidai*, Tokyo: Shinchosha, 1993.

Sato, Toshiki (2000), *Fubyodo Shakai Nihon: Sayonara Sochuryu* (Japan the Unequal Society: The End of the Massive Middle Class), Tokyo: Chuo Koron Sha.

Sedgwick, Mitchell W. (2001), 'The Globalization of Japanese Managers', in J.S. Eades, Tome Gill and Harumi Befu (eds), *Globalization and Social Change in*

Contemporary Japan, Melbourne: Trans Pacific Press, pp. 41-54.

Shukan Rodo Nyusu, (1997), **17**, p. 3.

Somu Sho (Ministry of Public Management, Home Affairs, Post and Telecommunications) (2001), *Joho Tsushin Hakusho: Joho Tsushin ni Kansuru Genjo Hokoku* (White Paper on the Communication of Information: A Report on the Transmission of Information), Tokyo: Somu Sho.

Sugishita, Tsuneo (2001), *NPO/NGO Gaido* (Guide to NPOs and NGOs), Tokyo: Jiyu Kokuminsha.

Tachibanaki, Toshiaki (1998), *Nihon no Keizai Kakusa* (Economic Inequality in Japan), Tokyo: Iwanami Shoten.

Tachibanaki, Toshiaki (2000), 'Nihon no Shotoku Kakusa wa Kakudai Shiteiruka – Gimon e no Kotae to Atarashii Shiten' (Is Economic Inequality Growing in Contemporary Japan? Some Answers to the Critics), *Nihon Rodo Kenkyu Zasshi*, **480**, July, 41-52.

Tominaga, Ken-ichi (2001), *Shakai Hendo no naka no Fukushi Kokka: Kazoku no Shippai to Kokka no Atarashii Kino* (The Welfare State in a Period of Change: The Failure of the Family and the New Functions of the State), Tokyo: Chuo Koronsha.

Tsuchiya, Shingoro (1995), *Ajia e no Kigyo Shinshutsu to Kaigai Fu-nin – Sono Keikaku to Jikko* (The Movement of Japanese Firms into Asia and Working Overseas), Tokyo: Nikan Kogyo Shinbumsha.

Vogel, Ezra (1979), *Japan as Number One: Lessons for America*, Cambridge, Mass.: Harvard University Press.

Yabuno, Yuzo (1995), *Rookaru-Inishiateibu – Kokkyo o Koeru Kokoromi* (Local Initiatives: Efforts to Go Beyond National Borders), Tokyo: Chuo Koron.

Yamada, Masahiro (1999), *Parasaito Shinguru no Jidai* (The Age of the Parasitic Singles), Tokyo: Chikuma Shobo.

Yamada, Masahiro (2000), 'Furiitaa Nihyakumannin ni Ashita wa nai sa' (Floating Casuals Have No Economic Future), *Bungei Shunju* (July), pp. 198-204 (translation available as 'No Future for the Freeters', in *Japan Echo*, **27**, (3), June 2001, 52-55).

10. Globalization, Late Industrialization and China's Accession to the WTO: A Critical Perspective on Close Integration

Gloria Davies and Russell Smyth[1]

INTRODUCTION

The progressive opening up of China since the late 1970s has been one of the most significant events for globalization. This chapter provides an overview of the main features of China's integration into the global economy and examines the challenges that further globalization will pose for China in relation to its future economic and socio-political well-being. We note that since the late 1990s several prominent members of China's intellectual elite have vigorously debated the pros and cons of further globalization. We locate their opposing arguments in the context of China's authoritarian political environment and the realities of state censorship, which has tended to discourage public debate on the range of problems that have arisen in the course of China's transition to a market economy. This includes problems of social injustice, the growing income gap between the rich and poor in China, massive unemployment and official corruption (as detailed for instance in He 1997; Wang, H. 2000; Wang, S. 2001; Davies 2002).

Following China's accession to the World Trade Organisation (WTO) there has been much positive comment about the benefits which globalization will bring for the Chinese economy (for instance Morck and Yeung 2000; Martin and Ianchovichina 2001). Advocates of greater globalization, such as the OECD (2002), argue that the discipline which international market forces will bring to bear will force China to reform its state-owned enterprises (SOEs) and fragile state-owned banking arrangements and become more competitive in international markets. This chapter adopts a more cautious view of the implications of further globalization for China than the optimistic vision of a fully marketized Chinese economy, delivering democracy along with the discipline of international market forces that is projected in much of this literature.

It is undeniable that the main economic manifestations of globalization such as inward foreign direct investment (FDI) and increased foreign trade have had a positive effect on China's economic growth since the introduction of marketization. However, globalization is at best a gilt-edged sword, which creates both winners and losers (Weisbrot 2001). As such, countries should be aware of 'the real costs and dangers of taken-for-granted forms of unregulated free-market globalization' (Wiseman 1998, p. 201). The fact is that the discipline of international market forces also carries costs for China's enterprise reforms and social stability. It will be argued in this chapter that these costs have tended to be downplayed among advocates of further globalization.

CHINA'S INTEGRATION INTO THE GLOBAL ECONOMY AND LATE INDUSTRIALIZATION

Inward foreign direct investment

As discussed elsewhere in this book by Richard Lee, inward FDI has had an important role in contributing to China's economic development. The level of inward FDI into China has been particularly impressive since the 1990s. China is now the largest recipient of FDI among both developing and transition economies, accounting for 25 per cent of all inward FDI into developing countries. In 2000, almost four-fifths of FDI bound for East Asia, excluding Japan, went to China (O'Brien 2001). Econometric studies using a range of methods confirm that there is a causal relationship between FDI and economic growth in China (see for example, Chen et al. 1995; Sun 1998; Shan et al. 1999; Sun et al. 2002).

It is important, though, to recognize that instead of the 'close integration' recommended by the reform orthodoxy consisting of free trade and free movement of capital, the Chinese government has adopted an approach of 'strategic integration' (Singh 1994; Nolan 1996). Foreign investment in China has never been a 'free-for-all'. Instead foreign investors have been subjected to a series of stringent government controls as to where and how they can invest, which is an ongoing source of complaint among multinationals. The lure of China's large potential market has been used to direct technological transfer into strategic sectors consistent with plan priorities (Nolan and Wang 1999);

> We shall guide the orientation of foreign investment in accordance with the state's industrial policies, directing foreign investment towards infrastructure and basic

industry construction, key projects and upgrading technology in existing enterprises (Chen 1994, cited in Nolan and Wang 1999, p. 182).

Consistent with the late industrialization perspective (Amsden 1989; 1992; Amsden and Hikino 1994), the focus of strategic integration has been on promoting technological catch-up through strategic joint ventures. Nolan (2001) presents a series of case studies for industries ranging from automobiles to white goods where major multinationals were required to transfer technologies as a precondition for getting market access. Zhao (1995) finds that imported technologies have significantly enhanced China's technological catch-up. This also extends to the transfer of management and marketing skills. Sit (1985) argues that FDI has acted as a catalyst for modernizing China's industries through the transfer of managerial expertise and international marketing skills.

China's strategy has also consisted of importing second-hand technologies, which have been adapted to suit local conditions. There are similarities in this respect with other late industrializing countries such as Japan. During the Meiji era in Japan (1868-1912), an important reason for high growth was the cultivation of so-called Meiji technologies from existing methods, which were better suited to local climatic conditions than their imported Western counterparts. After the Second World War Japanese enterprises also imported technologies from Europe and the United States, making improvements through incremental innovation. The practice of importing and reverse engineering second-hand foreign technologies to meet local conditions has been well documented in a number of large Chinese SOEs. For example, Nolan and Yeung (2001, pp. 446-447) and Steinfeld (1998, pp. 201-202) discuss how the massive steel producer Capital Iron and Steel (Shougang) made large purchases of low-price second-hand equipment from Europe and the United States (circa 1950) and then updated it with a four-stage investment process.

This positive scenario resulting from the Chinese government's adoption of a 'strategic integration' approach to inward FDI must be measured against the adverse consequences of rapid marketization in a socio-political environment that had, in the first three decades of the People's Republic, suffered the impact of ambitious and often seriously flawed Maoist central planning. In the 1980s this environment still lacked an adequate infrastructure and laws to ensure transparency and accountability in commercial conduct and to safeguard the interests of ordinary consumers. Even as late as 1998, the 'bad news' included at least the following:

People died from drinking phoney liquor; fake fertilizers killed crops; there were growing markets for illicit drugs, for sweatshop labor, and even for the sale of young women for wives and male infants for sons. Corruption was rampant. Industrial pollution was serious and growing fast. State enterprises were failing, unpaid workers were striking, and banks were mired in bad debt. The gap between rich and poor became much wider. During 1997 and 1998 average personal income growth has fallen off sharply, and for large portions of both urban and rural poor it has reversed (Liu and Link 1998).

In *China's Descent into a Quagmire*, a 1997 book-length critical survey of the impacts and consequences of China's entry into the global market economy since 1979, He Qinglian writes of a looming crisis in China's economic and fiscal well-being brought about primarily by corruption on the part of 'power holders and their hangers-on' within an increasingly decentralized one-party state machinery as well as by the exploitative and illicit means that these people used to accrue personal wealth at the expense of the People's Republic that they were meant to serve.[2] In their late 1998 review of He's work, Liu Binyan and Perry Link note that He exposes, among other things, the use of public funds for speculation in real estate or local and foreign stocks, with profits from such illicit investments being directly appropriated by these politically powerful speculators, who would pass all their losses on to the state accounts. Liu and Link observe that 'at least 500 billlion yuan – about US$60 billion' of state funds 'intended for the purchase of state grain, for education, and for disaster relief' had been misappropriated for speculation by corrupt officials in the course of the 1990s. They also point out He's grim assessment of the apparent success of joint enterprises with foreign or overseas Chinese business concerns in the 1990s, in which the mainland Chinese partner, in exchange for foreign currency deposited in overseas accounts held in his or her name, would use his or her local political power 'strategically' to allow the joint enterprise the use of property and the procuring of materials and licenses 'at well below fair prices' (Liu and Link 1998).

According to He Qinglian and several other prominent Chinese intellectuals who have observed their greatly altered social environment of the 1980s and 1990s with both hope and concern, these negative developments should not be explained away as mere growing pains resulting from China's transition from an inefficient state system and flawed centralized planning to a market economy. Rather, they suggest – often by resorting to figurative language, being mindful of the state's effective powers of censorship – that the fundamental problem rests with the abuse and misuse of power in China's authoritarian and often arbitrary political culture. In this regard, the Shanghai-based economic historian Zhu Xueqin uses the evocative Smithian figure of the 'invisible hand' to advocate the necessity of the further development of market mechanisms within China's economy, but counterposes to it the spectre of the 'arbitrary foot' of political power which, as he puts it, has 'trampled . . . and left a filthy imprint' on an otherwise clean 'hand' (Zhu X. 2000). For Zhu, the solution was to be found in a decisive separation of the spontaneous workings of the market from the personal interests of power-holders within the one party state, with a resultant drastic shrinkage of the state's role in the economic sector. Zhu's implicit faith in market forces and mechanisms as the harbinger of broader democratic reforms is predicated to a large extent on the neoclassical assumption of the market's spontaneous efficacy, and his view is shared by many others within the academy and government who have, since the 1990s, been dubbed as or claimed themselves to be China's 'liberals'.

Critics of this view, labelled by their 'liberal' detractors as 'leftists,' have focused conversely on the necessity of the state as a significant player in China's economic development as well as on the need for wide-ranging political reforms and the provision of a sound economic and industrial infrastructure whose magnitude and degree of complexity would require financing from the state (Wang, H. 2000; Wang, S. 2001). These critics are also wary of the optimistic prognosis for China on the part of advocates of further globalization. For them, the human 'costs' of globalization are of particular concern.

It has been predicted that inward FDI will increase significantly as a result of China's accession to the WTO (Ma and Wang 2001; see also R. Lee in this book) and that this will further boost China's already huge foreign exchange reserves. Developments in China's FDI are watched closely by the US government. The US-China Security Review Commission's Report to the US Congress of July 2002 suggests, among other things, that China's rapid accumulation of foreign exchange reserves through FDI and its trade surplus with the US should be studied in relation to the Chinese government's increased spending on defence, especially in the purchase of 'foreign weapons, technology and other components for its (that is the People's Liberation Army's) modernization program' (US-China Security Review Commission 2002).[3] The fear of rising Chinese nationalism and militarism is a theme often rehearsed in the US-dominated international news media and one which continues to produce tensions in US-China relations.

Many Chinese intellectuals have expressed concern about what they regard as prejudicial and negative representations of China in the international media. For instance, the Beijing-based historian Wang Hui observes that Chinese protests held in the wake of the 'accidental' NATO bombing of the Chinese embassy in Belgrade during the Kosovo war of 1999 were reported in the Western media as instances of 'anti-foreignism and nationalistic fanaticism', with 'the response of ordinary Chinese citizens against violence' as a motivating cause of the protests being left out of account. Without naming the US directly, Wang avers that 'those who monopolize the strength of the whole world in the name of globalism are actually the biggest nationalists' (Wang, H. 2003). Indeed the highly visible coupling of economic interests and military power on the part of the US since 11 September 2001, as noted by Vivienne Wee in her chapter, confirms Wang's critical observation.

Some critics of globalization have linked it to the doctrine of 'neoliberalism' – the positive vision of a global level playing field at the end of history, subject only to the discipline of international market forces and the arbitrations of the WTO, and 'freed' from the constraints of the nation-state (Bourdieu 1999;   Wang, H. 2000).   As a kind of ideological lure, 'neoliberalism' obscures social inequities in lived everyday experience by readily justifying these as 'costs' incurred in the grand project of an ever-expanding global free market.   A 'neoliberal' perspective anticipates that China's further globalization would yield only positive outcomes in the form of the state's reduced role, concomitant with the greatly enlarged significance of market forces.   Yet inward FDI is one key area of China's economic growth that requires the active involvement of the state to safeguard the interests of investors and workers alike.

The Beijing-based economist Fu Jun notes the remarkable speed with which the Chinese government has established a substantial institutional framework for facilitating and regulating FDI, starting from scratch in the late 1970s when the Maoist prohibition against foreign investment was finally overturned. In his 2001 analysis he lists market size, labour costs and infrastructure as significant variables in assessing the capacity of the different Chinese provinces to attract inward FDI. He also notes that progressive policy liberalization, legal reforms and the Chinese government's participation since the 1990s in a range of international conventions to safeguard foreign investment have all helped to facilitate the provision of a relatively more equitable playing field based mainly on economic advantage (since the late 1990s) as opposed to policy and cultural variables (dominant in the early phase of 1980s FDI) (Fu 2001). The crucial importance of a sound infrastructure and a comprehensive institutional framework for the purposes of attracting inward FDI underscores the necessity for state intervention.

For Wang Shaoguang, 'if investment and innovation are the two wheels of development . . . the invisible hand is not adequate in guiding an economy along those two dimensions' (Wang, S. 2001, p. 135). In this context, he recommends that state extractive capacity be maintained and strengthened for the purposes of developing China's market system, with the state (namely 'the capacity of the central government') playing a crucial role in developing 'education, financial systems, communications networks and other forms of physical and institutional infrastructure' (Wang, S. 2001, p. 135). From this perspective, euphoric claims that further globalization will eclipse the state in inverse proportion to the ascendancy of the free market become evidently problematic: globally, the massive economic power of TNCs and wealthy nation-states ensures that there is no level playing field while locally, rampant corruption in China is symptomatic of the central government's relatively weak extractive capacity for infrastructure building, the provision of public goods and services and adequate safety nets for the disadvantaged (Wang, S. 2001, pp. 137-145).

FOREIGN TRADE AND INDUSTRIAL POLICY

In 1999, the total external trade of 'Greater China' (China, Hong Kong and Taiwan) was $US810 billion, far exceeding the total trade of Japan ($US731 billion), and almost half that of the United States. This is after netting out $US137 billion of intra-regional trade (Wang 2002, p. 2). Lardy (2002, p. 116) predicts China 'almost seems certain in the next few years to overtake Canada, France and the United Kingdom to become the fourth largest trading country in the world. Within a decade, China's trade is likely to surpass that of Japan and Germany, making China the world's second largest trader'.

From the late 1970s China's exports have increased rapidly, buoyed by a series of devaluations to the *renminbi* designed to create the right incentives for exporters. The approach of the Chinese government has been to increase foreign exchange reserves in order to import foreign technologies. However, while China promoted exports, its attitude to imports from the 1970s to the mid-1990s was distinctly mercantilist. The Chinese government maintained a battery of protective measures, including high tariffs and quantitative import restrictions such as import inspection measures and import quotas, which were designed to promote import substitution (Vogel 1989, p. 375).

In this respect China's protectionist policies contradicted the 'more pain more gain' transition orthodoxy advocated by the IMF (1990) and World Bank (1996). However, China was in no position to open its markets to the full impact of international market forces. Nolan and Wang (1999, pp. 182-183) describe the whole of the Chinese large-scale upstream state-owned sector in the late 1970s as an 'infant industry'. Under these circumstances China could not hope to compete on a level playing field with the world's major multinationals. Thus, China developed an industrial policy centred on building large enterprise groups in the absence of open competition from foreign producers.

The central tenet of this industrial policy was the *zhuada fangxiao* ('grasp the big and let go of the small') reform program, which was reaffirmed at the

Fifteenth Congress of the Chinese Communist Party in September 1997. Following the Fifteenth Congress, the central government announced three major policies to develop large and medium-sized SOEs. First, the government is developing a number of enterprise groups (*qiye jituan*) including 120 groups, known as the 'national team', which are the 'generals' of the *zhuada* program (Sutherland 2001). Second, it wants to develop a modern enterprise system in large-scale SOEs by the year 2010. As part of the Ninth Five-Year Plan (1996-2000), the central government selected 100 large SOEs to form the 'core' of the 'modern enterprise system'. At least 20 of these large SOEs are also core members of the 120 national team enterprise groups (Huang et al. 1998). Third, it hopes to entrench three to five large firms in the world's biggest 500. To this end, in 1997, the central government announced preferential financial support for six large SOEs in key, strategic sectors.

The late industrialization perspective suggests that there is considerable precedent for building large firms and diversified business groups based on the experience of other late industrializing countries (Amsden and Hikino 1994). Amsden (1989, 1992) stresses that the development path of conglomerates in late industrializing countries has been different from that in industrialized countries. Large firms in industrialized countries first specialized in producing a narrow product line based on core competences and then diversified into related industries. This was possible because large industrial enterprises that developed in Europe and the USA achieved Schumpeterian organizational and technological breakthroughs, which created international oligopolies. However, as its definition suggests, 'late industrialization is a process devoid of innovation' (Amsden 1992). Hence, in contrast to firms in industrialized countries, firms in late industrializing countries have been forced to import and adapt foreign technologies and depend on learning through doing to compensate for the absence of core innovation.

A common criticism of the *zhuada* process is that enterprises have been forced together via administrative mergers and, as a result, lack specific business strengths. For example, Shieh (1999, p. 54) states:

> There have been a number of reports that government authorities have pressured successful conglomerates to acquire loss-making enterprises – raising concerns that conglomerates are, in some cases, being formed on the basis of political considerations rather than economic ones.

However, it can equally be argued that these sorts of concerns misconstrue the real economic rationale for merging big business groups with smaller loss-making firms in transitional economies, which is precisely to foster business strengths. Nolan and Wang (1999, p. 190) observe:

> Merger can be an especially powerful process of advancing business capabilities in a transitional economy, since business and technical skills are not so widely available as in an advanced economy. The merger process led by capable firms with advanced technological and management skills can have a powerful positive externality effect, spreading business capability more rapidly than would be the case in the absence of merger. Moreover, the pressure for mergers is reinforced in a poor transitional economy such as China. [In China there are] especially large incentives for merger that are consequent upon the underdeveloped state of market institutions, which inhibits the capacity to obtain needed inputs easily and reliably through contracts mediated by the market mechanism.

This last point has been stressed more generally by Khanna and Palepu (1997), who emphasize the knowledge-augmenting function of diversified business groups in overcoming institutional deficiencies in developing countries. Khanna and Palepu (1997) argue that business groups add value through diversification because they are better able to imitate the functions of institutions in advanced capitalist economies. Thus, while there has been a shift to more focused strategies in recent times in advanced capitalist economies, it does not follow that focused strategies will give the best results in emerging markets given institutional voids. Khanna and Palepu (1997, p. 51) point out:

> [Groups] should not break up simply because their competitors are focused foreign companies from advanced economies. Western companies have access to advanced technology, cheap financing and sophisticated managerial know-how. In the absence of institutions providing these and other functions in emerging markets, diversification may be the best way to match-up with the competition.

China's accession to the WTO

In the mid-1990s China's mercantilist approach started to change and it began to reduce protection. This was in response to pressure from the United States for greater market access and as part of China's bid to gain access to the WTO. In November 1999, China and the United States signed an agreement clearing the way for China to join the WTO (White House 2000). Under the agreement, China agreed to dismantle its mercantilist policies and with them the industrial policies underpinning its attempts to build large enterprise groups. The range of measures slated for implementation include the phasing out of quotas and local content requirements already under way and the substantial reduction of tariffs by 2005. China has also agreed to eliminate technology transfer requirements and offsets as a condition for investment or importation (see Nolan 2001).

A large literature has emerged which attempts to quantify the benefits to China from freer trade and more efficient allocation of resources. The consensus among most of these studies is that China will benefit from joining the WTO (see for example McKibbin and Tang 2000; Walmsley and Hertel 2001; Martin and Ianchovichina 2001; Tongzon 2001; Lim 2002; and Wang 2002). Gilbert and Wahl (2002) review more than 30 studies and conclude that most estimate that the welfare gains will be between 0.5 and 2.4 per cent of GDP. The only study which estimates a net welfare loss for China is Chow et al. (1999).

These potential gains, however, are long-run effects, where the modelling is forced to make a series of assumptions; and, as with any long-run effects, they are uncertain. When asked about the effects of the French Revolution almost 200 years after the event, Chairman Mao is said to have quipped that it was 'too early to tell' (Martin and Ianchovichina 2001). The long-run effects of China's accession to the WTO also involve a fair bit of guesswork given that the counterfactual is unclear and that the ultimate outcome depends on a complex interaction of factors, most of which are not transparent at this stage. Putting the long-run effects to one side, even the strongest advocates of China's accession to the WTO recognize that it will involve a J-curve effect, in which there will be substantial short-term costs. These will take the form of bankruptcies and mounting unemployment in the state-owned sector, placing further pressure on China's embryonic social security system as protection is lowered in industries such as agriculture, automobiles and some capital-intensive sectors.

The real debate is about how long it will take for the J-curve effect to bottom out and for things to improve. It is likely that those who stress the benefits to China from further trade liberalization and opening-up to market forces tend to understate the period of time needed before the economic situation improves. It should also be said that these are often the same individuals, and organizations, who had supreme faith in the operation of international market forces following the introduction of big bang reforms in Central and Eastern Europe. The IMF's (1990, p. 17) view was typical of the transition orthodoxy on Central and Eastern Europe which espoused the virtues of 'close integration':

It is . . . essential to move as rapidly as possible to a transparent and decentralized trade and exchange rate system, in order to hasten the integration . . . into the world economy. . . . The exchange rate [needs] to be moved to market clearing levels. [Only] a few sectors [need] to be protected for a short time [such as two or three years] from the intense competition of international markets.

Kornai (1990), who was one of the most prominent advocates of big bang reforms in Central and Eastern Europe, suggested at the start of the reforms that the process could be completed in 'one stroke' and that the J-curve would bottom out and start to improve within a few years. Other advocates of breaking up the 'state-owned dinosaurs' and bringing about trade liberalization in Central and Eastern Europe such as Lipton and Sachs (1990) made similar confident predictions. The reality, though, was rather different, with international trade in Central and Eastern Europe coming close to collapse following rapid falls in protection. As a result, from the mid 1990s a stream of more sober assessments started to emerge (see for example Rapaczynski 1996) and now it is largely conceded that the big bang price and trade liberalization reforms designed to engineer competition were a failure.

Wang Hui (2000; 2003) has noted that China's accession to the WTO, accompanied by much fanfare in the international media, was hardly a topic of public debate in China during the negotiations leading up to the event. The state-owned Chinese media largely echoed the positive views expressed in the US-dominated international media, while scholarly analyses of the costs and benefits of China's accession to the WTO authored by Chinese intellectuals published on the Internet and in select academic journals did not make their way into the public arena. Wang also observes that:

> because China's rural population lacks any real representation at the level of state policy making, the state, in the course of its negotiations with the WTO, made huge concessions on agricultural questions to the United States, Europe and other nations, demonstrating the close links between the reduction of the role of the state and the global economic order (Wang, H. 2003).

Increased unemployment leading to a further increase in the ranks of China's already vast mobile population of the working poor, the growing income gap between urban and rural China and between 'haves' and 'have-nots' in both urban and rural settings, deforestation and environmental pollution are some of the evident 'costs' of China's rapid marketization that continue to pose a formidable challenge for effective governance both locally and nationally. In its bid to suppress 'negative' media coverage on issues of local, national and global significance, the Chinese government has, in many ways, actively hindered the flow of information necessary for economic life within globalization. Thus, even though China has formally been brought into 'close integration' with the global economic order via its accession to the WTO, the Chinese public's curtailed access to the diverse range of information flows available outside China presents a striking picture of poor integration. It goes without saying that within the highly competitive local or global marketplace, poorly-informed Chinese citizens are placed at a distinct disadvantage in their dealings with well-informed members of the Chinese elite and foreigners.

In its 15 February 2002 report, Human Rights Watch documents numerous instances of Chinese state censorship that have resulted in the closure of offending media and publishing concerns or severe penalties (including jail sentences) for their editors and authors (Human Rights Watch 2002). This has fostered a tendency towards self-censorship on the part of officials and ordinary Chinese citizens alike, which has, in turn, impeded the government's own concerted attempts at encouraging accountability and transparency as basic values in the Chinese workplace. Since information as knowledge is a form of cultural capital, one can regard the asymmetry between the US and China, among other things, as the disparity between the 'information-rich' and the 'information-poor' in the moment of global economic 'integration'. This contrast is strikingly brought out in the provocative prose of the Slovenian cultural theorist Slavoj Zizek, who writes that:

> Today, the two superpowers, the USA and China, relate more and more as Capital and Labour. The USA is turning into a country of managerial planning, banking, servicing, and so on, while its 'disappearing working class' (except for migrant Chicanos and others who work predominantly in the service economy) is reappearing in China, where a large proportion of US products, from toys to electronic hardware, is manufactured in conditions that are ideal for capitalist exploitation: no strikes, limited freedom of movement for the work force, low wages . . . Far from being simply antagonistic, the relationship between China and the USA is therefore, at the same time, deeply symbiotic. The irony of history is that China fully deserves the title 'working-class state': it is the state of the working class for American Capital (Zizek 2001, p. 134).

CHALLENGES OF GLOBALIZATION

Addressing China's bad debts

China's banking system has a significant overhang of bad loans. At the end of 2001, the official estimate was that non-performing loans held by Chinese banks were worth 1.8 trillion RMB ($US 217 billion) or 25.4 per cent of bank lending.[4] However, an Ernst & Young study estimates the total value of unprofitable loans to be $US480 billion or 44 per cent of bank lending (Chandler 2002). Some see China's accession to the WTO as an opportunity to clean up the bad debt problem. Holz and Zhu (2000) propose that the financial sector be opened up to international ownership. They suggest (at p. 90) that:

WTO membership should provide the leaders of the PRC with a powerful instrument to overcome formidable social and political obstacles on their way to achieving the final success in reforming the country's inefficient banking and enterprise systems.

There is some precedent for introducing international involvement in cleaning up the bad debts of SOEs as part of the recent equity-for-debt swap (EDS). The EDS was first announced in 1999 and came into operation in 2000 when the State Council promulgated regulations on the operation of the Asset Management Companies (AMCs).[5] The four big state-owned banks have each set up one AMC to handle their bad loans. The four AMCs are Xinda (attached to China Construction Bank), Great Wall (attached to the Agricultural Bank of China), Orient (attached to the Bank of China) and Huarong (attached to the Industrial and Commercial Bank of China). As part of this scheme, one innovative development which Huarong has pioneered is to put together asset packages to sell to foreign investors. In November 2001 Huarong AMC sold asset packages to international investment consortiums led by Morgan Stanley (with a face value of 10.8 billion RMB) and Goldman Sachs (with a face value of 1.97 billion RMB).[6] At the same time as selling the assets, Huarong signed separate agreements with the Morgan Stanley and Goldman Sachs consortiums to set up joint ventures to dispose of these assets. Morgan Stanley proposed a two-tier structure, consisting of a joint venture that owns the debts and an offshore entity that charges a service fee to dispose of the assets (McGregor 2002). The Ministry of Foreign Trade and Economic Cooperation (MOFTEC) gave approval for the separate joint ventures to proceed in December 2002 (Kynge 2002).

The view that there can be a complete overhaul of China's banking system (including a quick sale of overvalued state-owned assets to foreign investors), however, is ultimately naive. For example, of the 100 billion RMB purchased by Huarong from the Industrial and Commercial Bank at face value under the EDS program, only about 0.5 per cent has been sold to third parties. Moreover, out of the 500 million RMB that has been sold to third parties, less than 10 per cent has been sold to foreign investors.[7] Most foreign investors are only interested in industries with growth potential, such as computers, electronics, food processing and telecommunications, and in assets in large and medium-sized cities. This would suggest that a flurry of foreign investment is not the solution.

One of the main reasons why it is difficult for the AMCs to sell debt/equity acquired under the EDS program is that it must be sold at par, unless the AMC gets special permission from the Ministry of Finance. The Ministry of Finance will grant permission for the AMCs to sell their equity at less than face value on a case-by-case basis. However, if this were to occur on a significant scale, in effect resulting in a fire sale of state-owned assets, it would force the AMCs to default on their bond commitments to the banks. Thus, the very banks whose non-performing loans were relieved by the EDS would see distressed assets reappear on their balance sheets (Steinfeld and Hulme 2000).

CHINA'S ENTERPRISE REFORMS

Nolan (2001, chapter 13; 2002) and Nolan and Zhang (2002) express concern about whether China's large SOEs are ready to compete on a level playing field now that China has joined the WTO. As Nolan and Zhang (2002) put it, while China's large-scale SOEs have undergone incremental *evolutionary* change, the world's leading firms have undergone a *revolutionary* transformation. Case studies conducted by Nolan (2001) in a wide range of industries suggest that after two decades of reform the competitive capability of China's large-scale SOEs is still weak relative to the global giants. The World Bank advocates downsizing of China's enterprise groups, but it is unlikely that privatization and liberalization will be sufficient to allow China to compete on the global 'level' playing field of wealthy developed nations.

This perspective runs counter to the orthodox view on post-socialist transition implemented in Central and Eastern Europe at the beginning of the 1990s. In Central and Eastern Europe, privatization was viewed as necessary 'to ensure a complete break with the old regime' (Borenzstein and Kumar 1991, p. 171). As part of this process, large-scale enterprises were privatized and downsized and emphasis was placed on small and medium-sized enterprises as an engine for post-socialist growth. No doubt coloured by the failure of Stalinist central planning, the orthodox view was, and perhaps still is, that large-scale enterprises in capitalist economies naturally evolved over time and that large-scale enterprises cannot be 'artificially constructed' through state sponsorship.

However, writing about the orthodox approach to reform followed in Central and Eastern Europe, Nolan (1996, p, 9) succinctly makes the point:

[Based on the experience of advanced capitalist economies] [t]he best policy was not passively to sell off individual plants to private buyers attempting to construct a textbook, perfectly competitive structure of small businesses in open competition with other countries' established firms. It would take a long time for large firms to emerge through the spontaneous play of market forces in the teeth of open competition from long established multinational corporations. In the meantime, in many sectors this would lead to efficiency losses stemming from failure to take advantage of economies of scale at the plant level as well as economies of 'scope' arising from multi-plant operation.

The focus on downsizing belies the fact that '[t]he large-scale "modern industrial enterprise" played a crucial role in the rise of the modern economy' (Nolan 1996, p. 4). As Chandler (1990, p. 593) puts it: '[The large-scale enterprise] provided an underlying dynamic in the development of modern industrial capitalism'. As a result, the reality of modern capitalism is that large firms dominate output in mature capitalist economies. The combined sales of the world's top 500 firms are responsible for more than 20 per cent of total world output. Sales of the biggest 500 enterprises in France, Germany, Japan, the United Kingdom and the United States account for between one quarter and one-third of their GDP. In contrast, sales of the largest 500 enterprises in China make up just 16 per cent of GDP with total sales less than the world's biggest firm, General Motors.[8]

The orthodox view overlooks a significant literature on the emergence of modern capitalism which suggests that the notion that large firms in mature capitalist economies evolved naturally in the teeth of global market forces is fallacious (see Chandler et al. 1997; Lake 1988; Lazonick 1991; Ruigrok and Van Tulder 1995). One of the great ironies of the stance that the United States has taken in the WTO on supposed barriers to free trade imposed by developing countries is that it was explicit in pursuing a mercantilist approach to promoting large-scale enterprises in its formative period throughout the nineteenth century. Nolan and Wang (1999, p. 178) point out:

> The United States in the nineteenth century unashamedly industrialized behind high protectionist barriers, 'free riding on free trade' (Lake 1988, chapter 3). As early as 1791, Alexander Hamilton argued for US industrialization behind tariff barriers (Ruigrok and Van Tulder 1995: 211) and for almost two centuries, US tariffs rarely were below 30 per cent (Ruigrok and Van Tulder 1995: 211-212). Despite the passage of antitrust laws, huge oligopolistic firms were allowed to grow. By the interwar period, US firms dominated big business globally, with around two-thirds of the world's top 50 companies (Schmitz 1993: 31). Government procurement spending has been a continuing strong influence on US big business, with an especially powerful effect on the aircraft, computer, semiconductor and electronics industries (Ruigrok and Van Tulder 1995: 211).

IMPLICATIONS FOR SOCIAL STABILITY, SOCIAL PROTECTION AND POLITICAL FREEDOM

China's enterprise reforms are at a delicate stage. One of the main implications of marketization is that there has been an escalation in the number of laid-off (*xiagang*) workers from the state-owned sector. According to official figures there were 26 million workers laid off between

1998 and 2002 (Armitage 2003). In addition, faced with an ageing population and rising health costs, in the mid-to-late 1990s SOEs increasingly found themselves unable to meet the cost of servicing their wage bill or provide basic social benefits such as healthcare and pensions to their workers. According to official statistics, in 1997 about 11 million workers in SOEs were receiving just a fraction of their wages or no wages at all, and there were 2.77 million retirees who were not receiving their pensions (Smyth 1998, p. 108). This situation necessitated a shift in the 1990s from the traditional iron rice bowl of the mini-welfare state to the establishment of an institutional welfare state based on welfare pluralism where the individual, enterprise, state and society share the costs of providing the social safety net (Gu 2001).

The opening up of China's markets to global competition has had an important role in necessitating the shift to an institutional welfare state. The issue of forced redundancies is a major social problem, which is being exacerbated by the process of globalization as China's SOEs are faced with increased levels of competition following China's accession to the WTO. The real issue is whether the social protection mechanism which China has in place is able to protect workers from the vicissitudes of global competition. Empirically-based analyses indicate that the government's introduction of social policy reform consistently lags behind social change (Woon 1999; Ye et al. 2002). As we have noted earlier, the one-party state's authoritarian style of governance has led to the censorship of dissenting views and 'bad news' as well as to strict controls being imposed on the flow of information within Chinese public culture, all of which contribute to the discouragement of the transparent accounting essential to the formulation of effective policy reform. Recent studies of labour migration and China's accession to the WTO suggest that it is highly questionable whether China's embryonic social security system has the capability to cope with the 'short-term' costs at the beginning of the J-curve, particularly in the worst affected areas in China's industrial north-east (see, for instance, Woon 1999; Ye et al. 2002; Prime 2002).

In the related area of labour standards and occupational health and safety (OHS), while the institutional and legal frameworks for protecting workers' rights exist, monitoring and enforcement is proving difficult (Nyland et al. 2003). Marketization and more flexible labour markets have created opportunities for migrant labour from rural areas to flood into China's cities and wealthier coastal regions in search of work and higher income. This trend is expected to increase. OECD (2002) estimates suggest that almost 70 million workers will exit agriculture between 2000 and 2010. This will place further pressure on urban labour markets, which are unable to allocate large amounts of surplus labour.

Migrants often receive lower wages than local workers, but are willing to accept these conditions because they can still earn much more than in their communities of origin (Hare 1999; Knight et al. 1999). The influx of foreign direct investment as the Chinese economy has opened up has facilitated this process through creating job opportunities.   The floating population of migrant workers in China is commonly estimated to be between 120 million and 150 million people (Pan 2002), with the state organ *People's Daily* admitting in October 2001 that 'some experts' have estimated that the number is 'at least 200 million' (*People's Daily* 2001b). Many of these work in collective township or village enterprises (CTVEs) or joint ventures in the coastal provinces in special economic zones (SEZs) such as Xiamen (Fujian) and Shenzhen, Zhuhai and Shantou (Guangdong).

While migrant workers provide cheap labour that fuels the globalization process, the existence of large pools of migrant labour makes it easier for firms to avoid their obligations under the OHS legislation. This is because migrants are either unaware of the legislation or are often willing to work without the correct occupational protection.   Though illegal, 'life or death contracts' where workers agree to work without OHS safeguards are prevalent in small CTVEs and private firms.   Where workers are injured, under-the-counter payments where injuries are not even recorded is a common occurrence.

This has more general implications for the success of the institutional welfare state and even the viability of the Chinese State. As globalization has increased competition, enterprises have been forced to curtail their costs through reducing protection offered to workers. This occurs at a time when the Communist Party is moving away from the rhetoric of the primacy of the working class to embrace the professional elite and capitalist segments of society.   As a result, workers feel squeezed between the state's failure to provide a new social safety net and the demise of the iron rice bowl system (Lee 1999, p. 66). This has led to a growing sense of betrayal reflected in mass demonstrations, in particular in the South West and North East of China (Zhao and Nichols 1996).

The Chinese Communist Party's constitutional metamorphosis into an organization that formally welcomes capitalists among its members was legitimated in 2001 on the imposed authority of former President Jiang Zemin's theory of the 'Three Represents'. This controversial move, justified as an 'advanced' version of Marxism, sparked much debate that the government quickly moved to censor, with Jiang going as far as to shut down the influential Party journal *The Pursuit of Truth* (*Zhenlide zhuiqiu*) for its negative evaluation of this political seachange in August 2001. Earlier, in June 2001, the editorial staff at *Southern Weekend* (*Nanfang zhoumo*), a Guangzhou-based Chinese news magazine with a reputation for critical independence, were replaced after the magazine published a series of exposé articles on rural socio-economic problems and an in-depth discussion of Jiang's 'Three Represents' (Human Rights Watch 2002). The Party, as the ideological bulwark of the state that it had controlled unchallenged since the founding of the People's Republic, had been engaged in an ongoing process of adaptive self-transformation throughout the 1990s, in the years leading up to the handover of Hong Kong in 1997. In order to allay widespread international scepticism about Hong Kong's political and economic future under Communist rule, the one-party state was keen to demonstrate both its commitment to abide by international agreements and its ability to maintain and further develop the free flow of goods and services in Hong Kong's fully fledged market economy (see, for instance, Oksenberg 1997; Huang, Y. 1997).

ECONOMIC INTEGRATION WITH HONG KONG

The return of Hong Kong to Chinese sovereignty was, as Jane Lee notes in her chapter, an integration fostered largely through economic rather than political means. As Lee also notes, cooperative efforts on the part of the central Beijing authorities and Hong Kong's local SAR administration in infrastructure planning and consolidation since 1997, in response to economic and market demands, constitute a positive aspect of integration between Hong Kong and China. The Beijing authorities have, for instance, sought to alleviate Hong Kong's recession woes – which began with the Asian financial crisis in 1997 – through a planned series of strategies that have been locally dubbed as 'moving water from north to south' ('water' being a metaphor for money), including new policies aimed at encouraging a far greater range of SOEs and other business enterprises (especially within the information technology sector) to invest in and to set up outlets in Hong Kong. Schemes have also been formulated to allow Hong Kong's unemployed workers to be retrained and to seek job opportunities north of the border in Shenzhen and other cities in the Pearl River Delta (Lam 2002).

Encouragement on the part of the Beijing authorities for greater flows of capital, goods and services as well as increased human mobility between Hong Kong and the mainland is viewed by several social commentators in Hong Kong, such as the highly regarded journalist and author Willy Wo-Lap Lam, as economic integration with a high political price tag. Lam observes that recent developments in Hong Kong-Beijing relations indicate that the 'one country, two systems' policy under which the Hong Kong handover took place in 1997 is being actualized in ways that show how 'the multisplendored possibilities of "two systems" could be sacrificed on the altar of the monolithic requirements of "one country"' (Lam 2002). In their public speeches of 2002, then President Jiang Zemin and Vice-Premier Qian Qichen implicitly queried the political loyalty of Hong Kong's senior civil servants by reference, among other things, to SAR Chief Executive Tung Chee-Hwa's first term as 'a one-man show'. Jiang also called on civil servants to 'conscientiously submit to and uphold the chief executive's leadership' while Qian publicly affirmed the SAR administration's newly introduced accountability or 'ministerial' system – a system much criticized by independent Hong Kong critics and members of the concerned public for its drastic undermining of the independence and integrity of the civil service – as one that would allow Tung to work with 'like-minded officials' (Lam 2002).

The 'ministerial' system, introduced in June-July 2002, saw the creation of a new administrative layer of political appointees drawn from the business, professional and academic sectors, to oversee Hong Kong's civil service and to set policies with the support of senior civil servants who would continue to play the role of Permanent Secretaries in relation to these politically appointed Secretaries on five-year contracts. The fourteen new Principal Officials appointed under this system are, in effect, the Chief Executive's Cabinet. Critics see this new system as a significant threat to the prospect of democracy in Hong Kong since it further concentrates power in the figure of the Beijing-appointed Chief Executive, who has now been empowered to nominate his allies from both public and private sectors to fill these powerful ministerial positions, subject only to Beijing's approval and without consultation with or accountability to either the legislature or the people of Hong Kong (Union Action 2002).

For now at least, organizations such as the Hong Kong Confederation of Trade Unions (HKCTU, founded in 1960, with a current membership of 151,600 in 58 affiliates) are able to promote workers' rights, expose exploitative and corrupt practices, organize strikes and publicly criticize the undemocratic aspects of Hong Kong's current political system. Yet it is clear that the Hong Kong SAR administration's proposed introduction of a new 'anti-subversion' law (based on Article 23 of the Basic Law that provides Hong Kong with its Constitution) is aimed at curtailing freedom of expression and other civil liberties that the people of Hong Kong have come to regard as their fundamental rights. Indeed the sinister implications of this new law on subversion and sedition led the European Union to pass a resolution in January 2003 calling explicitly for:

> a self-governing Hong Kong, where opposition parties are free to voice their opinion, where freedom of speech and the press is not constrained, where people are free to attend assemblies, religious activities and demonstrate, where people

have the right to form and join trade unions, and where people can engage in scientific research, art, literature and other cultural activities (Global Coalition Against Article 23 Legislation 2003).

The resourcefulness of the concerned Hong Kong public in organizing mass protests (including street protests in December 2002 with up to 60,000 marchers) and in lobbying for international support against the new 'anti-subversion' law (including the establishment of the Global Coalition Against Article 23 Legislation website) provides ample evidence of the commitment of ordinary citizens to the protection of their civil liberties under law. That opposition to the proposed law was and continues to be voiced in both Hong Kong's corporate sector and the international business community has made it one of the most unpopular proposals that the Tung SAR administration has pursued against the counsel of overwhelmingly negative public opinion (*Wall Street Journal* 2003).

The controversy surrounding the evolution of this proposed law provides a striking instance of concerted popular resistance to the coercive politics of 'integration' imposed on Hong Kong by Beijing. Moreover, it also indicates that due process and civil liberties are valued in the corporate sector as fundamental rights, and that integration between Hong Kong and China will continue to be troubled by the gulf between the demands of the Hong Kong public for the consolidation of democratic principles under Hong Kong law on the one hand, and the authoritarian politics of the mainland Chinese one-party state on the other hand. This is not to say that the one-party state has not gradually implemented and institutionalized reforms in administration and governance in the course of the last two decades that have produced a greater degree of accountability and transparency in government practice. But it is important to note that such reforms remain largely a form of 'accountability without democracy,' as *Union Action* (2002) puts it. Indeed while the Chinese government has been relatively successful in suppressing dissent on the mainland, it has not been quite so effective in doing so in Hong Kong where independent organizations such as the HKCTU (which funds the publication of *Union Action*) continue to have an influential voice in public culture and local politics. It will be interesting to see whether the mainland Chinese government is prepared to risk both its own political credibility and social stability in Hong Kong by adopting draconian measures to suppress popular opposition to its will, as translated into the policies of the unelected and increasingly unpopular Tung SAR administration. In this regard, the Tung administration's insistence on pushing through its proposed Article 23 legislation despite the strength and diversity of public opposition is viewed with pessimism in academic and corporate quarters both internationally and in Hong Kong.

Managing regional inequality

One of the most recent and significant reforms undertaken by the Chinese government in recent times is the overhaul of its residential system in October 2001, aimed at providing China's massive floating population of displaced peasants and unemployed workers with basic rights and services in the cities and towns where they find work. Under the former residential (*hukou*) registration system, the Chinese population was divided into two distinct sectors of urban and rural, with movement between the sectors strictly prohibited. Indeed there was little possibility of any movement under the former system since all citizens were entitled to receive public goods and services only in the places where their 'households' (*hukou*) had been registered. Now that it is actively engaged in reforming its residential system, the Chinese government readily acknowledges the injustices of the former system, pointing out that it provided the urban sector with housing, educational, health and employment benefits that were denied the rural sector, making the life of an urban resident into 'an object of envy' among 'several hundred million' members of the rural population (*People's Daily* 2001b).

The comprehensive household registration system in place during the years of the Maoist era became obsolete and ineffective as a framework for providing welfare and for maintaining social stability once the numbers of China's floating population began to swell in the late 1980s and especially throughout the 1990s. In this regard, the reform of China's residential system provides some level of social protection for many within China's enormous floating workforce who have long had to cope with the risks and additional costs of living and working as unregistered non-local residents in the various Chinese towns and cities undergoing urbanization. But since the reform only allows 'those who have a legal and static dwelling place, a stable occupation and source of income' to become eligible for permanent residence in the towns and cities where they live and work (*People's Daily* 2001a), large numbers of transient workers, hired informally and thus illegally, will continue to remain unprotected.

The Chinese government has admitted that, given the enormous size of the floating work population, the reform of the residential system will not translate into immediate benefits for all non-local working residents (*People's Daily* 2001b). But it is clear that this reform represents an important step in addressing urgent needs of social protection that will also have the effect of liberalizing the flow of human resources to different regions in China. Through the provision of non-discriminatory rights of abode to locals and non-locals alike, the present reform of the residential system is expected to make it easier for developing areas in China to attract skills and labour, alleviate the problems of overcrowding in the major cities, and thus provide better economic integration between the different regions. The disparity between rich and poor regions in China remains stark, as is evident in the pattern of inward FDI over the last two decades, a problem to which, as Fu Jun notes, the government has been fairly responsive, making policy adjustments to facilitate the development of the Chinese hinterland and thus progressively equalizing FDI policy advantages that were once exclusive to the SEZs (Fu 2001).

To date, however, the benefits of FDI have not been balanced, with most FDI occurring in the coastal region rather than the central or western regions. One effect of globalization worldwide has been that there is a growing level of income inequality within most societies. While the poor are generally living better than before, the gap between rich and poor has widened. The same process is occurring in China with a growing imbalance in the level of development among China's regions and between urban and rural areas.

Studies of regional income inequality in the market reform period, predominantly using data up to the mid 1980s, initially showed regional convergence (Hsueh 1994; Gundlach 1997; Raiser 1998). However, a number of studies have found evidence of an increase in cross-region income inequality in the late 1980s and 1990s (Knight and Song 1993; Rozelle 1994; Yao 1997; 1999). Using data for the period 1978 to 1995 Yao and Zhang (2001) find evidence of intra-zonal income convergence between provinces in the eastern, central and western zones, but income divergence between zones. Yao and Zhang (2001) argue that regional income inequality in China initially declined following market reforms because initial productivity gains in agriculture favoured the poorer regions, but increased after 1985 when the reforms shifted to the urban sector.

Regional income inequality is now widely regarded as a major political and social problem (O'Brien 2001; OECD 2002). Yang (1997, p. 92) suggests that the problem is manifest in two areas. First, relative economic stagnation in the interior makes it difficult for these provinces to generate employment activities, contributing to the migrant flow to the coastal provinces. This transient population is now seen as the source of a growing social problem. Second, domestic liberalization and the collapse of socialism in Central Asia has resulted in an increase in separatist activities in Xinjiang and Inner Mongolia.

CONCLUSION: IS FURTHER GLOBALIZATION THE RIGHT COURSE TO FOLLOW?

This chapter has taken a critical view of China's recent rush to tackle globalization head-on through the WTO, which has seen it move away from its traditional approach of strategic integration towards the kind of close integration that is more consistent with transition orthodoxy. Since its recent accession to the WTO, China has put its energies into 'getting on track with the international community' (*gen guoji jiegui*), which indicates China's preparedness to have its economy and society further subjected to the discipline of global markets. No one in the debate over China's accession to the WTO argues that China should not engage with the complexities of globalization. Even Chinese critics who warn against deepening socio-economic problems as a result of China's accession to the WTO are not opposed to further development of the Chinese market economy. It is obvious that over the last three decades globalization has made an immense contribution to lifting the living standards of the Chinese people. What this chapter has tried to argue, though, is that through strategic integration these benefits have come, to some extent, on China's terms. China's leadership has never taken much notice of what transition orthodoxy prescribes as the 'correct' reform path, yet it has still been successful when compared with the dismal record of most of the transition economies in Central and Eastern Europe.

Corruption and the authoritarian and arbitrary nature of the one-party state have, however, exacerbated already significant problems of socio-economic dislocation arising out of China's still relatively fragile market economy. It is questionable whether the Chinese government's attempts at reform, aimed at improving China's economic performance through policy liberalization under one-party state rule, will be adequate to meet the complex needs of social stability, human mobility, industrial growth and market expansion that further globalization will produce. In this context, the relative lack of transparency in government practice, excessive state control of information flows and the imposition of severe penalties on dissenting groups and individuals foster mistrust in the Chinese government both locally (among Chinese citizens) and internationally (among investors). These have been and will continue to be impediments to China's successful management of its economic growth: a poorly-informed and inadequately democratic society is placed at a distinct disadvantage in its ability to respond to or to manage new situations or crises, creatively and effectively. Moreover, the evidence to date of Hong Kong's integration with mainland China is, by most accounts, not encouraging. The challenge for China now is to reap the benefits from globalization through the WTO while dealing with the inevitable heightened level of adjustment costs which close integration will bring. As we have argued in the course of this chapter, integration is a complex process that involves not merely economic but broader social and political reforms. Whether China is able to do this in an effective manner remains to be seen.

REFERENCES

Amsden, A. (1989), 'Diffusion of Development: The Late Industrializing Model and Greater Asia', *American Economic Review Papers and Proceedings*, **81** (2), 282-286.

Amsden, A. (1992), 'A Theory of Government Intervention in Late Industrialization', in L. Putterman and D. Rueschemeyer (eds), *State and Market in Development: Synergy or Rivalry*, Boulder, Co.: Lynne Rienner.

Amsden, A. and T. Hikino (1994), 'Project Execution, Capability, Organizational Know-how and Conglomerate Corporate Growth in Late Industrialization', *Industrial and Corporate Change*, **3** (1), 111-147.

Armitage, C. (2003), 'China's "Iron Rice Bowl" gets the Chop', *The Australian* (Sydney), 13 January, p. 12.

Borenzstein, E and M. Kumar (1991), 'Proposals for Privatization in Central Europe', IMF Staff Papers, No. 38, Washington, D.C.: IMF.

Bourdieu, P. (1999), *Acts of Resistance: Against the Tyranny of the Market* (translated by R. Nice), New York: New Press.

Chan, J. M. (2003), 'New Security Laws in Hong Kong', *Daily Times*, 20 January, at <http://www.dailytimes.com.pk/default.asp?page=story_19-1-2003_pg3_4>.

Chandler, A. (1990), *Scale and Scope, The Dynamics of Industrial Capitalism*, Cambridge Mass.: Harvard University Press.

Chandler, C. (2002), 'Trying to Make Sense of Bad Debt Reform: China Selling Bank Assets to Solve the Problem', *Washington Post*, 15 January, p. E01.

Chandler, A., F. Amatori and T. Hikino (eds) (1997), *Big Business and the Wealth of Nations,* New York: Cambridge University Press.

Chen, J. (1994), 'Report on the Implementation of the 1993 Plan for National Economic and Social Development', *Beijing Review*, **37** (15), 11-17.

Chen, C., L. Chang and Y. Zhang (1995), 'The Role of Foreign Direct Investment in China's Post-1978 Economic Development', *World Development*, **23** (4), 691-703.

Chow, L.K., M.K.Y. Fung and L. Zhu (1999), 'Distributional Effects of Tariff Reductions in the Transforming Chinese Economy', *Pacific Economic Review*, **4** (2), 115-135.

Davies, G. (2002), 'Anticipating Community, Producing Dissent: The Politics of Recent Chinese Intellectual Praxis', *The China Review*, **2** (2), 1-35

Dornbusch, R. (1999), 'Don't Devalue the Renminbi', *Far Eastern Economic Review*, 26 August, p. 30.

Fernald, J., H. Edison and P. Loungani (1999), 'Was China the First Domino? Assessing Links between China and other Asian Economies', *Journal of International Money and Finance*, **18**, 515-535.

Fu, J. (2001), 'Institution Building and FDI', paper presented at *Financial Sector Reform in China* (11-13 September 2001, Fairbank Center, Harvard University), available at <http:// www.ksg.harvard.edu/cbg/ Conferences/financial_sector/ InstitutionandBuildingandFDI.pdf>.

Gilbert, J. and T. Wahl (2002), 'Applied General Equilibrium Assessments of Trade Liberalisation in China', *The World Economy*, **25** (5), 697-731.

Global Coalition Against Article 23 Legislation (2003), 'Interview with Michael Gahler, German representative on the EU's Human Rights and Foreign Relations Committee', 23 January, at <http://www.againstarticle23.org/en/newsdetail.php?id

=290>.

Gu, E.X. (2001), 'Dismantling the Chinese Mini-welfare State? Marketization and the Politics of Institutional Transformation, 1979-1999', *Communist and Post-Communist Studies*, **34**, 91-111.

Gundlach, E. (1997), 'Regional Convergence of Output per Worker in China: A Neoclassical I nterpretation', *Asian Economic Journal,* **11**, 423-442.

Hare, D (1999), '"Push" versus "Pull" Factors in Migration Outflows and Returns: Determinants of Migration Status and Spell Duration among China's Rural Population', *Journal of Development Studies*, **35**, 45-72.

He, Q. (1997), *Zhongguode xianjing* (China's Descent into a Quagmire), Hong Kong: Mirror Books.

Holz, C. and T. Zhu (2000), 'Banking and Enterprise Reform in the People's Republic of China after the Financial Crisis: An Appraisal', *Asian Development Review*, **18** (1), 73-93.

Hsueh, T-T. (1994), 'Patterns of Regional Development in the People's Republic of China', *Asian Economic Journal,* **8**, 1-38.

Huang, F. (1999), 'The Current Economic Situation and Trends in China – with a Discussion of Employment Related Issues in the Process of Industrialization', *Journal of Asian Economics,* **10**, 279-289.

Huang, L., Z. Wu and Y. Yao (1998), 'Bai hu shidian zhidu chuangxin chengxiao xianzhu', *Modern Enterprise Herald*, **1**, 35-39.

Huang, Y. (1997) 'The Economic Integration of Mainland China and Hong Kong' NBR Analysis (National Bureau of Asia Research), **8** (3), 15-26, available online at <http://www.nbr.org/publications/analysis/vol8no3/v8n3.pdf>.

Human Rights Watch (2002), 'China Human Rights Update', *Human_Rights Watch Press Backgrounder*, 15 February at <http://www.hrw.org/backgrounder/asia/china_update.htm>.

IMF (1990), *The Economy of the USSR: Summary and Recommendations*, Washington, D.C.: IMF.

Khanna, T. and K. Palepu (1997), 'Why Focussed Strategies Might be Wrong for Emerging Markets', *Harvard Business Review*, **75** (4), 41-51.

Knight, J. and L. Song (1993), 'The Spatial Contribution to Income Inequality in Rural China', *Cambridge Journal of Economics,* **17**, 195-213.

Knight, J, L. Song and H. Jia (1999), 'Chinese Rural Migrants in Urban Enterprises: Three Perspectives', *Journal of Development Studies*, **35**, 73-104.

Kornai, J. (1990), *The Road to a Free Economy*, New York: Norton.

Kynge, J. (2002), 'China Mulls New Transfer of Bank's Bad Loans', *Financial Times,* 19 November, p. 14.

Lake, D. (1988), *Power, Politics and Trade*, London: Cornell University Press.

Lam, W.W. (2002), 'Economic Recovery, at a Price', *China Brief,* 8 July, **2** (14), at <http://www.jamestown.org/pubs/view/cwe_002_014_002.htm>.

Lardy, N. (2002), *Integrating China into the Global Economy*, Washington, D.C.: Brookings Institute.

Lazonick, W. (1991), *Business Organization and the Myth of the Market Economy*, Cambridge: Cambridge University Press.

Lee, C.-K. (1999), 'From Organized Dependence to Disorganized Despotism: Changing Labour Regimes in Chinese Factories', *China Quarterly*, **57**, 44-71.

Lim, D. (2002), 'China: WTO Reforms and Macroeconomic Management',

Unpublished Manuscript, Department of Economics, ANU.

Lipton, D. and J. Sachs (1990), 'Creating a Market in Eastern Europe: The Case of Poland', *Brookings Papers on Economic Activity*, **1**, 75-147.

Liu, B. and P. Link (1998), 'A Great Leap Backward?' *The New York Review of Books*, 8 October, archived at <http://www.nybooks.com/articles/717>.

Ma, J. and Z. Wang (2001), 'Winners and Losers of China's WTO Entry', *The China Business Review*, **28** (2), 22-25.

Martin, W. and E. Ianchovichina (2001), 'Implications of China's Accession to the World Trade Organisation for China and the WTO', *The World Economy*, **24** (9), 1205-1219.

McGregor, R. (2002), 'China Moves on Debt Sales', *Financial Times*, September 16, p. 15.

McKibbin, W. and K.K. Tang (2000), 'Trade and Financial Reform in China: Impacts on the World Economy', *The World Economy*, **23** (8), 979-1003.

Morck, R. and B. Yeung (2000), 'Bring China into the WTO', *Japan and the World Economy*, **12**, 289-294.

Nolan, P. (1996), 'Large Firms and Industrial Reform in Former Planned Economies: The Case of China', *Cambridge Journal of Economics*, **20** (1), 1-29.

Nolan, Peter (2001), *China and the Global Business Economy*, Basingstoke: Palgrave.

Nolan, P. (2002), 'China and the Global Business Revolution', *Cambridge Journal of Economics*, **26**, 119-137.

Nolan, P. and X. Wang (1999), 'Beyond Privatization: Institutional Innovation and Growth in China's Large State-owned Enterprises', *World Development*, **27** (1), 169-200.

Nolan, P. and G. Yeung (2001), 'Big Business with Chinese Characteristics: Two Paths to the Growth of the Firm in China under Reform', *Cambridge Journal of Economics*, **25**, 443-465.

Nolan, P. and J. Zhang (2002), 'The Challenge of Globalization for Large Chinese Firms', *World Development*, **30** (12), 2089-2107.

Nyland, C., R. Smyth and C. Zhu (2003), 'Globalization and Occupational Health and Safety Regulation in China', Unpublished Manuscript, Monash University.

OECD (2002), *China in the World Economy: The Domestic Policy Challenges*, Paris: OECD.

O'Brien, K. (2001), 'Globalization and China', Studies in Globalization, *Working Paper No. 3*, Centre for Applied Economics, University of South Australia.

Oksenberg, M. (1997), 'Preserving Hong Kong's Political Autonomy', *NBR Analysis* (National Bureau of Asia Research), **8** (3), 5-14, available online at <http://www.nbr.org/publications/analysis/vol8no3/v8n3.pdf>.

Pan, P. (2002), 'Poisoned back into Poverty: As China Embraces Capitalism, Hazards to Workers Rise', *Washington Post*, 4 August, p. A01.

People's Daily (2001), 'Breaking Barrier: China Reforms Residence System', *People's Daily*, 28 August, available online at <http://english.peopledaily.com.cn/200108/28/eng20010828_7851>.

People's Daily (2001), 'Residence System Reform Speeds Up Human Resources Flow' *People's Daily*, 31 October, available online at <http://english.peopledaily.com.cn/20011031_83627>.

Prime, P.B. (2002), 'China Joins the WTO: How, Why and What Now?' *Business Economics*, April, **37** (2), 26-32. Also available online at <http://www.

chinacenter.net/PBPpdffiles/WTOPrime3.pdf>.

Raiser, M. (1998), 'Subsidizing Inequality: Economic Reforms, Fiscal Transfers and Convergence across Chinese Provinces', *Journal of Development Studies*, **34**, 1-26.

Rapaczynski, A. (1996), 'The Roles of the State and the Market in Establishing Property Rights', *Journal of Economic Perspectives*, **10**, 87-103.

Roberts, I. and R. Tyers, 'China's Exchange Rate Policy: The Case for Greater Flexibility', Unpublished Manuscript, Department of Economics, ANU.

Rozelle, S. (1994), 'Rural Industrialization and Increasing Inequality: Emerging Patterns in China's Reforming Economy', *Journal of Comparative Economics*, **19**, 362-391.

Ruigrok, W. and R. Van Tulder (1995), *The Logic of International Restructuring*, London: Routledge.

Schmitz, C. (1993), *The Growth of Big Business in the United States and Western Europe, 1850-1939*, Basingstoke: Macmillan.

Shan, J., G. Tian and F. Sun (1999), 'Causality Between FDI and Economic Growth' in Y. Wu (ed.), *Foreign Direct Investment and Economic Growth in China*, Cheltenham, U.K.: Edward Elgar.

Shieh, S. (1999), 'Is Bigger Better?' *China Business Review*, May-June, 50-54.

Singh, A. (1994), 'The Plan, the Market and Evolutionary Economic Reform in China', UNCTAD Discussion Paper No. 76.

Sit, V. (1985), 'The Special Economic Zones of China: A New Type of Export Processing Zone?', *Development Economics*, **23** (1), 69-86.

Smyth, R. (1998), 'Toward the "Modern Corporation": Recent Developments in the Institutional Reform of State-owned Enterprises in Mainland China', *Issues and Studies*, **34** (8), 102-131.

Song, L. 'China', in R.H. McLeod and R. Garnaut (eds), *East Asia in Crisis: From Being a Miracle to Needing One*, London: Routledge.

Steinfeld, E. (1998), *Forging Reform in China: The Fate of State-owned Industry*, Cambridge: Cambridge University Press.

Steinfeld, E. and V. Hulme (2000), 'Free Lunch or Last Supper? China's Debt-Equity Swaps in Context', *China Business Review*, July/August, 22-27.

Sun, H. (1998), 'Macroeconomic Impact of Foreign Direct Investment in China: 1979-1996', *The World Economy*, **21**, 675-694.

Sun, Q., W. Tong and Q. Yu (2002), 'Determinants of Foreign Direct Investment across China', *Journal of International Money and Finance*, **21**, 79-113.

Sutherland, Dylan (2001), 'Policies to Build National Champions: China's "National Team" of Enterprise Groups', in P. Nolan, *China and the Global Business Revolution*, London: Palgrave.

Tongzon, J. (2001), 'China's Membership in the WTO and the Exports of the Developing Economies of East Asia: A Computable General Equilibrium Approach', *Applied Economics*, **33**, 1943-1959.

Tyers, R. (2000), 'China after the Crisis: The elemental Macroeconomics', *Asian Economic Journal*, **15** (2), 173-199.

Union Action (2002), '"Rule by Tycoon Consolidated": the new ministerial system promises accountability without democracy', *Union Action* (HKCTU), June, at <http://hkctu.org.hk/english/unionaction/ua602-1.html>.

US China Security Review Commission (2002), 'Report to Congress of the US-China

Security Review Commission – The National Security Implications of the Economic Relationship between the United States and China', July, at <http://www.uscc.gov/ch9_02.htm>.

Vogel, E. (1989), *One Step Ahead in China*, London: Harvard University Press.

Wall Street Journal (2003), 'Still a Bad Bill' *Wall Street Journal Online*, 14 February, at <http://online.wsj.com/article_email/0,, SB1045172659893867263,00.html>.

Walmsley, T. and T. Hertel (2001), 'China's Accession to the WTO: Timing is Everything', *The World Economy*, **24** (8), 1019-1049.

Wang, H. (2000), '1989 shehui yundong yu Zhongguo "Xin ziyouzhuyi" de lishi genyuan: zailun dangdai Zhongguo de sixiang zhuangkuang yu xiandaixing wenti' ('The 1989 Social Movement and the Historical Roots of China's "Neoliberalism": further comments on the state of contemporary Chinese thought and modernity'), *Zhongguo xiandai wenxue*, **19**, 451-501.

Wang, H. (2003), *The 1989 Social Movement and the Historical Roots of China's Neoliberalism* (trans. with introduction by T. Huters), Cambridge, Mass. and London: Harvard University Press.

Wang, S. (2001), 'The Changing Role of Government in China', in X. Zhang (ed.), *Whither China? Intellectual Politics in Contemporary China*, Durham, NC and London: Duke University Press.

Wang, Z. (2002), 'WTO Accession, "Greater China" Free Trade Area and Economic Relations Across the Taiwan Strait', Unpublished Manuscript, Economic Research Services, United States Department of Agriculture.

Weisbrot, M. (2001), 'Gobalisation: A Primer', <http://www.cepr.net/GlobalPrimer.htm>.

White House (2000), United States Government Web Site on the China-US WTO Accession Agreement <http://www.chinapntr.gov>.

Wiseman, J. (1998), *Global Nation? Australia and the Politics of Globalization*, Cambridge: Cambridge University Press.

Woon, Y. (1999), 'Labor Migration in the 1990s', *Modern China*, **25** (4), 475-512.

World Bank (1996), *World Development Report: From Plan to Market*, Washington, D.C.: Oxford University Press.

Yang, D. (1997), *Beyond Beijing: Liberalization and the Regions in China*, Routledge: London.

Yao, S. (1997), 'Industrialization and Spatial Income Inequality in Rural China, 1986-1992', *Economics of Transition*, **5**, 97-112.

Yao, S. (1999), 'Economic Growth, Income Inequality and Poverty in China under Economic Reforms', *Journal of Development Studies*, **35**, 104-130.

Yao, S. and Z. Zhang (2001), 'Regional Growth in China under Economic Reforms', *Journal of Development Studies*, **38**, 167-186.

Ye, Z., J. Young, and V.A. Hulme (2002), 'Hope for China's Migrant Women Workers', *The China Business Review*, **29** (3), 30-36.

Zhao, H. (1995), 'Technology Imports and their Impacts on the Enhancement of China's Indigenous Technological Capability', *Journal of Development Studies*, **31**, 585-602.

Zhao, M. and T. Nichols (1996), 'Management Control of Labor in State-Owned Enterprises: Cases from the Textile Industry', *China Journal*, **36**, 1-21.

Zhu X. (2000), '1998: Ziyouzhuyide yanshuo' ('1998: the discourse of liberalism'), *Huaxia wenzhai*, 10 January, zk0001a1 at <http://www.cnd.org/HXWZ/ZK00/

zk202-1.hz8.html>.

Zizek, S. (2001), *Did Somebody Say Totalitarianism? Five Interventions in the (Mis)use of a Notion*, London and New York: Verso.

NOTES

1   Thanks to Bram Basavanand and Peter Micic who provided research assistance in the writing of this chapter.
2   It is worth noting that He Qinglian's book, first published in Hong Kong, was subsequently approved for publication in mainland China with the support of powerful establishment intellectuals within the party-state bureaucracy. She was quickly hailed as an important critical voice both in China and internationally. But while the Chinese government had accepted He's 1997 critique of official corruption − a problem that it was keen to address at the time − the one-party state soon found He's subsequent critiques of its coercive politics intolerable. By March 2000, along with others accused of being 'rightists' and 'liberals'. He had been censured and penalized. Banned from publishing in mainland China and living under surveillance from that time onwards, He finally left China in June 2001 for the United States to continue her research (see also Davies 2002).
3   Yet, as Wang Shaoguang argues, the PLA suffered from inadequate funding throughout the 1980s and early 1990s, demonstrating the weakness of the central government's ability to provide financial support for the improvement and professionalization of China's defence forces. This led the PLA to engage in commercial activities to make up for chronic budget shortfalls with adverse consequences that finally forced the government 'to take the military out of business' in July 1998 (Wang, S. 2001, pp. 139-140).
4   'Banks, Auctioneers Team Up for Non-performing Assets', Xinhua News Agency, 23 August 2002.
5   'Regulations Governing Asset Management Companies' People's Republic of China State Council Document No. 297, 10 November 2000, <http://www.jscq.com.cn/next/zcfg/zhongjin/007.htm> (in Chinese).
6   'Foreign Capital Allowed to Handle Non-performing Assets in China', Xinhua News Agency, 2 December 2002.
7   Interview conducted by the author with a representative of Huarong AMC, December 2002.
8   *Jingji Ribao* (Economic Daily), 12 February 1998, p. 5 (in Chinese).

11. (Case Study 2) A Glimpse of FDI in China and Related Issues[1]

Richard Lee York Wo

CAPITAL FLOW INTO CHINA: THE FDI INFLOW TREND

Ever since its adoption of the Open Door policy in 1979, China has attached importance to attracting foreign capital into China, and has achieved remarkable success in this regard. Statistics show that up to the end of 2001 the accumulated Foreign Direct Investment (FDI) actually invested in China amounted to US$394.127 billion while the contracted amount was US$744.25 billion.[2] The country has been the largest recipient of FDI among developing countries for nine consecutive years. It is also the sixth largest recipient of FDI on a worldwide basis.[3] According to the latest FDI Confidence Index by A.T. Kearney Inc., China has replaced the US to become the most popular Investment Destination of Choice.[4]

In fact, FDI is the most significant form of foreign capital flowing into China. Figure 1 shows that FDI inflow into China grew rapidly from the early 1990s and reached its peak at US$45.4 billion in 1998. It came down in 1999 because of the Asian financial crisis but rebounded in the following year and reached an all-time high of US$46.8 billion in 2001, an increase of 14.9 per cent over the previous year. Following China's accession to the WTO in November 2001, it was expected that FDI inflow into China for 2002 would pick up new momentum.[5]

THE MIX OF CAPITAL INFLOW

Figure 2 shows that the mix of capital inflow before and after 1990 was quite distinct. In the 1980s capital inflow into China mainly took the form of loans, and FDI inflow was maintained at a relatively low level. For instance, in the three years between 1988 and 1990, total foreign capital flowing into China amounted to around US$10 billion per year, with loans making up two-thirds of this annual amount. However, the pattern has clearly changed since the early 1990s. FDI inflow increased rapidly while the total amount of loans was maintained at between US$10 and 12.6 billion. In 2001, the total foreign capital inflow amounted to US$59.4 billion, with FDI representing over 78 per cent of the aggregate total.

Figure 1. FDI flow into China
(US$ in 100 Million)

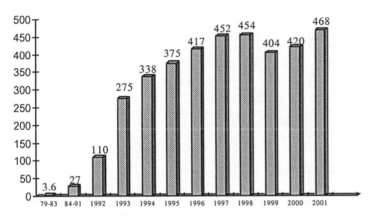

Note: The figures for years 1979-83 and 1984-91 are annual averages for the respective periods.
Source: Figures drawn from the statistics for the Ministry of Foreign Trade & Economic Cooperation, PRC.

This demonstrates that China has adopted a cautious borrowing policy all along. As a result, its external debt level has always been relatively low and stable. By the end of 2001, the balance of China's total external debt amounted to only US$170.1 billion, well within the internationally accepted safety level.[6]

Other forms of capital flows into China, which include international leasing, international IPO and suchlike, are beginning to grow. However, they are still very insignificant.

THE ROLE OF FDI IN CHINA'S ECONOMIC DEVELOPMENT

FDI has been playing a critical role in China's modernization and development. It has not only brought badly needed capital into China, but has brought with it technology, management skills, access to international markets and so on.

Figure 2. Capital flows into China

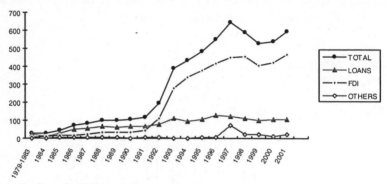

Note: The figure for 2000 is an estimated one.
Source: Figures drawn from statistics by National Bureau of Statistics and other related government departments, PRC.

FDI and GDP growth

China's GDP recorded an average of over 8 per cent growth per year for the past decade. It reached a record high of RMB 9.59 trillion in 2001.[7] The influx of FDI into China for the corresponding period played a significant part in China's growth. FDI alone accounted for 4 per cent of China's GDP in 2001.

FDI and foreign trade

From the 1990s onward, China's foreign trade has also been growing rapidly. China's total import and export stood at the modest amount of US$115.44 billion in 1990. However, the corresponding figure in 2001 was US$509.6 billion, almost 4.5 times larger.[8] If the Asian financial crisis slowed down the growth rate of China's foreign trade to some extent, this was neither detrimental nor permanent. China's share in international trade increased from 2.9 per cent in 1997 to 4.3 per cent in 2001. China was the world's tenth biggest foreign-trading country in 1997, and its ranking advanced to sixth in 2001.[9]

While it is difficult to pinpoint the exact contribution of FDI to China's foreign trade, some estimate that 48 per cent of China's exports and 18 per cent of its tax revenues come from FDI-related sectors, and China's exports account for 23 per cent of China's GDP.[10]

Figure 3. China's GDP growth

(RMB in hundred million)

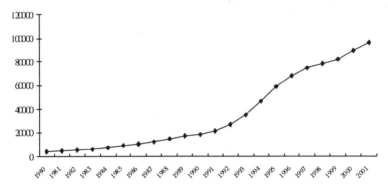

Source: Statistics by National Bureau of Statistics, PRC.

FDI and foreign exchange reserves

The figures for China's foreign exchange reserves show the same growth pattern. The total foreign exchange reserves in 2001 stood at US$212.2 billion, about 11 times that of ten years ago.[11]

Some other aspects of FDI impact on Chinese economy are worth noting. Up to 2001, there were over 390,000 joint venture companies and subsidiaries wholly owned by foreign capital in China. They have provided over 21 million jobs, and contributed 20 per cent of the national tax return. The share of foreign capital in China's total fixed investment for the year 1999 amounts to 11.17 per cent.[12]

In line with the globalization trend China, with its impressive economic development, has demonstrated its appeal as a rising 'global factory'. It has been reported that nearly 400 of the Fortune 500 enterprises have invested in more than 2,000 projects in China. The world's major manufacturers of computers, electronic products, telecommunications equipment and petrochemicals have expanded their production networks into China.[13]

In summary, China has been very successful in attracting FDI in the past decades. Its capabilities in absorbing and digesting such amounts of capital influx are also impressive. The effective use of FDI has helped China to achieve sustained growth over the years.

Figure 4. Growth of China's import & export and foreign exchange reserves

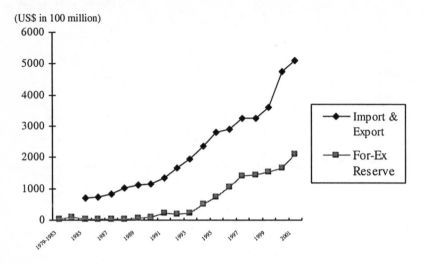

(US$ in 100 million)

Sources: Statistics by National Bureau of Statistics and Ministry of Foreign Trade & Economic Cooperation, PRC.

CHINA FDI: AN INTERNATIONAL PERSPECTIVE

The total international FDI flow in 2001 was US$735 billion, about a 51 per cent drop from the previous year due to a sluggish economy worldwide and international instability. However, the flow of FDI into China has picked up momentum. As mentioned above, with a total investment of US$46.8 billion, China is the largest recipient of FDI among the developing countries, and ranks 6th on a worldwide basis.[14]

In the same year, China FDI accounted for 6.37 per cent of the total FDI flowing into developing countries. It is reported that 80 per cent of FDI flowing into Asia (except Japan) between 1996 and 2000 actually flowed into China, as compared with the corresponding figure of 20 per cent ten years ago.[15]

On a regional level, statistics show that within the period between 1990 and 1998, China picked up 72 per cent of the total FDI that flowed into China and four Southeast Asian countries (namely Indonesia, Malaysia, Thailand and the Philippines).

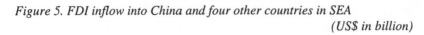

Figure 5. FDI inflow into China and four other countries in SEA

(US$ in billion)

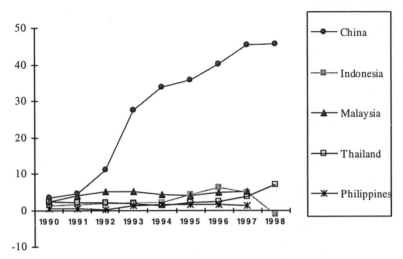

Source: Statistics by Ministry of Foreign Trade & Economic Cooperation, PRC.

It should be noted that although the absolute amount of FDI flowing into China is large, the relative figure (that is on a per capita basis) is low, only US$240 on an accumulated basis (up to 1999). Furthermore, according to the UNCTD World Investment Report of 2002, China ranked only 84th in the worldwide FDI Potential Index. Given China's vast population and huge market potential, as well as the rapidly growing economy, there is a good chance for China to attract more FDI in the years to come, and to make better and more efficient use of it.

CHINESE INVESTMENT OVERSEAS ON THE RISE

It is perhaps worth noting that in line with its 'go-out strategy' China is beginning to encourage domestic enterprises to invest overseas, in the hope of pushing its export-oriented economy along. It was reported that by June 2002 there were 6,758 joint venture projects overseas, with Chinese capital amounting to US$8.9 billion. Areas of overseas investment expanded from trade, shipping and the restaurant business to manufacturing processing, resources exploration, project contracting, agricultural cooperation, R & D and so on.[16] However, this is still very much in the initial stages and the capital outflow amount is far from significant. Given the tight control of foreign exchange by the central government, it would not be realistic to expect that China would make substantial investment abroad in the near future.

Figure 6. Global FDI input (on per capita basis up to 1999)

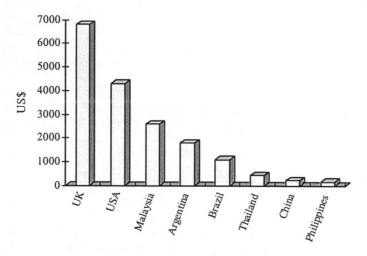

Source: Figures drawn from 'International Comparison of China FDI Inflow' by the Study Group of China FDI Inflow, <DRCNet.com.cn>, 8 October 2001.

CHINA'S ACCESSION TO THE WORLD TRADE ORGANISATION (WTO): A NEW ERA

Although China has been opening up its economy for more than twenty years, its accession to the WTO is generally considered to be a milestone with far-reaching significance not only for its economic development, but also for its political reform. With its accession to the WTO, China is prepared to integrate with the worldwide market and participate actively in the international division of labour. This will help to strengthen its economic reforms and accelerate its growth through a more efficient allocation of resources.

On a policy level, China's opening-up policy would change from one with limited scope and sectors into a comprehensive one. The policy would no longer be carried out on a trial basis but be implemented in a systematic way within a well-defined legal framework and a given time schedule. Also, China would deal with its international economic issues more on a multilateral basis within the WTO framework than on a bilateral basis.

China's accession to the WTO has given a big impetus to FDI flowing into China. It is expected that the overall investment environment will become more stable, transparent and relatively fair for FDI. New opportunities in services and other formerly closed sectors are expected to attract new FDI flowing in. Already there appears to have been a shift of focus of overseas capital from general manufacturing to basic industries, infrastructure, and new and high-technology sectors, as well as a growing inflow of investment from large multinational corporations.[17]

A new trend is likely to emerge for the FDI pouring into China. FDI is expected not only to take the traditional way of greenfield investments, but also to look for other forms of investments such as merger and acquisition. This has become possible because China is reforming its financial market. FDI will also be involved more in rationalization programmes, that is the process of privatizing SOEs (state-owned enterprises), and will participate in the management of NPAs (non-performing assets). More FDI will go into service sectors, such as financial services, telecommunications, distribution and retail, tourism and so on, which were formerly closed to FDI. Geographically, FDI will spread to inner areas, that is the less developed parts of China. This is in line with China's National Strategy on Development of the Western Region. At the same time, the existing favourable policies towards FDI enjoyed by the coastal region will gradually fade away.

However, this new trend can take place only if the obstacles associated with the lack of an adequate legal and regulatory framework (as well as with opposition) are progressively lifted.

THE ASIAN FINANCIAL CRISIS

The Asian financial crisis which began in 1997 swept most Asian countries with devastating effects. One by one, the economies of the region collapsed, with their currencies depreciating and foreign exchange dwindling. China, however, though also seriously affected, responded to the crisis from a position of strength and kept its currency stable. There are many reasons contributing to this. First, China has a carefully tailored foreign exchange administration regime. Second, prudent external borrowing policy resulted in a relatively low debt level. Third, China had a back-up of substantial foreign exchange reserves and an international trade surplus.[18] Fourth, the success of the Macroeconomic Adjustment Program since mid-1993 had helped to slow down domestic demand and set a realistic growth rate without excess inflation. More important was the fact that the *Renminbi* depreciated over 50 per cent at that time, thus providing a certain buffer for the currency during the crisis. Fifth, as the main source of capital inflow into China, FDI also played an important role in helping China through the crisis. By its very nature, FDI flow is relatively stable compared with other forms of capital flow, such as loans and portfolio flows.

For China, one of the lessons learnt from the crisis was the issue of national security for its own financial and monetary systems. With China's further opening up to the world, it will be necessary to facilitate the interflow of capital between China and foreign countries. Under such circumstances, however, China's own financial and monetary systems would also become vulnerable to external factors which are beyond the control of national policies. Too much haste in making the *Renminbi* convertible would result in a potentially high price for China's economic development during an emergency situation like the Asian financial crisis. Therefore, it is generally accepted that the restricted flow of capital across the border in the meantime is a necessary evil. After the Asian financial crisis, it is believed that the Chinese government reprioritized the agenda for its monetary and financial reform program, particularly with regard to the convertibility of the currency.

NOTES

1   This is an amended and updated paper based on the author's presentation at the 2002 ARIACO Conference, Kuala Lumpur, 6 March 2002.
2   Statistics by the Ministry of Foreign Trade and Economic Cooperation (PRC) and also the Speech to the International Investment Forum 2002 by Shi Guangsheng, Minister of Foreign Trade and Economic Cooperation, Xiamen, 8 September 2002.
3   'UNCTAD Statistics in Brief', from *World Investment Report* 2002, at <www.unctad.org/>.
4   *21st Century Economic Journal*, 29 September 2002, Electronic News.
5   The newly released figure for FDI flowing into China in 2002 is US$527.43 billion, another 12.31 per cent increase over 2001. Statistics by the Ministry of Foreign Trade and Economic Cooperation, PRC.
6   Statistics by the State Administration of Foreign Exchange, PRC.
7   China's GDP increased by 8 per cent in 2002 and amounts to RMB10.2 trillion (approximately US$1.23 trillion).
8   The figure in 2002 was US$620.79 billion, another increase of 21.8 per cent over 2001. Statistics by Ministry of Foreign Trade and Economic Cooperation, PRC.
9   Speech by Shi Guangsheng, Minister of Foreign Trade & Economic Cooperation, PRC. Xinhua News Agency, 24 December 2002.
10 *21st Century Economic Journal*, 29 September 2002, electronic news.
11 China's foreign exchange reserves stood at US$286.4 billion by the end of 2002, an increase of 35 per cent over 2001. Statistics by National Bureau of Statistics, PRC.
12 Statistics by National Bureau of Statistics and other related departments, PRC.
13 UNCTAD report on global investment in 2001, quoted by *Time* (Asia) online 13 November 2001.
14 UNCTAD, The World Investment Report 2002, quoted by *21st Century Economic Journal*,

30 September 2002.

15 *Hong Kong Economic Journal*, 14 March 2002.

16 Speech to the International Investment Forum 2002, Shi Guangsheng, Minister of Foreign Trade and Economic Cooperation, Xiamen, 8 September 2002.

17 Shi Guangsheng, speech to press conference, 13 November 2002, <MOFTC.gov.cn>, accessed 2 January 2003.

18 By the end of 1997, China's foreign exchange reserves stood at US$139.89 billion and its international trade surplus was US$46.2 billion.

12. (Case Study 3) The Movement of People: Interflows between Hong Kong and Mainland China[1]

Jane C.Y. Lee

INTRODUCTION

This chapter analyses the changing patterns of the movement of people between Hong Kong and mainland China in the first five years after Hong Kong was returned to Chinese sovereignty in 1997. It incorporates an account of people flows before 1997. Changes to relevant government policy will be highlighted, in relation to their implications for Hong Kong's economic development and integration with the mainland.

CHANGES IN THE PATTERN OF SOCIO-ECONOMIC RELATIONSHIP BETWEEN HONG KONG AND MAINLAND CHINA AND MOVEMENT OF PEOPLE

Hong Kong's economic and social relationship with the mainland underwent dramatic changes in the few years immediately before and after its reunification with China. Before 1997, Hong Kong was regarded as a society of immigrants. For historical reasons, the then colonial government assumed that it did not have a hinterland, and thus all physical and economic planning had to be considered within the confines of the colony's territorial boundaries with reference to Hong Kong's very limited supply of flat land. The movement of people between Hong Kong and South China was rigidly controlled and discouraged. Since the domestic market of Hong Kong was very small, its success was highly dependent on maintaining an open economy by encouraging the free flow of capital and people, including both permanent and transit residents. Such a principle, however, did not apply to those travelling to and from mainland China. From 1979 the economy of the mainland began to grow steadily and social and economic exchanges with Hong Kong increased without interruption. By 1997, however, control over flows of people and capital between Hong Kong and mainland China was not significantly adjusted to account for new situations arising from the higher levels of economic exchange between the two sides.

In the 15 years before 1997, Hong Kong's socio-economic relationship with the Pearl River Delta also underwent significant changes. First, about 52 per cent of Hong Kong's manufacturing and trading firms were economically active in the mainland in 2001, employing around 10 million workers in the Pearl River Delta (*Made in PRD* 2002). Second, the economy of mainland China (and South China in particular) grew rapidly, and quickly became the hinterland of Hong Kong. Third, there remained a huge gap in the economic level between the people of Hong Kong and the Pearl River Delta, yet at the non-government level more and more social and marriage relationships were established. By 1998, the government of Hong Kong estimated that there could be as many as 1.7 million mainland children born of Hong Kong parents.[2] The immigration policy of the Hong Kong government, which fundamentally assumed that mainland people continued to be socio-economically backward, imposed rigid control and restrictions over people coming from the mainland. The then policy of the PRC government also did not allow its people to travel freely between provinces; even at the time of writing, individual citizens were not permitted, theoretically speaking, to travel outside mainland Chinese territory without giving 'proper reasons' categorized by the central government. As a result, the movement of people between Hong Kong and the mainland grew in the 1990s with a one-way traffic flow, that is, principally from Hong Kong to the mainland.

The socio-economic relationship between mainland China and Hong Kong was transformed soon after 1997. First, the bubble economy in Hong Kong burst during the financial turmoil of 1998-1999. Second, the effect of globalization together with a new stage of economic growth in the mainland accelerated a fundamental restructuring of Hong Kong's economy. The immediate impact on Hong Kong was price suppression in such areas as individual salaries, property values and consumer goods. The socio-economic gap between Hong Kong and the mainland quickly narrowed. More Hong Kong families began choosing to live in the Pearl River Delta region and to commute to Hong Kong to work or study on a daily basis. Between January and November in 2002, the most commonly used border post (namely Lo Wu) recorded a head count of 87.2 million (an average of 247,000 per day); the number during the peak seasons could be up to 3 million a week.[3] The SAR government conducted a survey in 2001[4] and came up with an estimate that about 7.9 per cent of households (or 163,000 households) owned properties in the mainland and 41,000 Hong Kong residents actually lived in the Pearl River Delta (though most people felt that the government had under-estimated the actual figures). The figures released by the Immigration Department were borne out by the fact that the number of Hong Kong visitors travelling to the mainland increased from 28.8 million in 1996 to 55.6 million in 2002, that is, an average per person of more than seven trips from Hong Kong to the mainland each year. Government controls on mainland-Hong Kong flows continued. A quota system was applied. The central government slightly relaxed the policy in 1999-2000 and the number of mainland visitors coming to Hong Kong reached 4.4 million in 2001, an increase of 15.8 per cent over the previous year. In January 2002 the policy was further relaxed, virtually permitting package tours to visit Hong Kong without a quota. By December 2002 the number of mainland visitors had increased dramatically to 6.8 million, which accounted for a further increase of 54.5 per cent compared to 2001 (see Figure 2). A few studies showed that the consumption power of the mainland tourist continued to rise, being second only to tourists from the USA.[5] Even so, the interflow remained unequal, being still fundamentally one-way traffic from Hong Kong to the mainland.

Figure 1. Total passenger arrivals and departures by control point (Jan. to Nov. 2002)

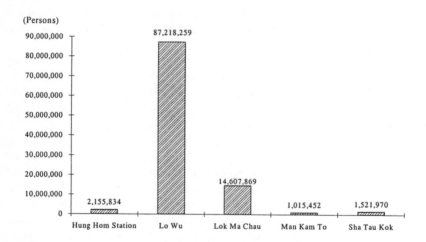

Source: Hong Kong Monthly Digest of Statistics.

Figure 2. Visitors between mainland and Hong Kong

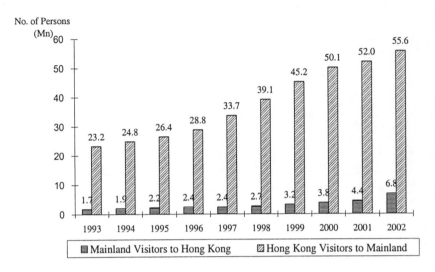

Source: Hong Kong Monthly Digest of Statistics.

The socio-economic relationship between Hong Kong and mainland China is also reflected in the increase in the volume of trade between the two sides over the past few years. In the eight years between 1994 and 2001, ocean cargo throughput between mainland China and Hong Kong was maintained at 15-19 million tonnes (see Figure 3). Hong Kong is the largest container terminal in the world, and trade relating to mainland China accounted for 44 per cent of Hong Kong's imports and 39 per cent of Hong Kong's exports respectively in 2002.[6] In 2001, 54 per cent of Hong Kong's overall cargo traffic was between Hong Kong and the mainland, either by air, sea or land.[7] The total number of goods vehicles crossing the territorial border, for example, was about 8.9 million[8] (trips) in the period between January and November in 2002 (an average of 27,000 per day). Hong Kong also played an important bridging role in trade exchanges between the mainland and Taiwan. By 2002, 26.8 per cent of cross-Strait trade went through Hong Kong (see Figure 4).

Figure 3. Ocean cargo throughput loaded and discharged between mainland China and Hong Kong

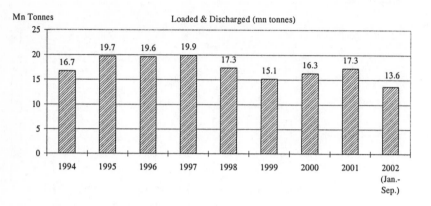

Sources: Hong Kong Shipping Statistics.

Figure 4. Cross-strait trade between mainland China and Taiwan

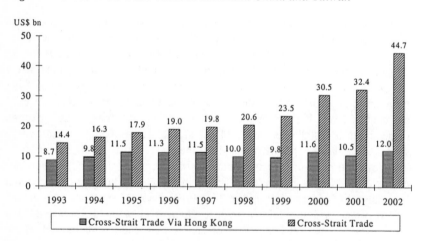

Source: Hong Kong External Trade.

IMPLICATIONS FOR FUTURE ECONOMIC DEVELOPMENT AND NATION BUILDING

After 1997, the development of stronger socio-economic ties between Hong Kong and the mainland was chiefly the result not of sovereign and political factors but of economic factors. The opening and liberalization of the mainland economy and relaxation of the policy on people's movements were the most critical points, implying that mainland political leaders were increasingly responsive to economic and market demands. In order to facilitate the free flow of people, goods, capital and information, continued improvements in infrastructure will be necessary, including more roads and bridges, more efficient and convenient train schedules, more efficient airports and seaports and air cargo servicing centres. In the long term, there is also a huge demand for high quality human resources for greater economic integration of both sides.

There are also threats facing greater economic integration between Hong Kong and the Pearl River Delta. First, there have been and will continue to be pressures on price integration, which virtually means suppression of property and labour costs in Hong Kong, resulting in short-to-medium-term economic suffering for both unskilled and lower-income workers as well as professionals. Problems of structural unemployment and the ageing population in Hong Kong will also be sustained for another few years. Second, a radical review of traditional assumptions about social policies in Hong Kong (such as those for housing, education and welfare) by incorporating a 'cross-border' concept will become increasingly necessary.

Greater socio-economic integration between Hong Kong and the mainland is making an important contribution to the function of nation building. The 'Chinese' identity of the Hong Kong people has been rapidly enhanced since 1997. More people are speaking *putonghua*, the national language, and have become interested in trying to seek employment in the mainland. Intermarriage has become more common. Obviously the most sensitive issues remain in political areas such as human rights and freedom of news reporting and speech.

There has been argument between mainland and Hong Kong Chinese over whether or not the role of Hong Kong should be confined to economic areas. Increasingly, however, people began to feel that Hong Kong was losing the uniqueness it had before 1997. In the concept of practising 'One country, two systems', the two economic systems would inevitably become integrated. If Hong Kong has no political role, then it will be just another Chinese city, or just a regional headquarters of Guangdong province in the South China region. Hong Kong should, however, continue to function like an international city, having political, cultural and economic influence in East

Asia as well as on global issues.

CONCLUSION

The above discussion suggests that people's interchange and movements have altered in accordance with changes in social and economic levels between the two territories. Public policies should respond to market needs and be adjusted efficiently to facilitate the free flow of people and hence information, capital and goods exchanges. As a society of immigrants, Hong Kong is taking time to adjust and revise its domestic policies in order to promote stronger ties and relationships with the mainland, and the Pearl River Delta in particular. What is important is a change of mindset, which requires not only economic but also cultural and political adjustments.

REFERENCES

Made in PRD - The Changing Face of Hong Kong Manufactures (2002), Hong Kong: Federation of Hong Kong Industries.
Hong Kong External Trade, Hong Kong: Census and Statistics Department, the Hong Kong Special Administrative Region Government, various issues.
Hong Kong Monthly Digest of Statistics, Hong Kong: Census and Statistics Department, the Hong Kong Special Administrative Region Government, various issues.
Hong Kong residents' Experience of and Aspirations for Taking up Residence in the Mainland of China (2002), Hong Kong: Planning Department, the Hong Kong Special Administrative Region Government.

NOTES

1 This chapter is based on the author's presentation at the 2002 ARIACO Conference in Kuala Lumpur, 6 March 2002.
2 'Speech by Secretary for Security in the Legislative Council on right of abode', Press Conference, Hong Kong Special Administrative Region Government, 28 April 1999.
3 Other border stations were Hung Hom, Lok Ma Chau, Man Kam To and Sha Tau Kok. The total passenger numbers arriving at and departing from Hong Kong-Guangdong control points reached 106,519,384 between January and November in 2002. See Figure 1.
4 *Hong Kong Residents' Experience of and Aspirations for Taking up Residence in the Mainland of China*, Hong Kong: The Planning Department, the Hong Kong Special Administrative Region Government, December 2001.
5 Two major studies have been conducted by the Hong Kong Policy Research Institute in 1997 and 1998 showing that there was huge potential for mainland tourist and business visitors coming to Hong Kong and that this should bring tremendous economic benefits to the territory.
6 *Hong Kong External Trade*, Hong Kong: Census and Statistics Department, the Hong Kong Special Administrative Region Government, various issues.
7 *Hong Kong Monthly Digest of Statistics*, Hong Kong: Census and Statistics Department, the Hong Kong Special Administrative Region Government, various issues.

8 *Hong Kong Monthly Digest of Statistics*, Hong Kong: Census and Statistics Department, the Hong Kong Special Administrative Region Government, various issues.

Index